POWER AND SECURITY IN THE INFORMATION AGE

Also of interest

The Resurgence of the State
Trends and Processes in Cyberspace Governance
Edited by
Myriam Dunn, Sai Felicia Krishna-Hensel and Victor Mauer
ISBN 978-0-7546-4947-2

Power and Security in the Information Age
Investigating the Role of the State in Cyberspace

Edited by

MYRIAM DUNN CAVELTY
Center for Security Studies, ETH Zurich, Switzerland

VICTOR MAUER
Center for Security Studies, ETH Zurich, Switzerland

SAI FELICIA KRISHNA-HENSEL
*Center for Business and Economic Development
Auburn University, Montgomery, USA*

ASHGATE

© Myriam Dunn Cavelty, Victor Mauer and Sai Felicia Krishna-Hensel 2007

All rights reserved. No part of this publication may be reproduced, stored in a retrieval system or transmitted in any form or by any means, electronic, mechanical, photocopying, recording or otherwise without the prior permission of the publisher.

Myriam Dunn Cavelty, Victor Mauer and Sai Felicia Krishna-Hensel have asserted their right under the Copyright, Designs and Patents Act, 1988, to be identified as the editors of this work.

Published by
Ashgate Publishing Limited
Gower House
Croft Road
Aldershot
Hampshire GU11 3HR
England

Ashgate Publishing Company
Suite 420
101 Cherry Street
Burlington, VT 05401-4405
USA

Ashgate website: http://www.ashgate.com

British Library Cataloguing in Publication Data
Power and Security in the information age : investigating
    the role of the state in cyberspace
    1. Computer security 2. Information society 3. Information
    technology 4. Cyberterrorism
    I. Dunn Cavelty, Myriam II. Mauer, Victor III. Krishna-Hensel, Sai
    Felicia
    005.8

Library of Congress Cataloging-in-Publication Data
Power and security in the information age : investigating the role of the state
in cyberspace / edited by Myriam Dunn, Victor Mauer, and Sai Felicia Krishna-Hensel.
        p. cm.
    Includes bibliographical references and index.
    ISBN 978-0-7546-7088-9
    1. Computer security. 2. Information society. 3. Information technology. 4.
Cyberterrorism. I. Dunn, Myriam. II. Mauer, Victor. III. Krishna-Hensel, Sai Felicia.

    QA76.9.A25P68 2007
    005.8--dc22

2007018839

ISBN 978 0 7546 7088 9

Printed and bound in Great Britain by TJ International Ltd, Padstow, Cornwall.

Contents

List of Contributors		*vii*
Preface by Sai Felicia Krishna-Hensel		*ix*
1	Introduction: Information, Power, and Security – An Outline of Debates and Implications *Myriam Dunn Cavelty and Elgin M. Brunner*	1
2	Is Anything Ever New? – Exploring the Specificities of Security and Governance in the Information Age *Myriam Dunn Cavelty*	19
3	Meta-power, Networks, Security and Commerce *J.P. Singh*	45
4	Cyberspace and Sovereignty: Thoughts on Physical Space and Digital Space *Geoffrey L. Herrera*	67
5	Terrorist Use of the Internet and the Challenges of Governing Cyberspace *Maura Conway*	95
6	Improving Information Security in Companies: How to Meet the Need for Threat Information *Manuel Suter*	129
7	Conclusion: The Role of the State in Securing the Information Age – Challenges and Prospects *Myriam Dunn Cavelty and Victor Mauer*	151
Index		*163*

List of Contributors

Elgin M. Brunner is a Ph.D. candidate and researcher at the Center for Security Studies (CSS), ETH Zurich (Swiss Federal Institute of Technology). She holds a degree in International Relations from the Graduate Institute of International Studies in Geneva. She specializes in Gender Issues in Security Studies, Information Operations, the changing nature of warfare, and the societal impact thereof.

Maura Conway is lecturer at the Department of Law and Government at the Dublin City University. Her research interests are in the area of terrorism and the Internet. She is particularly interested in cyberterrorism and its portrayal in the media, and the functioning and effectiveness of terrorist websites. Along with a number of book chapters, she has also published in *First Monday*, *Current History*, the *Journal of Information Warfare*, and elsewhere.

Myriam Dunn Cavelty is head of the New Risks Research Unit at the Center for Security Studies (CSS), ETH Zurich and coordinator of the Crisis and Risk Network (CRN). Her field of expertise is the impact of the information revolution on security policy issues. Myriam holds a degree in political science, modern history, and international law from the University of Zurich.

Geoffrey L. Herrera is Visiting Research Fellow at the Center for the Study of Force and Diplomacy at Temple University, in Philadelphia, USA. He is the author of a number of articles on technology, international transformation, and international systems theory and of *Technology and International Transformation: Railroads, the Atom Bomb, and the Politics of Technological Change* from SUNY Press.

Sai Felicia Krishna-Hensel is Director of the Interdisciplinary Global Studies Research Initiative, Center for Business and Economic Development, Auburn University, Montgomery, and President and Program Chair of the Comparative Interdisciplinary Studies Section of the International Studies Association, United States.

Victor Mauer is Deputy Director and Head of Research of the Center for Security Studies (CSS), ETH Zurich, and heads the Center's European Security and Defence Policy (ESDP) project. He specializes in European security, European integration, and transatlantic relations and has published on European and transatlantic affairs. He studied at the Universities of Bonn, Oxford, and Cambridge.

J.P. Singh is Assistant Professor in the Communication, Culture and Technology Program at Georgetown University and Editor of *Research Policy Review*. Singh authored *Leapfrogging Development? The Political Economy of Telecommunications Restructuring* and co-edited (with James N. Rosenau) *Information Technologies and Global Politics*. His current book project is titled *Negotiating the Global Information Economy*. He has authored nearly thirty journal articles and book chapters. He is Chair of the Science, Technology and Environmental Politics section of the American Political Science Association; President of the International Communication Section of the International Studies Association; and Vice President of the Policy Studies Organization.

Manuel Suter is a Ph.D. candidate and researcher at the Center for Security Studies (CSS), ETH Zurich. He specializes in information security and Critical Information Infrastructure Protection (CIIP). Manuel holds a degree in political science, modern history, and constitutional law from the University of Zurich.

Preface

Cybersecurity: Perspectives on the Challenges of the Information Revolution

Sai Felicia Krishna-Hensel

The concept of world politics as essentially a struggle for power between nation-states marked the intellectual dialogue of the post war period as scholars sought to understand the forces that had resulted in the transformational conflicts that had changed the world as they had known it. Disillusioned with idealistic interpretations of the world order, greater emphasis began to be placed on a 'realistic' approach where conflict and power plays were a dominant feature of world politics. The political realism of scholars such as Edward Hallett Carr, George Kennan, Hans Morgenthau, and Robert Gilpin among others, have reflected a general disenchantment with the prevalent tradition of scholarship which had confidence that rational human beings could construct effective institutions to promote order in the international system.[1] Realist theory emphasized the importance of military strength as an index of state power. The principal actors in this competitive international system were states that were engaged in ensuring their own security, wealth, and power. Simultaneously, however, historians focused on the wars and the interwar periods as proof that the nation-state was increasingly finding itself challenged for supremacy and control over events that originated beyond its borders and whose impact transcended national boundaries. The idea of an international society gained momentum from the experiences of this period. The communication between peoples, the movement in ideas and cultural contacts, as well as in trade and commerce, had become easier and more rapid. Just as the national order replaced the localism of the medieval system, the study of politics in the twentieth century moved toward the idea of global cooperation and interdependence. This perspective recognizes that there has been an on-going evolution in the recognition by many national governments, international institutions, and non-governmental actors that they would need to work together to confront global problems. This constructive approach reflected an optimistic attitude concerning the ability of states to engage in cooperative efforts and presented a viable alternative to political realism.

---

1   Edward Hallett Carr, *The Twenty Years' Crisis, 1919–1939: An Introduction to the Study of International Relations* (London, 1939, 1964); George Kennan, *Realities of American Foreign Policy* (New York, 1966); Hans J. Morgenthau, *Politics Among Nations: The Struggle for Power and Peace* (New York, 1948, 1985); Robert Gilpin, *War and Change in World Politics* (Cambridge, 1981).

The contemporary international order is characterized by economic interdependency and is subject to serious vulnerabilities from global events over which no single nation has control. A critical challenge confronting the nation-state in a globalizing world is its ability to provide protection and prosperity within its borders as the forces of integration within the international system continue to multiply. There is no well developed theory or paradigm that has emerged from this evolving analytic approach. Instead, the discourse has revolved around identifying global problems, strategies, and structures for addressing transnational challenges. Scholars, such as David Mitrany, have adopted a functionalist perspective and argued that over time, a 'web of international activities and agencies' would emerge with jurisdiction transcending that of states in specific instances.[2] This perspective presupposes that integrated institutions and policies would replace the existing policy divisions of nation states in situations where cooperative responses were in order.[3]

Scholars who situate risk at the center of contemporary social change reinforce the basic concerns that lie at the center of integrative theory. Suggesting that the challenges are not essentially new but that it is how we typify them that determines the risk that they pose, they propose that 'Risk may be defined as a systematic way of dealing with hazards and insecurities induced and introduced by modernization itself'.[4] We are becoming increasingly conscious of risks which both technologically and politically include threats emanating from individuals, groups, and rogue states that cause long term irreversible and invisible damage to communication networks and interrupt transmissions. These vulnerabilities are qualitatively different from the hazards and dangers experienced in previous periods of history. The current threats to the security environment are the direct consequence of technological progress and are a seemingly implicit and unavoidable corollary. Further, many of these risks inhabit cyber space and are not perceptible to the senses. Indeed, as technology continues to enable the transfer of a wide range of activities to the cyber forum and on a global scale, the risks multiply. The contemporary threat environment is not bound by local origins but expands to include the global networks, and thus is technologically and politically reflexive. The risk environment transcends the limits of time and space boundaries, and presents a continuous and general challenge. Cyber threats globalize because they universalize and equalize. They affect all users, transactions, and dataflows regardless of location or political persuasion. Since networks are cross border organisms, security of networks is only possible through supra national solutions.

This is dramatically illustrated in the globalised world of internet communications. An ironic corollary to the expanding reach of information is that it has become necessary to secure the information to ensure that it cannot be misused or modified by unauthorized users. Not only has it become essential to protect the information itself, but it has also become important to protect the networks

---

2   David Mitrany, *A Working Peace System* (Chicago, 1966), pp. 10–11.

3   Karl Deutsch et al., *Political Community and the North Atlantic Area* (Princeton, 1957); Ernst B. Haas, *The Uniting of Europe: Political, Social, and Economic Forces, 1950–1957* (Stanford, 1958).

4   Ulrich Beck, *Risk Society* (London, 1992), p. 21.

over which information travels. This challenge, difficult in itself, becomes even more complex as the rapidly changing technological environment moves at a rate that often exceeds that of the ability to respond. As the global communications network continues to develop at a rapid pace driven by innovative developments in technology, the ability of the nation state to secure the networks is increasingly based on interdependence between agencies and cooperating governments. The growing reliance on the internet has raised serious policy concerns of regulation, privacy, copyright, and access. The policy process has been placed in a position of responding to challenges and has yet to have a framework that can anticipate problems and have a built-in response mechanism. This is partially explained by the reality that technology moves ahead unfettered, while policy is dependent on deliberation, debate, and agreement before any guiding principles can be put in place. Two primary challenges face the policy maker in the cyber world. One is that the internet is being used in creative and unexpected ways to propagate criminal activity and the other is that a response to control or regulate would impact the very freedom that underlies the cyber revolution. Consequently, policy is confronted by new threats that are often difficult to identify, while simultaneously, traditional criminality is moving on-line. Thus the globally interconnected information network demonstrates the limitations of cybersecurity efforts that are solely reliant on individual nations, groups of industrialized countries, or private enterprise. It underlines the importance of a combined effort by government, industry, law enforcement, and the global population with access to the networks. Systemic vulnerabilities are encountered on a frequent basis as the networks continue to replace traditional forms of interaction, The global cybersecurity effort involves both regulatory policy as well as technical standardization. Policy initiatives often entail a slower decision making process while the response time for technical solutions tends to be much faster. The reality of this environment is that the infrastructure is designed to incorporate basic security considerations that can operate independently of the policy development process. Standardization of security initiatives has been central to the communications revolution since its inception. The rapid spread of the communications network has focused attention on the need for integration of national, regional, and international security standards. The threat environment is perceived as a global phenomenon so that attacks on a segment of the network can have wider implications. International cooperation is seen as the solution to developing and implementing network standards.

The location and sophistication of various elements of technology complicates the task of the policy maker, although it affects the technician/standard setter somewhat differently. The positioning of satellites such as the DBS (Direct Broadcasting Satellite) in realms that are not constrained by territorial boundaries, impacts on the ability to block or regulate incoming information. The same holds true for information outflows. Not only is there a fear that unregulated information flows can compromise political goals, but there is also a concern that information as propaganda, or cultural imperialism, cannot be restrained. Many governments share the fear that their ability to influence and govern their populations is undermined by a free flow of information. Iran has exhorted ISP's to block thousands of sites that have been identified by the government as problematic.[5] China has a similar policy in effect and at its most extreme, it was reflected in the government's crack down on sites reputed to be spreading false information on the SARS outbreak E-Mail screening, and chat room censorship is routine. The government is also working on ways to control SMS (short messaging service) that can be received via mobile phone units.[6] The issues surrounding TDF's (Trans Border Data Flows) represent a category in themselves. Corporate datasets involving a variety of operations, medical records, financial/credit information etc are often transmitted to other countries which provide outsource services, but which often lack the same stringent privacy laws and protective regulations that prevail in the originating country. On an entirely different level, there is the genuine concern in an age of terrorism that free channels support the objectives of terrorists and provide a convenient means of communication.

The post 9/11 threat environment has led to a series of worldwide government responses towards net and information controls, such that net content was blocked and removed. Some of the actions were justified, such as the scrubbing of the NRC (Nuclear Regulatory Commission) website that contained sensitive material which could be used by terrorists.[7] If this were characteristic of all net scrubbing it would be quite understandable, however, the panic mode that ensued resulted in the censorship of harmless matter. Part of the justification was that any information, however innocuous could be put to nefarious use. As we shall see, this cuts into the fundamental issue of net freedom. The leading legislation was the U.S. Patriot Act, followed by U.N. Security Council Resolution 1373 designed to protect against terrorism. The provisions of the Patriot Act alarmed internet professionals who objected to the expansive classification of 'protected computers' to include machines located outside territorial borders. The legality of this expanded jurisdiction raised troubling implications for sovereignty issues.[8] European governments and others worldwide appeared to have had similar responses toward information control. France, for example, gave judges the power to order the retrieval of e-mail databases and gave freer access for messages to be decoded. Encryption firms were required to hand over their data to authorities. Police were given the authority to make remote online searches of ISP records. Similarly, Germany authorized its intelligence services to enable unlimited police access to internet records of suspicious individuals. Great Britain eased barriers for the police to monitor financial transactions and private e-mail online by dispensing with the prior approval of judges. Italy, India, and Denmark, similarly relaxed the rules for internet surveillance and greatly increased the powers of the police and security officials, with specific legislation such as India's Prevention of Terrorism Ordinance.[9]

---

5   BBC News, 12 May 2003, 09:18:04 GMT.

6   AP News, 14 May 2003, 10:09 PM ET.

7   Mike M. Ahlers, 'Nuke Agency Takes Website Offline', CNN.com, 25 October 2004, <http://www.cnn.com/2004/US/10/25/terror.nrc/index.html>, accessed 20 March 2007.

8   John Hines, 'Jurisdiction: Should Nations extend their legal reach beyond their borders?' no date, <http://www.isoc.org/pubpolpillar/juris.shtml>, accessed 20 March 2007.

9   Minwalla, Shabnam, 'Net Policing Comes to India', *Times News Network*, 1 August 2003, 12:51:07 AM.

The range and degree of state controls and censorship has varied based on the openness of the societies, as well as the specific threat environment in which the controls were imposed. China, for example, has routinely interfered with public access to western news sites, such as the *New York Times* and the BBC. Since almost all of internet access is through one conduit ChinaNet operated by the state Telecomm agency, it is easier to block traffic. In its pursuit of its conflicting aims to economic integration with the freer West from a closed and centrally planned economy, China has tried to balance access with control. The introduction of Google and other search engines has, however, posed problems for an administration concerned about public access to subversive information as well as a public whose information sources cannot be controlled. The government decided that this posed a new kind of threat prompting blockage of the search engines.[10]

Since it was established in 1988, the European Telecommunications Standards Institute (ETSI) leader has been a principal in setting security standards. As nations acknowledged their increasing dependence on technology infrastructures, Critical Information Infrastructure Protection (CIIP) became an important component of national security policy in many countries. The measures developed to combat cybercrime and protect information infrastructures included procedures for evaluating threats and vulnerabilities and anticipating, responding to, and recovering from cyber attacks. Cooperation between states and the private sector revolved around sharing of information. An interesting development is the acknowledgement by private industry that government intervention is necessary to encourage the technology companies to focus on security solutions. This change in attitude reflects an awareness that market forces cannot be the sole driver of industry improvements. Government incentives and policies were especially important for securing infrastructure networks that ensured the operation of essential services like water and electricity.

Greater emphasis is being placed on the need for developing a global culture of cybersecurity in response to the recognition that network security undertaken in advanced societies to ensure economic survival has to be counterbalanced by an even more fundamental need to ensure that the global information society will continue to operate for the benefit of developing economies as well.

References

Ahlers, Mike M., 'Nuke Agency Takes Website Offline', *CNN.com*, 25 October 2004, <http://www.cnn.com/2004/US/10/25/terror.nrc/index.html>, accessed 20 March 2007.

Beck, Ulrich, *Risk Society* (London: Sage Publications, 1992).

Carr, Edward Hallett, *The Twenty Years' Crisis, 1919–1939: An Introduction to the Study of International Relations* (London: Macmillan, 1939, 1964).

Deutsch, Karl et al., *Political Community and the North Atlantic Area* (Princeton: Princeton University Press, 1957).

---

10 Peter S. Goodman and Mike Musgrove, 'China Blocks Web Search Engines', *Washington Post*, 12 September 2002, p. E01.

Gilpin, Robert, *War and Change in World Politics* (Cambridge: Cambridge University Press, 1981).

Goodman, Peter S. and Mike Musgrove, 'China Blocks Web Search Engines', *Washington Post*, 12 September 2002, p. E01.

Haas, Ernst B., *The Uniting of Europe: Political, Social, and Economic Forces, 1950–1957* (Stanford: Stanford University Press, 1958).

Hines, John, 'Jurisdiction: Should Nations Extend Their Legal Reach Beyond Their Borders?' no date, <http://www.isoc.org/pubpolpillar/juris.shtml>, last accessed 20 March 2007.

Kennan, George, *Realities of American Foreign Policy* (New York: W.W. Norton and Company, 1966).

Minwalla, Shabnam, 'Net Policing Comes to India', *Times News Network*, 1 August 2003, 12:51:07 AM.

Mitrany, David, *A Working Peace System* (Chicago: Quadrangle, 1966).

Morgenthau, Hans J., *Politics Among Nations: The Struggle for Power and Peace* (New York: Alfred A. Knopf, 1948, 1985).

Chapter 1

Introduction: Information, Power, and Security – An Outline of Debates and Implications

Myriam Dunn Cavelty and Elgin M. Brunner

> Governments of the Industrial World, you weary giants of flesh and steel, I come from Cyberspace, the new home of Mind. On behalf of the future, I ask you of the past to leave us alone. You are not welcome among us. You have no sovereignty where we gather.
>
> John Perry Barlow, *A Declaration of the Independence of Cyberspace*, 1996

John Perry Barlow's utopian manifesto of an independent cyberspace envisages a world in which governments hold little if any power over the people, in which new information and communication technologies (ICT) allow a free market to thrive without government intervention, and where communities are bound by common beliefs and values rather than geographical location. Technology changes everything, so the credo goes. And the 'new' information technologies change things very rapidly and fundamentally, so that society is undergoing an enormous structural change, a revolution from an industrial society to a 'super-industrial society'. As futurist Alvin Toffler put it, humankind has passed through the first wave of the agricultural revolution and the second wave of the industrial revolution, and is now in the midst of a third wave of turmoil, where technology drives an information society free from traditional economic, political, and cultural constraints.[1] Thus, according to Toffler, 'the political technology of the Industrial Age is no longer appropriate technology for the new civilization taking form around us. Our politics are obsolete.'[2]

Indeed, who has not often felt that technology is fundamentally changing our way of life? Who can escape the 'suggestive power of virtual technologies'?[3] We are reminded almost constantly that we live in the information age – we communicate through the internet, we use mobile phones, we get immediate worldwide news, we download music and movies, we buy merchandise online, and we reserve plane tickets and book hotel rooms on the web. And it is not only as individuals that we feel the impact of this development daily: Entire segments of public life,

---

1 Alvin Toffler, *Third Wave* (New York, 1980).
2 Alvin Toffler, 'Introduction', in Clement Bezold (ed.), *Anticipatory Democracy* (New York, 1978), pp. xiv–xv.
3 Term used by Paul Virilio, 'Speed and Information: Cyberspace Alarm!', *Ctheory*, 18 March 1995.

including such diverse sectors as culture, business, entertainment, and research, have been revolutionised by the new technology. The marriage of computers and telecommunications, the integration of these technologies into a multimedia system of communication that has global reach, and the fact that they are available worldwide at low cost seem to be bringing about a fundamental transformation in the way humans communicate and interact.

But however much consensus there may be on the growing importance of ICT today, agreement is far more elusive when it comes to pinning down the impact of this development on security or other issues. In this introduction, we therefore aim to broadly discuss the 'information revolution' in relation to security matters. In particular, we want to outline the current debates and the possible implications of current developments. This undertaking is complicated by the fact that the 'information revolution' is a very fuzzy concept: Many different parties currently use the term for many different facets of an elusive phenomenon, leaving the researcher with a confusing diversity of usually poorly defined concepts. A clarification of terms and concepts is thus much needed, but so is a discussion of possible consequences.

What Information Revolution?

Undoubtedly, the information revolution is closely linked to the relatively recent technological development in information processing and communication technologies and to the rapid global dispersion of these technologies – most significantly, to the ascent of 'the internet', a global decentralised communication network of computer networks. For many observers, it is the most popular and most amazing manifestation of ICT, and it enjoys a phenomenal growth rate. In only very few years, it has become the bloodstream of the information revolution.

The internet's success story is truly dazzling: not only has it transformed the way business is done and how people interact, but it has also given rise to new socio-cultural patterns such as hacker communities. It has given birth to new forms of art, stimulating the imagination of designers, writers, and the movie industry. Overall, the internet has come to be an essential part of many lives and a source of inspiration. It creates a new dimension, a detached place that has come to be called 'cyberspace', a term that stands for the fusion of all communication networks, databases, and sources of information into a huge, tangled, and diverse blanket of electronic interchange; this global fusion of networks creates a 'network ecosystem', a place that is not part of the normal, physical world: it is 'virtual', or in other words:

> Cyberspace is a bioelectronic environment that is literally universal, it exists everywhere there are telephone wires, coaxial cables, fiber–optic lines or electromagnetic waves. This environment is inhabited by knowledge, existing in electronic form.[4]

---

4 John Arquilla and David F. Ronfeldt, 'Cyberwar is Coming!', in John Arquilla and David F. Ronfeldt (eds), *In Athena's Camp: Preparing for Conflict in the Information Age* (Santa Monica, 1997), p. 41.

There can be no doubt that the recent technological development has been an indispensable trigger for change. The decreasing costs and increasing performing power of computers 'have led to the application of information technologies (IT) in virtually all corners of society'.[5] In other words, with the advent of the internet, there has been a vast increase in speed, capacity, and flexibility in the collection, production, and dissemination of information. This technologically deterministic approach, which, according to the major theorist of information society, Frank Webster, is only one among five possible analytical definitions of this 'revolution',[6] emphasises the most commonly accepted feature of this current period.

Nevertheless, neither the breakthroughs in information technologies nor their ubiquitous application can *per se* be considered a revolution. In fact, it is questionable whether we are experiencing any revolution at all. The term 'revolution' usually designates a sudden, radical, or complete change.[7] Indeed, in subjective perception, the changes and developments all around us may seem rapid enough to be called sudden, radical, or fundamental. A closer look, however, reveals transformations that are less sudden, violent, and fast. From this perspective, the alleged 'revolution' instead resembles a gradual process with neither a clear beginning nor a foreseeable end, making the applicability of the term 'revolution' in the narrower sense somewhat questionable. The term 'evolution' would seem much more appropriate: it better describes the gradual adjustment and the non-linearity of the development. Nevertheless, in the context of scientific-technical transformation, the term 'revolution' has been used less strictly:[8] its definitions also include concepts that can be applied to our case, for example understood as a 'fundamental change in the way of thinking about or visualizing something: a change of theorems', or, even more aptly, as a 'changeover in use or preference especially in technology'.[9]

Be it a revolution or an evolution, in order to arrive at a meaningful analysis of the consequences, it is crucial to take into account that technology is not an abstract, exogenous variable, but is rather inherently endogenous to politics.[10] Computer networks and the communications they carry are produced by people, and people live in physical space, under the rule of law. This embeddedness means that ICT and people can only be fully examined from an overarching perspective that encompasses

---

5 Ibid., p. 52.

6 Frank Webster, 'What Information Society?', in Daniel S. Papp and David Alberts (eds), *The Information Age: An Anthology on its Impact and Consequences, Vol. I* (Washington, 1997), pp. 51–71. The others are economic, occupational, spatial, and cultural.

7 Definition as given by Merriam-Webster's Collegiate Dictionary.

8 For example the 'Agricultural Revolution', 'The Industrial Revolution', or 'The Long Revolution' that took place from 1800–1945. Mitchell M. Waldrop, 'Is There an Information Revolution?', in Ryan Henry and Edward Peartree (eds), *The Information Revolution and International Security* (Washington, 1998), pp. 1–9.

9 Definition as given by Merriam-Webster's Collegiate Dictionary.

10 Daniel Chandler, 'Technological or Media Determinism' (1995), <http://www.aber.ac.uk/media/Documents/tecdet/tdet02.html>; Geoffrey Herrera, 'Technology and International Systems', *Millennium*, 32/3 (2003): 559–94; Donald Mackenzie and J. Wajcman (eds), *The Social Shaping of Technology: How the Refrigerator Got its Hum* (Buckingham, 1994), reprint.

an understanding of the social, economic, political, and technical dimensions. Or, as one author in this volume aptly puts it: '[T]he political implications emerge when physical objects fuse with human rules and institutions.'[11] Hence, for the purposes of this volume, we define the information revolution as a phenomenon whose consequences are unfolding in a space already shaped by thousands of other influences, such as institutions, traditions, cultures, etc., even though it was initiated by the recent technological development in information technologies, leading to the application of these technologies in 'all corners of society'.

The range of stakeholders and issues potentially affected by the information revolution is exceptionally wide, encompassing individual human beings as well as nation-states and the international system at large. The focus of this book will mainly be on the nation-state as the fundamental unit and building block of the international system, even though cyber-security is a multi-dimensional and multi-disciplinary public policy issue area, not to mention multi-stakeholder participation in policy initiatives.[12] The reason for this is that we are primarily interested in the role of the state in securing the information age. However, we do not and cannot focus on all states; the reason being that 'the multiple imbalances that characterise the diffusion of novel information and communication technologies [...] along income, gender, age and many other socioeconomic categories',[13] commonly discussed under the heading of the 'digital divide', have created a world of haves and have-nots when it comes to the information revolution. In other words, there is a considerable disparity between rich societies and low-income countries in terms of access to ICT. In fact, this digital divide also has concrete implications for security matters, which we will address further below. When we develop our arguments about the potential consequences of the information revolution for security in this volume, it is important to be conscious of the fact that most of the debate only applies to high-income states. Through its selection of authors, topics, and approaches, the collection at hand perpetuates the Western views on ICT and information age security, which are in some cased not relevant to the developing countries.

What Consequences?

Having defined the phenomenon and discussed the usefulness of various definitions, we will now move on the consequences. How, then, does the information revolution relate to and affect the state and the international system more generally? Various arguments are advanced in the literature: the transnational architecture of the global information network has made territorial borders less significant; the application of information technologies to both the military and the civilian realm leads to a blurring

---

11 Geoffrey Herrera in this volume.

12 Milton Mueller, *Ruling the Root: Internet Governance and the Taming of Cyberspace* (Cambridge, 2003); William J. Drake, *Reforming Internet Governance. Perspectives from the Working Group on Internet Governance (WGIG)* (New York, 2005); D. MacLean (ed.), *Internet Governance: A Grand Collaboration* (New York, 2004).

13 Dieter Zinnbauer, 'Internet, Civil Society and Global Governance: The Neglected Political Dimension of the Digital Divide', *Information & Security*, 7 (2001), p. 45.

of boundaries between the political, military, and civilian spheres; as a consequence of the empowerment of an ever growing number of actors with information, the distribution of power has become increasingly volatile and complex not only among states as parts of the international system, but also with regard to private businesses and politicians, as well as transnational and non-governmental entities.[14]

'Cyber-libertarians' like John Perry Barlow tout the information revolution as a technological leap forward that will inevitably and irrevocably transform all aspects of life.[15] However, this view met with resistance almost as soon as it made its appearance. More sceptical observers point to the limited economic and social impact of information technologies and argue, as we have above, that the process of change is more evolutionary than revolutionary. They point to the superficial impact of ICT in enhancing productivity or transforming industrial economies; they also warn against adopting a technological deterministic approach to the changing nature of society and politics.[16] Those who enthusiastically preach the many advantages of the 'Information Age' and who see a broad array of new options opening up thus find themselves opposed by others who give more emphasis to major threats and substantial dangers arising as a consequence of the application of the new ICT to the whole spectrum of society. In between these two extremes, there are others who regard the new developments both as an opportunity and as a risk.

Cyber-enthusiasts and the Positive Consequences of the Information Revolution

Cyber-enthusiasts concentrate on the growing opportunities that the worldwide application of the new information and communication technologies has opened for all societal actors – individual, economic, political, and cultural – and emphasise that access to all sorts of information, and the ability to diffuse it broadly, leads to an empowerment of these societal actors vis-à-vis the state. At the same time, they believe that the applications of the very same technological developments have the potential to enhance the efficiency of government agencies and help to establish closer cooperation between the state and society.

In connection with the concept of the 'information society', many information age theorists and politicians claim that the internet has a democratising effect.[17]

---

14 Daniel S. Papp and David Alberts, 'The Impacts of the Information Age on International Actors and the International System', in Papp and Alberts (eds), *The Information Age: An Anthology of its Impacts and Consequences*, pp. 285–96.

15 Alvin Toffler and Heidi Toffler, *War and Anti–War* (New York, 1993). Nicolas Negroponte's *Being Digital* and George Gilder's *Microcosm* are especially vivid examples.

16 Rob Kitchin, *Cyberspace: The World in the Wires* (Chichester, 1998); Robert O. Keohane and Joseph S. Nye, 'Power and Interdependence in the Information Age', *Foreign Affairs* 77/5 (1998): 81–94.

17 See for example Brian D. Loader, 'The Governance of Cyberspace: Politics, Technology, and Global Restructuring', in Brian D. Loader (ed.), *The Governance of Cyberspace* (London/ New York, 1997), pp. 1–19; Alinta Thornton, *Does Internet Create Democracy?*, Master Thesis, University of Technology (Sydney, 1996), <http://www.wr.com.au/democracy/index.html>; William H. Dutton (ed.), *Society on the Line: Information Politics in the Digital Age* (Oxford, 1999), pp. 174–201.

These thoughts have also triggered a debate over 'teledemocracy' and the use of the internet to support increased civic participation in the democratic process.[18] Scholars usually maintain that the internet may suppress democracy as well as promote it, depending on many determining factors: future development, attractiveness, accessibility, availability, regulation of ICT, the unhindered flow of information, and human behaviour, which is a very important variable.[19] However, the overly euphoric prophets of the internet's many virtues again seem to forget that it is entirely shaped by human beings, and by itself is no more than a vessel, or a means of distributing content. The internet will never be able to change human basic psychology, and thus, the human factor remains the most challenging, uncertain, and most important part of the equation.

Among the advocates of the 'Information Age', we also find those who tout the opportunities of the information technology for the military. Those who stress the importance of the current Revolution in Military Affairs (RMA), which is due to the application of the recent technological developments to the whole range of weapons systems, information-gathering, communication, and surveillance, regard the global information environment as having become a '*battlespace* in which [...] technology is used to deliver critical and influential content in order to shape perceptions, manage opinions, and control behaviour.'[20] Under such a paradigm, due to the hallmarks of the information revolution, such as the transparency of events and the global immediacy of coverage, the concepts of information warfare and information operations play an increasingly important role to the extent that, for some, 'the most – perhaps only – effective weapon in this battlespace is information.'[21] In proclaiming all these supposedly positive implications of the emerging 'Information Age', many scholars (predominantly from the US) rely on the assumption that 'fortunately, the information revolution strengthens our hand'.[22]

Cyber-pessimists and the Negative Consequences of the Information Revolution

The other side emphasises the 'negative' implications of the so-called information revolution by indicating the multiple dangers and major threats that arise from the application of the new technologies to the entire spectrum of societal activity. The dangers and threats originate from varying sources, depending on one's perspective and the subject matter that is considered to be at risk. While some futurists expect a blending of technology and culture that not only threatens identity, but leads to the migration of entire societal strata of the information society towards the so-called

---

18 Edward Schwartz, *NetActivism: How Citizens Use the Internet* (Sebastopol, 1996).

19 Andrew L. Shapiro, 'Think Again: The internet', *Foreign Policy*, Summer (1999), pp. 14–27; The Benton Foundation, 'Telecommunications and Democracy, in Papp and Alberts, *The Information Age: An Anthology on its Impact and Consequences*, pp. 167–80.

20 Dan Kuehl, 'Foreword', in Edwin L. Armistead (ed.), *Information Operations: The Hard Reality of Soft Power* (Washington, 2002), p. 4 (Emphasis ours).

21 Ibid.

22 Joseph S. Nye, 'Foreword', in Henry and Peartree (eds), *The Information Revolution and International Security*, p. ix.

'infosphere',[23] others more cautiously warn that the internet is not an inherently democratising factor[24] or that the whole revolutionary undertaking could become a 'control revolution'.[25] While David Shenk, for example, warns that 'information overload threatens our ability to educate ourselves, and leaves us more vulnerable as consumers and less cohesive as society,'[26] David Rothkopf points to the potentially disastrous consequences of disinformation practices in an economically globalised world.[27]

Others emphasise that the smooth, reliable, and continuous operation of key sectors of modern society, including those vital to national security and the essential functioning of industrialised economies, depends on a range of highly interdependent national and international software-based control systems. Vulnerabilities in these infrastructures are believed to be on the rise due to increasingly complex interdependencies. In addition, the overall capability of malicious actors to do harm is seen to be enhanced by inexpensive, ever more sophisticated, rapidly proliferating, and easy-to-use tools in cyberspace.[28]

Warnings are frequently sounded concerning the consequences of applying the new information and communication technologies to the military realm: Experts generally reject the notion that information warfare is less violent than conventional conflicts, a dangerous misperception that is compounded by a blurring of the boundaries between the civilian and the military realms, with important implications for international humanitarian law. On the one hand, Michael Ignatieff, for example, points out that the supposedly surgical strikes of information warfare are not *a priori* less bloody than conventional operations, but that the 'bloodiness' of a war depends on the perspective; e.g., Kosovo was the first war with no fatalities for the West due to its technological omnipotence and risk-averse political culture; nevertheless, the 'technological superiority is [...] not a guarantee of national security and there is no reason to believe that zero-casualty, zero-risk, zero-defect warfare will actually result in a safer world, or even a world safer just for Americans. Virtual war, therefore, is a dangerous illusion.'[29] On the other hand, certain observers identify important tendencies towards convergence between military and the civil technologies, leading to the militarisation of society at large and turning every conflict into information warfare and, as a consequence thereof, point to the 'sham humanitarian nature of information weapons'.[30] Charles Dunlap points to the need for both state leaders and soldiers to recognise the potential of modern technology. More important, he argues,

---

23 Michael Vlahos, 'Entering the Infosphere', *Journal of International Affairs*, 51/2 (1998): 497–525.

24 Andrew L. Shapiro, 'Think Again: The Internet'.

25 Andrew L. Shapiro, *The Control Revolution* (New York, 1999).

26 David Shenk, *DATA SMOG: Surviving the Information Glut* (New York, 1997), p. 15.

27 David J. Rothkopf, 'The Disinformation Age', *Foreign Policy*, 114/Spring (1999): 82–96.

28 David Mussington, *Concepts for Enhancing Critical Infrastructure Protection: Relating Y2K to CIP Research and Development* (Santa Monica, 2002).

29 Michael Ignatieff, *Virtual War. Kosovo and Beyond* (London, 2000), p. 212.

30 A. Krutskikh, 'Information Challenges to Security', *International Affairs*, 45/2 (1999), p. 32.

is the realisation that such technology 'will never substitute for answering the kind of 'hard questions' of law, ethics, and policy that will continue to re-complicate moral life on the 21st century battlefields.'[31]

Information as a Resource of Power

A common feature of most of the literature on the information revolution, and of many of the points made above, is the particular belief that in the 'information age', information is becoming the major resource of power. The famous notion of 'soft power', for example, rests on the contention that 'power is passing from the capital-rich to the information-rich.'[32] This conception of power is founded largely on the classical economic reasoning that, in an era of increasing economic interdependence and ever-increasing market liberalisation, the party with an informational advantage (both as a consumer and as a producer) is in a better position to generate profit – which can be transformed into whatever 'commodity' is deemed most appropriate for consolidating power – at the expense of, and relative to, competitors. Consequently, such reasoning implies that 'the one country that can best lead the information revolution will be more powerful than any other.'[33] However, it is of course also worth considering that this very country may also, as a consequence of its 'Information Edge', become increasingly vulnerable to asymmetric and – in the broadest sense – IT-induced challenges.

Others, such as Jeffrey Hart and Singbae Kim,[34] analyse the information revolution as part of a perpetual technological development and, therefore, identify a recently increasing linkage between technological power and informational power, which they call 'technoledge'. This, they argue, constitutes a qualitative change. This qualitative change could be due to the fact that 'information everywhere is seen and used as a state's strategic resource' on the one hand, while, simultaneously, information is increasingly becoming an object of mass consumption in all countries.[35]

One of the core arguments in the literature on the information revolution, intertwined with the argument about information as a resource of power (or even as the resource of power *par excellence*), is that the technological development enhances two trends that diminish the importance of the state, both of which have implications for security: increasing internationalisation and increasing privatisation. It is evident that both tendencies have security implications for the state and its powers. Two central conflicts reveal the nature of the ongoing redistribution of power: first, the notion that the information revolution empowers new forms of international actors,

---

31 Charles J. Dunlap Jr., *Technology and the 21st Century Battlefield: Recomplicating Moral Life for the Statesman and the Soldier* (Honolulu, 1999), p. 34.

32 Joseph Nye, 'Soft Power', *Foreign Policy*, 80 (1990): 153–71.

33 Joseph S. Nye and William A. Owens, 'America's Information Edge', *Foreign Affairs*, March/April (1996), p. 20.

34 Jeffrey A. Hart and Kim Sangbae, 'Power in the Information Age', in Jose V. Ciprut (ed.), *Of Fears and Foes: Security and Insecurity in an Evolving Global Political Economy* (Westport, 2000).

35 A. Chernov, 'Global Information Society', *International Affairs*, 006 (2004), p. 27.

such as NGOs and activists, thus challenging the state's status as the major player in the international system; and second, the idea that the emergence of a global electronic marketplace would inevitably imply a collapse of the state's economic pillar of power as companies increasingly become global citizens and economic boundaries no longer correspond to political ones. Both of these trends have particular implications for nation-states' room for manoeuvre when it comes to security.[36]

Whether or not the information revolution presents a challenge to the function and status of the state as a prime actor is one of the most extensively discussed topics among information revolution scholars. The most extreme view is that 'global villages' and non-territorial actors will make the nation state obsolete altogether.[37] Even though such radical changes are implausible in the short term, the state's primacy as the central actor in international affairs is indeed being challenged by ICT: it experiences difficulties in retaining its role as provider of security and economic well-being to the public, thus jeopardizing two of the state's main duties. For example, states face difficulties in providing substantial security against the threats of information warfare and 'cyber-terrorism', and since economic activity is increasingly being conducted beyond the confines of individual states, their ability to secure and control it is being further reduced. Because of ICT, international actors not restricted by geography, such as multinational corporations (MNCs) and some non-governmental organisations (NGOs), are increasingly able to act internationally with little regard for the demands of individual states.[38] Demands for transparency in the political process force governments and state-like organisations to provide information in an easily accessible format, causing states and their institutions to lose their traditional monopoly on information.

Furthermore, because economic relations between states, as well as a shift towards the service sector in most developed countries, seem to have such a significant effect on the current conduct of international relations, the changing economic substructure becomes exceedingly important for considerations of change in the operating environment. The importance of knowledge and information as a source of wealth has led to the idea that the future might belong to 'virtual states' that have little military power and natural resources, and hardly any agriculture or manufacturing sectors, but are highly skilled in using managerial, financial, and creative tools to manage assets in foreign countries.[39]

In accordance with this view, interstate violence is likely to decline, mainly because the information revolution knits countries closely together, but also because

---

36 David J. Rothkopf, 'Cyberpolitik: The Changing Nature of Power in the Information Age', *Journal of International Affairs*, 51/2 (1998): 321–56.

37 See so-called modernist or 'prophetic' writings, Peter F. Drucker, *The New Realities: In Government and Politics, in Economics and Business, in Society and World View* (New York, 1989); and Alvin and Heidi Toffler publications.

38 Papp and Alberts, 'The Impacts of the Information Age on International Actors and the International System'; Brian Nichiporuk and Carl H. Builder, 'Societal Implications', in Arquilla and Ronfeldt, *In Athena's Camp: Preparing for Conflict in the Information Age*, pp. 295–314.

39 Richard Rosecrance, *The Rise of the Virtual State: Wealth and Power in the Coming Century* (New York, 1999), p. 4.

traditional conquest using military hard power seems incongruous in such an environment; armies can only seize real estate, which does not confer knowledge or capital and is basically worthless to the virtual state.[40] The most remarkable aspect of this idea is the notion that ultimately, these entities will compete for information resources: developed nations will no longer struggle for political dominance, but for their share of global information output. These states do not need or desire additional territory, because their skilled workforce, capital, and information trump the traditional territorial factor.[41] However, this view clearly fails to address new threats that arise from increased dependence on ICT and the increased vulnerabilities that can be exploited by other actors. New dimensions of mercantile and economic conflict, concerning, for example, intellectual property issues, will become more and more important in the future. An arsenal for 'information warfare' would constitute an excellent tool at any level of conflict, particularly between 'virtual states', which we will discuss in the following.

Information, Power, and the Implications for Security

More specifically, the information revolution has dramatically increased the importance of information in the strategic world, alongside existing traditional physical military capabilities, and the information domain has moved to centre stage in combat operations. This has given rise to new forms of warfare. Many aspects of modern wars are shaped by new doctrines for conducting so-called 'information operations', with substantial implications for military affairs, politics, and society as a whole.[42] This military doctrine contains the candid announcement of the intention to exploit information operations as a tool for international politics detached from military battlefield operations – e.g., to conduct computer espionage and computer sabotage as well as 'truth projection' over electronic mass media at all times. In addition, information operations concepts are directed at civilian targets at the physical, psychological, and virtual levels.[43]

This change in the scope and space of warfare brings new challenges for the protection of society. The development towards wilful integration of civil infrastructure and stronger shift towards the deception of entire societies is alarming. Scenarios for future warfare assume that combat will no longer be an act of last resort; because of the low likelihood of incurring combat casualties, the reduced cost of engaging in conflict, and the anonymity enjoyed by the actual combatants

---

40 Ibid., pp. 15–18.

41 Ibid.

42 Joint Chiefs of Staff, JP 3–13, Joint Doctrine for Information Operations (Washington, 2006); Donald H. Rumsfeld, (Original Signed), *Information Operations Roadmap* (30 October 2003), <http://www.gwu.edu/~nsarchiv/NSAEBB/NSAEBB177/info_ops_roadmap.pdf>; Headquarters, Department of the Army, *Field Manual No. 3–13, Information Operations: Doctrine, Tactics, Techniques, and Procedures* (2003).

43 Chris Hables Gray, 'Perpetual Revolution in Military Affairs, International Security, and Information', in Robert Latham (ed.), *Bombs and Bandwidth: The Emerging Relationship Between Information Technology and Security* (New York, 2003), pp. 199–212.

in delivering strikes, it becomes much easier to commit acts of war. The expansion of the battlefield to include human perception and the 'virtual space' threatens to result in even more civilian involvement in conflicts. This is likely to be reinforced by the dual-use nature of most targets in the information infrastructure as well as the dual-use character of new weapons and information tools used in information operations.[44]

Information operation concepts enhance the focus of security policy on the vulnerability of civil infrastructures, and thus ultimately raise an array of questions about the nature, scale, and management of future international conflicts. The information infrastructure – the complex combination of computer networks and communications systems that serve as the underlying infrastructure for organisations, industries, and the economy – has become a key asset in today's security environment.[45] All critical infrastructures are increasingly dependent on the information infrastructure for a variety of information management, communications, and control functions. This dependence has a strong national-security component, since information infrastructure enables both economic vitality and military and civilian government operations. In particular, the information infrastructures of the government and the military depend on commercial telecommunications providers for everything from logistics and transport to various other functions.[46] Current trends, such as the opening and liberalisation of markets, globalisation processes that stimulate the cross-national interconnection of infrastructures, and widespread access to telecommunications networks, are heightening the security requirements of the infrastructures in countries across the entire world.

In addition, there are also dangers arising from society's dependence on information and communication technology systems. For one thing, many of the networks and systems were built piecemeal by many different people and organisations using a wide assortment of information technologies, and with a wide range of functionalities in mind. Very few have been designed or implemented with assurance or security as primary considerations.[47] There is also a historic lesson to be learned: It is a recurring phenomenon that the conveniences of a new technology are embraced long before its unwanted side-effects are systematically dealt with. The resulting 'convenience overshoot' may last for decades.[48] Today, this approach might just be a trifle too dangerous: Too much depends on the smooth, reliable, and continuous operation of the CII. Furthermore, on the technical level, security

---

44 Edwin L. Armistead (ed.), *Information Operations: The Hard Reality of Soft Power* (Washington, 2004).

45 Computer Science and Telecommunications Board, National Research Council, *Trust in Cyber-space* (Washington, 1999).

46 Stewart D. Personick and Cynthia A. Patterson (eds), *Critical Information Infrastructure Protection and the Law: An Overview of Key Issues* (Washington, 2003), p. 1.

47 Seymour E. Goodman, 'The Protection and Defense of Critical Information Infrastructures', paper presented at the 43rd Annual IISS Conference, *The Strategic Implications of the New Economy* (Geneva, 2001), pp. 3–4.

48 Examples are: The introduction of the Ford Model T in 1909 and the widespread use of seat belts; the 70–year delay between the introduction of steam locomotives and the first use of pneumatic brakes.

will hardly evolve naturally or be generated by the forces of the free market alone, because there are substantial obstacles to IT security: there is no direct return on investment, time-to-market impedes extensive security measures, and security mechanisms often have a negative impact on usability.[49] In his book on 'Normal Accidents', Charles Perrow argues that in an interactively complex system, two or more discrete failures can interact in unexpected ways, thereby affecting supposedly redundant sub-systems. A sufficiently complex system should in fact be *expected* to have many such unanticipated failure mode interactions, making accidents inevitable, even without external triggers.[50] Even as our knowledge and competence as regards system reliability increases, demands for new functionality will likewise increase, further increasing system complexity. An inevitable 'ingenuity gap' arises.[51]

In addition, states will have to address potential threats to security that will likely emerge as a result of an unequal distribution of soft power. Countries, regions, and various groups already suffering economic hardship and political and cultural alienation are unlikely to feel the benefits of information technology easily.[52] Thus, while developed states may be tempted to exploit the opportunities afforded to them by information technologies in order to gain advantages over their rivals, they will have to weigh this against the cost of ignoring their vulnerability to asymmetrical threats. A reduction of security risks will not only entail increased multilateral cooperation, but also increased engagement with non-state actors – most notably those in the private sector who own information systems – and with people, states, and regions that already feel marginalised.

Structure of the Book

Considering all this, we still are left with an exceptionally broad field of enquiry because of the all-embracing omnipresence of ICT. When we look at the consequences of the information revolution for states and the international system in this volume, we particularly focus on the aspects of security. We are certainly aware of the fact that the concept of security is not easily defined in a manner satisfactory to a wide array of stakeholders.[53] But we do not want to delve into the

---

49 Michael Näf, 'Ubiquitous Insecurity? How to "Hack" IT Systems', *Information & Security: An International Journal* 7 (2001): 104–18.

50 Charles Perrow, *Normal Accidents: Living with High-Risk Technologies* (New York, 1984).

51 An ingenuity gap is a shortfall between rapidly rising need of complex societies for initiative and innovation and the inadequate supply of it. See Thomas Homer-Dixon, *The Ingenuity Gap* (New York, 2000), p. 1.

52 Andreas Wenger, 'Editorial: The Internet and the Changing Face of International Relations and Security', *Information & Security: An International Journal*, 7 (2001), pp. 7–8.

53 The term and concept of security has been discussed by a great many scholars. Examples of this debate include: Barry Buzan, *People, States and Fear. An Agenda for International Security Studies in the Post–Cold War Era* (Harlow, 1991); David Baldwin, 'Security Studies and the End of the Cold War', *World Politics*, 48/1 (1995): 117–41; Stephen Walt, 'The Renaissance of Security Studies', *International Studies Quarterly*, 35 (1991):

discussion on the delimitation of 'security issues' here, and are even less eager to define 'security studies'. In our context, security is closely connected to the new vulnerabilities arising from the application of the information and communication technologies to nearly the whole spectrum of political and societal undertakings. These vulnerabilities may arise *from* the whole range of (newly) empowered actors – the individual, private, corporate, commercial, and political, governmental and intergovernmental, inter- and transnational entities – and apply *to* these very same actors. The new vulnerabilities include the wide array of technological applications on the one hand, and the potentially destabilising societal implications thereof on the other. Obviously, security increases when these diffuse vulnerabilities decrease.

Therefore, the question of whether a new conception of security is needed due to the information revolution is also addressed in one of the chapters in this book. Concerning what Myriam Dunn calls 'information age security', a conceptually dichotomous move has become discernible – namely, a distinction between 'offensive activities such as information warfare, cyber-crime, or cyber-terrorism; and defensive activities such as information assurance or critical information infrastructure protection'. But what is the essence of this change? Do we in fact need completely new conceptions of security due to the information revolution? This volume will caution against hasty suppositions, and like all concepts in use in the information age, the concept of 'information age security' requires careful scrutiny. Therefore, as Dunn and others in this volume argue, it is important to adopt a historical perspective on the continuity of change and technological development and its informational dimensions, so as not to overshoot the mark. Indeed, there have been other information and communication revolutions in earlier times, all of which have significantly shaped history, human activities, and their institutions. What this shows is that the current efforts to grasp the meaning of challenges created by the information age for security should be seen in an appropriate context. Only when we know what it is that sets security in the information age apart from security in other ages can we begin to approach the topic theoretically.

Such efforts inevitably lead us to be cautious about far-reaching assertions concerning the changes supposedly caused by the forces of the information revolution. In accordance with a constructivist mindset, security in the information age is set apart from security in other ages mainly due to aspects that we, or rather, the key political players, perceive and construct as being new. Indeed, the information revolution has not changed the core values of society, nor has it changed the essential nature of security. Nonetheless, the conditions and practices of creating security have changed. This has a direct impact on state practices when it comes to securing efforts. A similar link between the dynamics of the information revolution and constructivist thinking is made in J. P. Singh's chapter. Focusing on the notion of changing power, Singh argues that most traditional concepts of power in political science – be they instrumental, structural, or soft-power notions – describe power in terms of the capacity to do particular things or to prevent others from certain behaviour. This, he argues, is completely opposed to what information technology allows people to do

---

211–39; Keith Krause and Williams, Michael C. (eds), *Critical Security Studies: Concepts and Cases* (Minneapolis, 1997).

and does not reflect any interaction between technology and individuals. Traditional concepts take actor identities and preferences as given. Information technologies, however, when understood as interactive technologies, are about the formation of preferences and identities. Central to this is the concept of 'meta-power', a kind of power that allows the redefining of other relations of power as well as the formation of preferences and identities. As the author argues, 'information networks change the very context – understood here as identities of issues and actors – within which interactions take place.'

Another modality of the power discussion that is central to the information revolution debate is the relation between the common conceptions of cyberspace and of territorial sovereignty. It is usually argued, according to Geoffrey Herrera, that 'territorially bound political authority will have a very difficult time controlling a non-territorial realm.' In this view, cyberspace, as compared to territorial sovereignty, does not relate to any physical place. Herrera challenges this notion. He cites a series of examples, from the allocation of domain names and the physical infrastructure of global information networks themselves to software controls that states have successfully imposed on their own national networks, to show to what extent the common wisdom misunderstands the nature of cyberspace. Herrera observes 'a simultaneous double-move: the territorialisation of cyberspace and the deterritorialisation of state security'.

Especially when the governance mechanisms, actors, and processes available for managing issues in the new security environment are elucidated, major challenges in connection with this deterritorialisation become obvious. Maura Conway's chapter analyses the difficulties of internet governance in the light of terrorists' increasing use of the medium. Both terrorism and the internet are significant global phenomena, reflecting and shaping various aspects of world politics. The political dynamic between these two might even be described as a 'transversal' phenomenon.[54] Detailed descriptions and analysis of the clampdown on terrorists' burgeoning internet presence, undertaken by both state-based and sub-state actors, in the wake of the events of 11 September 2001 in the US and the July 2005 bombings in London, serve to illustrate manifold governance challenges, such as the debates over the role of various actors in the governance process, including national governments and internet service providers; the appropriate legislative response to the terrorist internet presence; and the debate over free speech vs. limits on speech.

In addition, there is a growing understanding that cooperation between the public and private sectors is a key element in making cyberspace more secure. As Manuel Suter's chapter shows, joint action is needed for at least two reasons: first, because firms are often stretched beyond their own limits in coping with incidents and in terms of risk management; second, because it is only by joint action that the numerous interdependencies can be studied adequately. However, joint action between companies is hard to establish, owing to obstacles like business competition or free riding. Thus, because cooperation is essential to cyber-security, states should

---

54 The term 'transversal' was used briefly by Michel Foucault to describe struggles against authority that were not limited to one country.

foster efforts to this end, including private/public collaboration through information-sharing associations.

In conclusion, this volume focuses on the role of the state in defending against cyber-threats and in securing the information age. It is about the state regaining its authority in the field of information technologies, but also about the state adapting to the challenges of the information age. The notion that is most uncritically accepted within the overall information security debate is that state power is eroding due to the effects of information and communication technology and that the state is unable to provide security in the information age. This volume challenges the unidimensionality of this statement. Without denying that new challenges for the state have arisen, all authors in this volume argue that too much credence is often given to the spectre of an erosion of sovereignty.

References

Armistead, Edwin L. (ed.), *Information Operations: The Hard Reality of Soft Power* (Washington: National Defense University, 2004).

Arquilla, John and David F. Ronfeldt, 'Cyberwar is Coming!', in John Arquilla and David F. Ronfeldt (eds), *In Athena's Camp: Preparing for Conflict in the Information Age* (Santa Monica: RAND, 1997), pp. 23–60.

Baldwin, David 'Security Studies and the End of the Cold War', *World Politics* 48/1 (1995): 117–41.

Barlow, John Perry, *A Declaration of the Independence of Cyberspace* (1996), <http://homes.eff.org/~barlow/Declaration-Final.html>, accessed 16 February 2007.

Buzan, Barry, *People, States and Fear. An Agenda for International Security Studies in the Post-Cold War Era* (Harlow: Pearson Longman, 1991).

Chandler, Daniel, 'Technological or Media Determinism' (1995), <http://www.aber.ac.uk/media/Documents/tecdet/tdet02.html>, accessed 16 February 2007.

Chernov, A., 'Global Information Society', *International Affairs*, 6 (2004): 22–8.

Computer Science and Telecommunications Board, National Research Council, *Trust in Cyber-space* (Washington, D.C.: National Academy Press, 1999).

Department of the Army, *Field Manual No. 3-13, Information Operations: Doctrine, Tactics, Techniques, and Procedures* (Washington, D.C.: Department of Defense, 2003).

Drake, William J., *Reforming Internet Governance. Perspectives from the Working Group on Internet Governance (WGIG)* (New York: United Nations ICT Task Force, 2005).

Drucker, Peter F., *The New Realities: In Government and Politics, in Economics and Business, in Society and World View* (New York: Harper Collins Publisher, 1989).

Dunlap, Charles J., Jr., *Technology and the 21st Century Battlefield: Recomplicating Moral Life for the Statesman and the Soldier* (Honolulu: University Press of the Pacific, 1999).

Dutton, William H. (ed.), *Society on the Line: Information Politics in the Digital Age* (Oxford: Oxford University Press, 1999).

Gilder, George, *Microcosm: The Quantum Revolution in Economics And Technology* (New York: Free Press, 1989).

Goodman, Seymour E., 'The Protection and Defense of Critical Information Infrastructures', paper presented at the 43rd Annual IISS Conference, *The Strategic Implications of the New Economy* (Geneva, 2001).

Gray, Chris Hables, 'Perpetual Revolution in Military Affairs, International Security, and Information', in Robert Latham (ed.), *Bombs and Bandwidth: The Emerging Relationship Between Information Technology and Security* (New York: The New Press, 2003), pp. 199–212.

Hart, Jeffrey A. and Kim Sangbae, 'Power in the Information Age', in Jose V. Ciprut (ed.), *Of Fears and Foes: Security and Insecurity in an Evolving Global Political Economy* (Westport: Praeger, 2000).

Herrera, Geoffrey, 'Technology and International Systems', *Millennium*, 32/3 (2003): 559–94.

Homer-Dixon, Thomas, *The Ingenuity Gap* (New York: Knopf, 2000).

Ignatieff, Michael, *Virtual War. Kosovo and Beyond* (London: Chatto & Windus, 2000).

Joint Chiefs of Staff, *JP 3–13, Joint Doctrine for Information Operations* (Washington, D.C.: Department of Defense, 2006).

Keohane, Robert O. and Joseph S. Nye, 'Power and Interdependence in the Information Age', *Foreign Affairs*, 77/5 (1998): 81–94.

Kitchin, Rob, *Cyberspace: The World in the Wires* (Chichester: Wiley and Sons, 1998).

Krause, Keith and Williams, Michael C. (eds), *Critical Security Studies: Concepts and Cases* (Minneapolis, 1997).

Krutskikh, A., 'Information Challenges to Security', *International Affairs*, 45/2 (1999): 29–37.

Kuehl, Dan, 'Foreword', in Edwin L. Armistead (ed.), *Information Operations: The Hard Reality of Soft Power* (Washington, D.C.: Joint Command, Control and Information Warfare School Joint Forces Staff College NDU, 2002).

Loader, Brian D., 'The Governance of Cyberspace: Politics, Technology and Global Restructuring', in Brian D. Loader (ed.), *The Governance of Cyberspace: Politics, Technology and Global Restructuring* (London: Routledge, 1997), pp. 1–19.

Mackenzie, Donald and J. Wajcman (eds), *The Social Shaping of Technology: How the Refrigerator Got its Hum* (Buckingham: Open University Press, 1994), reprint.

MacLean, Don (ed.), *Internet Governance: A Grand Collaboration* (New York: United Nations ICT Task Force, 2004).

Mueller, Milton, *Ruling the Root: Internet Governance and the Taming of Cyberspace* (Cambridge: MIT Press, 2003).

Mussington, David, *Concepts for Enhancing Critical Infrastructure Protection: Relating Y2K to CIP Research and Development* (Santa Monica: RAND, 2002).

Näf, Michael, 'Ubiquitous Insecurity? How to "Hack" IT Systems', *Information & Security: An International Journal*, 7 (2001): 104–18.

Negroponte, Nicholas, *Being Digital* (New York: Alfred A. Knopf, 1995).
Nichiporuk, Brian and Carl H. Builder, 'Societal Implications', in John Arquilla and David Ronfeldt (eds), *In Athena's Camp: Preparing for Conflict in the Information Age* (Santa Monica, RAND: 1997), pp. 295–314.
Nye, Joseph S. and William A. Owens, 'America's Information Edge', *Foreign Affairs* March/April (1996): 20–36.
Nye, Joseph S., 'Foreword', in Ryan Henry and Edward Peartree (eds), *The Information Revolution and International Security* (Washington, D.C.: The CSIS Press, 1998), pp. vii–xiv.
Nye, Joseph, 'Soft Power', *Foreign Policy* 80 (1990): 153–71.
Papp, Daniel S. and David Alberts (eds), *The Information Age: An Anthology of its Impacts and Consequences, Vol. I* (Washington, D.C.: National Defense University Press, 1997).
Papp, Daniel S. and David Alberts, 'The Impacts of the Information Age on International Actors and the International System', in Daniel S. Papp and David Alberts (eds), *The Information Age: An Anthology of its Impacts and Consequences*, Vol. I (Washington, D.C.: National Defense University Press, 1997), pp. 285–296.
Perrow, Charles, *Normal Accidents: Living with High-Risk Technologies* (New York: Basic Books, 1984).
Personick, Stewart D. and Cynthia A. Patterson (eds), *Critical Information Infrastructure Protection and the Law: An Overview of Key Issues* (Washington, D.C.: National Academies Press, 2003).
Rosecrance, Richard, *The Rise of the Virtual State: Wealth and Power in the Coming Century* (New York: Basic Books, 1999).
Rothkopf, David J., 'Cyberpolitik: The Changing Nature of Power in the Information Age.' *Journal of International Affairs*, 51/2 (1998): 331–56.
Rothkopf, David J., 'The Disinformation Age', *Foreign Policy*, 114/Spring (1999): 82–96.
Rumsfeld, Donald H., (Original Signed), *Information Operations Roadmap* (30 October 2003), <http://www.gwu.edu/~nsarchiv/NSAEBB/NSAEBB177/info_ops_roadmap.pdf>, accessed 18 April 2007.
Schwartz, Edward, *NetActivism: How Citizens Use the Internet* (Sebastopol: Songline Studios, 1996).
Shapiro, Andrew L., 'Think Again: The Internet', *Foreign Policy*, Summer (1999): 14–27.
Shapiro, Andrew L., *The Control Revolution* (New York: PublicAffairs™, 1999).
Shenk, David, *DATA SMOG: Surviving the Information Glut* (New York: HarperEdge, 1997).
The Benton Foundation, 'Telecommunications and Democracy', in Daniel S. Papp and David Alberts (eds), *The Information Age: An Anthology on its Impact and Consequences, Vol. I* (Washington: National Defense University Press, 1997), pp. 167–80.
Thornton, Alinta, *Does Internet Create Democracy?*, Master Thesis, University of Technology (Sydney, 1996), <http://www.wr.com.au/democracy/index.html>, accessed 16 February 2007.

Toffler, Alvin and Heidi Toffler, *War and Anti–War* (New York: Warner Books, 1993).

Toffler, Alvin, 'Introduction', in Clement Bezold (ed.), *Anticipatory Democracy* (New York: Vintage Books, 1978).

Toffler, Alvin, *Third Wave* (New York: Bantam Books, 1980).

Virilio, Paul, 'Speed and Information: Cyberspace Alarm!', *Ctheory*, 18 March 1995.

Vlahos, Michael, 'Entering the Infosphere', *Journal of International Affairs*, 51/2 (1998): 497–525.

Waldrop, Mitchell M., 'Is There an Information Revolution?', in Ryan Henry and Edward Peartree (eds), *The Information Revolution and International Security* (Washington, D.C.: The CSIS Press, 1998), pp. 1–9.

Walt, Stephen, 'The Renaissance of Security Studies', *International Studies Quarterly*, 35 (1991): 211–39.

Webster, Frank, 'What Information Society?', in Daniel S. Papp and David Alberts (eds), *The Information Age: An Anthology on its Impact and Consequences*, Vol. I (Washington, D.C.: National Defense University Press, 1997), pp. 51–71.

Wenger, Andreas, 'Editorial: The Internet and the Changing Face of International Relations and Security', *Information & Security: An International Journal*, 7 (2001): 5–11.

Zinnbauer, Dieter, 'Internet, Civil Society and Global Governance: the Neglected Political Dimension of the Digital Divide', *Information & Security: An International Journal*, 7 (2001): 45–64.

Chapter 2

Is Anything Ever New? – Exploring the Specificities of Security and Governance in the Information Age

Myriam Dunn Cavelty

Introduction

There is not much doubt among experts that the basic conditions of international relations have changed in the last decade, with the information revolution often being named as one major driver of change.[1] The seeming dominance and prevalence of information in many aspects of modern life has caused this age to be dubbed the 'information age'. Along with 'information society', 'cyber-terrorism', 'cyberspace', 'e-business', etc., 'information revolution' and 'information age' are expressions that only entered our vocabulary a few decades ago[2] but are now commonplace in the press, political speeches, popular books, scholarly journals, and everyday conversations.

It is common knowledge, however, that the significance of information is not unique just to our time, but that it has always been vital to humankind. It is also commonly understood that throughout history, advances in scientific-technical fields have played major roles in changing human affairs recurrently, and that there have been other information and communication revolutions, all of which have significantly shaped history as well as human activities and their institutions.[3] The

---

1 Mark W. Zacher, 'The Decaying Pillars of the Westphalian Temple: Implications for International Order and Governance', in James N. Rosenau and Ernst-Otto Czempiel (eds), *Governance Without Government, Order and Change in World Politics*, Cambridge Studies in International Relations Nr. 20 (Cambridge, 1992), pp. 58–9; Manuel Castells, *The Rise of the Network Society* (Oxford, 1996).

2 Bruce Kushnick, *The Unauthorized Biography of the Baby Bells & Info-Scandal* (New York, 1999).

3 Daniel S. Papp, David S. Alberts, and Alissa Tuyahov, 'Historical Impacts of Information Technologies, An Overview', in David S. Alberts and Daniel S. Papp (eds), *The Information Age, An Anthology of Its Impacts and Consequences* (Washington D.C., 1997); Ronald J. Deibert, 'Exorcismus Theoriae, Pragmatism, Metaphors and the Return of the Medieval in IR Theory', *European Journal of International Relations*, 3/2 (1997): 167–92; Michael E. Hobart and Zachary S. Schiffman, *Information Ages, Literacy, Numeracy, and the Computer Revolution* (Baltimore, 2000); Albert Borgmann, *Holding on to Reality, The Nature of Information at the Turn of the Millennium* (Chicago, 1999).

key issue, therefore, is to identify the defining characteristics and special qualities of the current 'revolution', and in our context, to analyse the implications for national and international security and governance.

The difficulties of studying the information age and its implications for international relations and security are considerable, not least because previous work on the subject is relatively sparse, disorganized, and hardly informed by International Relations theory or other theoretical approaches. In addition, due to the vocabulary of clichés that inhabits the information-age debate, we must strive particularly for conceptual precision to arrive at meaningful analysis. There are three major semantic cornerstones of the information-age vocabulary: 'information', 'cyber-', and 'digital', all of which are so important that they have come to represent the age we live in. The information-age vocabulary is created by simply placing these prefixes before familiar words, thus creating a whole arsenal of new expressions. The nature of these terms is such that their meaning has never been precise – nowadays, however, they have been used so extensively that they can basically mean everything, and thus ultimately nothing. To put it mildly, a 'definition quagmire' has arisen in terms of information-age vocabulary so that it is often difficult to know what one is talking about.[4]

Furthermore, more often than not, technology is seen as an abstract, exogenous variable rather than something that is inherently endogenous to politics.[5] As a result, the majority of scholars fall into the trap of over-interpretation and technological determinism when exploring the characteristics of technology and the implications of the current information revolution.[6] Technological determinism has always been an alluring temptation: The conviction that the world is subject to change and is about to enter into a new phase of history is a near-permanent feature of modern life, mirroring a belief in an unbroken line of constant progress closely linked to technological development.[7] Europeans began the last century optimistically, thinking that the railroad and telegraph had made advanced nations too interdependent to afford armed conflict. By mid-century, it seemed clear that radio, cinema, and the mass media were transforming society as profoundly as steam power and factories had transformed industry in the 1700s.[8] Today, it seems beyond dispute that humankind

---

4 Geoffrey S. French, 'Shunning the Frumious Bandersnatch, Current Literature on Information Warfare and Deterrence', TRC Analysis (The Terrorism Research Center, 2000).

5 Geoffrey Herrera, 'Technology and International Systems', *Millennium*, 32/3 (2003): 559–94; Merritt Roe Smith and Leo Marx (eds), *Does Technology Drive History? The Dilemma of Technological Determinism* (Cambridge, 1994).

6 Cf. Alvin Toffler, *Third Wave* (New York, 1980); Alvin Toffler, *Power Shift* (New York, 1981); Peter F. Drucker, *The New Realities In Government and Politics, in Economics and Business, in Society and World View* (New York, 1989); Nicholas Negroponte, *Being Digital* (New York, 1995).

7 J.G. de Beus, *Shall We Make the Year 2000?* (London, 1985), p. 5.

8 Karl W. Deutsch, 'Mass Communications and the Loss of Freedom in National Decision-Making, A Possible Research Approach to Interstate Conflicts', *Journal of Conflict Resolution*, 1/2 (1957): 200–11.

has progressed from the agricultural age through the industrial age to arrive at the information age.[9]

Next to this feeling of novelty and uniqueness, issues connected to the increasing complexity and rapid rate of change in modern society are often cited to underscore that the information revolution is fundamentally changing modern life. However, complexity and change are not at all new to our times, but were already widely discussed in the 1960s and 1970s.[10] Back then, as now, developments in the technical sphere continually seem to outpace the capacity of individuals and social systems to adapt. Thus, the notion of 'out-of-control' technology and fears of vulnerabilities due to dependency on technology are recurring themes in political and philosophical thought.[11]

What this shows us is that the current efforts to grasp the meaning of challenges to security created by the information age should be seen in an appropriate context, so that prevalent feelings and assumptions may turn into informed understanding of causes and effects of the latest technological and policy developments. In this paper, we endeavour to identify and describe what it is that sets security in the information age apart from security in other ages, and explore how to best approach the topic theoretically. This will help us to understand key characteristics of the information age and show possible solutions for overcoming the challenges states are faced with today.

The Information Infrastructure as Society's Achilles Heel

In order to theorise about security in the information age, we need to come to a conclusion as to what is essentially new – and also, and more difficult, concerning what has fundamentally changed due to these novel foundations. It is clear that the scope and nature of how we perceive and interpret the magnitude and depth of the current transformations greatly impacts on how we start thinking about the issue and ultimately, how we approach it theoretically. If we believe that nothing fundamental has changed, then we are either not looking at the issue in the way that most realists do, or we may come to the conclusion that it is enough to revamp older approaches or adapt them to slightly changing circumstances. On the other hand, if we believe that the information revolution has brought about a more fundamental change in the international system, old approaches are no longer sufficient.

It is considerably easier to answer what is new than to pin down what has changed. In this chapter, we argue that two points are indeed 'new', in the sense that they are unprecedented: the technology (which, as we will show, is inherently insecure) that fuels the current information revolution is new; and the dependency of

---

9 Toffler, *Power Shift*; John Naisbitt, *Megatrends, Ten New Directions Transforming Our Lives* (New York, 1982).

10 Todd R. LaPorte (ed.), *Organized Social Complexity, Challenge to Politics and Policy* (Princeton, 1975); Alvin Toffler, *Future Shock* (New York, 1970).

11 Langdon Winner, *Autonomous Technology: Technics-out-of-control as a Theme in Political Thought* (Cambridge, 1977).

society on this technology is new. Before we turn to these two issues separately, we try to establish what information-age security actually is.

Setting the Stage: Defining Information-Age Security

Due to the newness of the topic and the attention it has attracted, few semantic walls have been erected around the relevant concepts in information-age taxonomy,[12] with the result that these terms have so many meanings and nuances, that the words quickly become confusing or lose their meaning altogether. In the absence of any satisfactory definition of 'information-age security', we can best fill the concept with meaning by designating issues that could be part of it. It makes sense to discern two categories: *offensive* activities such as information warfare, cyber-crime, or cyber-terrorism; and *defensive* activities such as information assurance or critical information infrastructure protection (CIIP).[13] The common denominator of these issues is their unspecified connection to the so-called information revolution and cyberspace, or, more specifically, their connection to the so-called information infrastructure.

It would, however, be misguided to restrict 'information-age security' to virtual means of attack or incidents: The means of attack against the information infrastructure can be physical, such as a hammer, a backhoe, or a bomb, but can also consist of cyber-based hacking tools. The same is true for the target: it is not that easy to understand what exactly the information infrastructure is. This is due to the fact that it not only has a *physical* component that is fairly easily grasped – such as high-speed, interactive, narrow-band, and broadband networks; satellite, terrestrial, and wireless communications systems; and the computers, televisions, telephones, radios, and other products that people employ to access the infrastructure – but also an equally important *immaterial*, sometimes very elusive (cyber-) component, namely the information and content that flows through the infrastructure, the knowledge that is created from this, and the services that are provided.[14]

Security in the information age is thus linked, on the one hand, to the technological side of the information revolution: information and communication technologies and the broader information infrastructure. Furthermore, it concerns threats against the information infrastructure, but also threats emanating from it. Mainly, it is about cyber-threats – a rather vague notion for which no definitions exist, but which signifies the malicious use of information and communication technologies (ICT) either as a target or as a tool by a wide range of malevolent actors – and countermeasures to thwart these cyber-threats. Since this 'definition' is still fairly imprecise, we want to look at specific aspects of the information infrastructure in the next chapter in more detail.

---

12 Uri Fisher, 'Information Age State Security: New Threats to Old Boundaries', *Journal for Homeland Security*, November 2001.

13 Andrei Krutskikh (1999), 'Information Challenges to Security', *International Affairs*, 45/2 (1999): 29–37.

14 Myriam Dunn and Isabelle Wigert, *The International CIIP Handbook 2004: An Inventory of Protection Policies in Fourteen Countries* (Zurich, 2004); Isabelle Abele-Wigert and Myriam Dunn, *The International CIIP Handbook 2006: An Inventory of Protection Policies in 20 Countries and 6 International Organizations, Vol. I* (Zurich, 2006).

The Apparent Insecurity of the Information Infrastructure...

To start with some basics, information can be understood as an abstraction of phenomena, or as a result of our perceptions and interpretations, regardless of the means by which it is gathered.[15] Consequently, information is distinct from technology. In contrast, however, what we can do with information, and especially how fast we can do it, is greatly dependent on technology. Thus, the tools of the current 'revolution', often subsumed under the heading of information and communication technologies (ICT) – among the most important of which are advanced computing, advanced networking, cellular/wireless technology, and digital transmission/compression[16] – are giving this age its distinct characteristics.

Some argue that the beginnings of the current information revolution go back to the invention of the telegraph,[17] but it was definitely only in the early 1990s that a confluence of events brought about what can be described as a 'techno-crescendo' of information revolution dreams, when computers became popular with the masses, and knowledge workers began to outnumber factory workers.[18] One of the most noteworthy features of this more recent technological environment is the tendency towards 'connecting everything to everything', thus creating vast open networks of different sizes and shapes.

From their modest beginnings some 20 years ago, computer networks have become a pivotal element of modern society[19] and networks in a more abstracted sense have even become a metaphor for many aspects of modern life.[20] The marriage of computers and telecommunications and the worldwide assembly of systems such as advanced computer systems, databases, and telecommunications networks has made electronic information widely available, and helped to turn the current revolution into a phenomenon of such grand proportions.

The tools of the information revolution are rapidly advancing and changing, even though the burst of the dot-com bubble has considerably dampened the hyper-tech euphoria of the late 1990s. Experts tend to agree that the major technological trends of the future are automation, mobility, miniaturisation, global networking, and

---

15 United States Joint Forces Command (2004), *United States Joint Forces Command Glossary*, <http://www.jfcom.mil/about/glossary.htm>; Department of the United States Air Force, *Cornerstones of Information Warfare* (Washington, D.C., 1995).

16 Alberts, David S., Daniel S. Papp, and W. Thomas Kemp III, 'The Technologies of the Information Revolution', in David S. Alberts and Daniel S. Papp (eds), *The Information Age, An Anthology of Its Impacts and Consequences* (Washington, D.C., 1997).

17 Ibid.

18 Kushnick, *The Unauthorized Biography of the Baby Bells & Info-Scandal*, p. 22.

19 R. J. Ellison, D. A. Fisher, R. C. Linger, H. F. Lipson, T. Longstaff, and N. R. Mead, *Survivable Network Systems, An Emerging Discipline*, Technical Report. CMU/SEI-97-TR-013. ESC-TR-97-013, November 1997.

20 John Arquilla and David F. Ronfeldt, *The Advent of Netwar* (Santa Monica, 1996); John Arquilla and David Ronfeldt (eds), *Networks and Netwars, The Future of Terror, Crime, and Militancy* (Santa Monica, 2001); Castells, *The Rise of the Network Society*.

the increasing ubiquity of computing and networking.[21] In our context, especially the security implications of this are of interest. Since cyber-threats are about the malicious use of the (global) information infrastructure, the (current and future) characteristics of the technological environment have a considerable impact on the perception of the threat. Especially the increasing number of disruptive occurrences in the cyber-domain plus the Microsoft monoculture on operating systems that show persistent security flaws has led to the impression that the IT-world has a severe security problem.

The internet as a key component of the networked global information infrastructure can be used to demonstrate the inherent insecurity of the technological environment. As every computer that is connected to a larger part of the global information infrastructure is part of the internet, this insecurity weighs particularly heavy: every such machine becomes, in theory, susceptible to attack and intrusion. It was also the extensive and widespread dependence on the information infrastructure, or at least the perception thereof, that has called new attention to the importance of information to national security in the first place.[22]

In order to understand the intrinsic insecurity of the internet, a historical 'detour' is most enlightening. As is well known, the internet began as ARPAnet in the 1960s, a US Department of Defense project to create a nationwide computer network that would continue to function even if a large portion of it were destroyed in a nuclear war or natural disaster. During the next two decades, the network that evolved was used primarily by academic institutions, scientists, and the government for research and communications. Nevertheless, all the early network protocols that now form part of the internet infrastructure were designed with openness and flexibility, not security in mind,[23] even though recognition of vulnerabilities date back at least to 1988 when a student called Morris created a worm that invaded ARPAnet computers and disabled roughly 6,000 computers by flooding their memory banks with copies of itself.[24]

In the early 1990s, the nature of the internet changed significantly as the US government began pulling out of network management and as commercial entities offered internet access to the general public for the first time, a development that

---

21 Batelle, The Business of Innovation, 'Technology Forecast – Strategic Technologies for 2020', <http://www.battelle.org/forecasts/technology2020.stm>.

22 Richard O. Hundley and Robert H. Anderson, 'Emerging Challenge, Security and Safety in Cyberspace', in John Arquilla and David Ronfeldt (eds), *In Athena's Camp, Preparing for Conflict in the Information Age* (Santa Monica, 1997), pp. 231–52; Gary Chapman, 'National Security and the Internet', paper presented at the Annual Convention of the internet Society (Geneva, July 1998); David Halperin, 'The Internet and National Security, Emerging Issues', in David S. Alberts and Daniel S. Papp (eds), *The Information Age, An Anthology of Its Impacts and Consequences, Vol. II* (Washington, 2000), pp. 137–73; Alan Campen, *The First Information Warfare* (Fairfax, 1992), Alan D. Campen, and Douglas H. Dearth (eds), *Cyberwar 2.0, Myths, Mysteries and Reality* (Fairfax, 1998).

23 General Accounting Office, *Computer Security, Hackers Penetrate DOD Computer Systems*, GAO/T-IMTEC-92-5 (Washington, D.C., 20 November 1991).

24 Marcel Dekker, 'Security of the Internet', in *The Froehlich/Kent Encyclopedia of Telecommunications, Vol. 15* (New York, 1997), pp. 231–55.

coincided with the advent of increasingly powerful, yet reasonably priced personal computers with easy-to-use graphical operating systems.[25] The commercialisation of the internet had a considerable impact on making the network inherently insecure, because there are significant market-driven obstacles to IT security: There is no direct return on investment, time-to-market impedes extensive security measures, and security mechanisms often have a negative impact on usability,[26] so that security is often sacrificed for functionality.

Beyond the various governing boards that work to establish policies and standards, the internet is bound by few rules and answers to no single organization. The internet is therefore a primary example of an unbounded system, a system characterised by distributed administrative control without central authority, limited visibility beyond the boundaries of local administration, and lack of complete information about the network.[27] While conventions exist that allow the various parts of the internet to work together, there is no global administrative control to assure that these parts behave according to these conventions.[28]

Another factor that contributes to the vulnerability of the internet is the rapid growth and use of the network, accompanied by rapid deployment of network services involving complex applications. Often, as seen above, these services are not designed, configured, or maintained securely. In addition, it is believed that the security problems of the technical subsystems of today will become worse in the future. We are facing an ongoing dynamic globalisation of information services, which – together with technological innovation, as described shortly above – will lead to a dramatic increase of connectivity and complexity of systems, causing ill-understood behaviour of systems, as well as barely understood vulnerabilities.[29]

...and Its Link to the Critical Infrastructure Protection Debate

Technological insecurity in isolation would most likely not cause the same amount of concern across such a variety of actors in a variety of policy fields if it were not for dependency – or more precisely, society's dependence on these technologies, which makes technological insecurity a potential threat to the functioning of highly developed societies. This is how cyber-threats came to be anchored firmly

---

25 Tim Berners-Lee, *Weaving the Web, The Original Design and Ultimate Destiny of the World Wide Web* (New York, 1999).

26 Michael Näf (2001), 'Ubiquitous Insecurity? How to "Hack" IT Systems', *Information & Security, An International Journal, Vol. 7* (2001): pp. 104–18.

27 Ellison et al., *Survivable Network Systems, An Emerging Discipline*.

28 Yaman Akdeniz, 'The Regulation of internet Content in Europe, Governance Control versus Self-Responsibility', *Swiss Political Science Review*, 5/2 (1999): 123–31; Kenneth Neil, 'Internet Governance and the Ancien Regime', *Swiss Political Science Review*, 5/1 (1999): 127–33; Zoë Baird, 'Governing the Internet, Engaging Government, Business, and Nonprofits', *Foreign Affairs*, 81/6 (2002): 15–20; Giampiero Giacomello, 'Taming the Net? The Issue of Government Control on the internet', *Swiss Political Science Review*, 5/2 (1999): 116–22.

29 Steven H. Strogatz, 'Exploring Complex Networks', *Nature*, 410 (8 March 2001): 268–76; Näf 'Ubiquitous Insecurity? How to "Hack" IT Systems'.

in the security political agenda: in connection with the larger context of critical infrastructure protection (CIP).[30]

CIP as a policy issue has risen to the top of the security agendas of many countries in the last couple of years. It is clear that protection concepts for strategically important infrastructures and objects have been part of national defence planning for decades, though at varying levels of importance. Towards the end of the Cold War and for a couple of years thereafter, however, the possibility of infrastructure discontinuity caused by attacks or other disruptions played a relatively minor role in the security debate – only to gain new impetus around the mid-1990s,[31] mainly due to the information revolution. The US – among other factors, due to its leading role as an IT nation – was the first state to reconsider the problem of CIP in earnest, augmented by a heightened perception of the threat after the Oklahoma City bombing of 1995. After Oklahoma City, government officials realised that an attack on a seemingly insignificant federal building, outside the 'nerve centre' of Washington, was able to set off a chain reaction affecting an area of the economy that would not have normally been linked to the functions of that federal building.

A direct outcome of the Oklahoma City blast was Presidential Decision Directive 39 (PDD-39), which directed the attorney general to lead a government-wide effort to re-examine the adequacy of US infrastructure protection. As a result, Attorney General Janet Reno convened a working group to assess the issue and report back to the White House with policy options. The review, which was completed in early February 1996, particularly highlighted the lack of attention that had been given to protecting the cyber-infrastructure: critical information systems and computer networks. The topic of cyber-threats was linked to the topics of critical infrastructure protection and terrorism. In 1996, President Bill Clinton started the process of developing a national protection strategy with his Presidential Commission on Critical Infrastructure Protection (PCCIP), and this has remained a high-priority issue ever since. In a clear case of policy diffusion by imitation,[32] numerous countries have drafted protection policies of their own.

This development has to be seen in connection with one of the biggest catchphrases of the time: 'asymmetric vulnerability'. Throughout the Cold War, asymmetry had already been an important element of US strategic thinking, but was seldom called by that name.[33] After the Cold War, the US began to fear that its huge conventional military dominance would force any kind of adversary – states or sub-state groups – to use asymmetric means, such as dirty bombs, information operations, or terrorism. The intention of asymmetric tactics is to circumvent an opponent's advantage in

---

30 Cf. The White House, *A National Security Strategy for a New Century* (Washington, D.C., 1997).

31 Eric Luiijf, Helen H. Burger, and Marieke H.A. Klaver, 'Critical Infrastructure Protection in the Netherlands, A Quick-scan', in Urs E. Gattiker, Pia Pedersen, and Karsten Petersen (eds), *EICAR Conference Best Paper Proceedings 2003*, <http://www.tno.nl/instit/fel/refs/pub2003/BPP-13-CIP-Luiijf&Burger&Klaver.pdf>.

32 Johan Eriksson (ed.), *Threat Politics, New Perspectives on Security, Risk and Crisis Management* (Aldershot, 2001).

33 Bruce D. Berkowitz, *The New Face of War: How War Will Be Fought in the 21st Century* (New York, 2002).

terms of capabilities by avoiding his strengths and exploiting his weaknesses.[34] This adjustment can be seen as part of the US Department of Defense's struggle to understand the post-Cold War security environment. Basically, since the global distribution of power was asymmetric, it followed that asymmetric strategies would evolve naturally.[35] The concept of an asymmetric threat or vulnerability connotes that 'the enemy', clearly doomed to fail against America's mighty high-tech war machine in any conventional conflict, will instead plan to bring the US to its knees by striking at vital points at home[36] – these points being fundamental to the national security and the essential functioning of industrialised societies as a whole, and not necessarily to the military in particular. These vital points are called 'critical infrastructures' (CI) in today's security debate.

The concept of critical infrastructures usually includes sectors such as information and telecommunications, financial services, energy and utilities, and transport and distribution, plus a list of additional elements that vary across countries and over time.[37] Attacking infrastructure has a 'force multiplier' effect, allowing even a relatively small attack to achieve a much greater impact. As the CI delivers a range of services that individuals, and society as a whole, depend on, any damage to or interruption of the CI causes ripples across the technical and societal systems. For this reason, CI structures and networks have historically proven to be appealing targets for a whole array of actors.[38]

A sense of urgency is created not only by society's ever-increasing dependence on ICT, but also by the way that ICT are becoming all-embracing, are connecting other infrastructure systems, and are creating interrelationships and interdependencies between the latter. The interdependency factor means that critical infrastructures do not need to be attacked in any physical manner, but might be targeted for electronic or cyber-attacks, the worst-case scenario being a concerted action of qualified hackers with hostile intentions that could force a whole nation to its knees.[39]

There are two sides to this particular cyber-threat image, which evolved in the 1990s: A new kind of vulnerability due to modern societies' dependency on inherently insecure information systems on the one hand, and an expansion of the threat spectrum on the other. The falling costs, increased and large-scale availability, greater utility, and ease of use of ICT have caused this technology to propagate and

---

34 Kristin S. Kolet, 'Asymmetric Threats to the United States', *Comparative Strategy*, 20 (2001): 277–92.

35 Stephen J. Blank, *Rethinking Asymmetric Threats* (Carlisle, 2003).

36 Bruce D. Berkowitz, 'Warfare in the Information Age', in John Arquilla and David Ronfeldt (eds), *In Athena's Camp, Preparing for Conflict in the Information Age* (Santa Monica, 1997).

37 John Moteff, Claudia Copeland, and John Fischer, *Critical Infrastructures, What Makes an Infrastructure Critical?* CRS (Congressional Research Service) Report for Congress RL31556, 30 August 2002.

38 Office of Critical Infrastructure Protection and Emergency Preparedness, 'Threat Analysis', Number, TbA03-001, 12 March 2003, <http,//www.ocipep-bpiepc.gc.ca/opsprods/other/TA03-001_e.pdf>.

39 President's Commission on Critical Infrastructure Protection, *Critical Foundations, Protecting America's Infrastructures* (Washington, D.C., 1997): pp. 5–8.

to permeate all aspects of life, with the result that societies in developed countries are becoming increasingly dependent on it for their well being, every-day life, work, economic transactions, comfort, entertainment, and many personal interactions.[40] In addition, the perception today is that there are a variety of actors in cyberspace who are willing to contravene national legal frameworks and hide in the relative anonymity of cyberspace. The growing prevalence and aptitude of these cyber-based threat actors is seen as considerable threat to national security, because they seem to have the capacity to inflict significant damage through tools that are readily available and relatively easy to use by those with even a cursory knowledge of, and skills in using, computer technologies.[41]

In this chapter, we have focused particularly on the inherent insecurity of the global networked information infrastructure, the rise of new actors, and the link to the critical infrastructure protection debate as key reasons for the emergence of cyber-fears. We have argued that the new factor in information-age security is mainly to be found in a changing technical foundation and society's dependency on it. In a next step, we would like to take this argument further and explore what this means for security and governance.

Implications of the Information Revolution for Security and Governance

To interpret what this technological expansion actually means for the individual, for society, for the state, or for international relations implies a great deal of speculation. For a number of reasons, which are conceptual and theoretical as well as empirical, there is no simple answer to what has changed to what degree. First, the developments triggered by the information revolution are recent and ongoing, and difficulties in grasping their true proportions are inevitable, because we ourselves are in the midst of the process. Second, the possible implications are far from straightforward: Many observe that the present epoch is marked by persistent opposites and derives its order from episodic patterns with very contradictory outcomes.[42] Nonetheless, to identify features of the information age, we first want to assess the main literature concerned with the information revolution and its impact on international security. On the basis of these arguments, we then venture to identify what can be called 'new' and transformative.

---

40 Myriam Dunn, *Information Age Conflicts, A Study on the Information Revolution and a Changing Operating Environment*, Zürcher Beiträge zur Sicherheitspolitik und Konfliktforschung, No. 64. (Zurich, 2002): pp. 62–5.

41 President's Commission on Critical Infrastructure Protection, *Critical Foundations, Protecting America's Infrastructures*.

42 James N. Rosenau, *Turbulence in World Politics, A Theory of Change and Continuity* (Princeton, 1990); Center for Strategic and International Studies, *The Information Revolution and International Security*, Robert F. McMormich Tribune Foundation Report (Washington D.C., 1996).

A Change in Power Structures?

One of the core arguments in the literature on the information revolution, which is strongly influenced by a liberalist world-view, is that the technological development leads to a shift in power structures, away from the state to a diversification of influential actors. Two central and interlinked developments are said to reveal the nature of the change: the changing nature of power and the redistribution of power.

The changing nature of power is seen as a result of the growing importance of information technologies; it is said that the main locus of power resources has been shifting from military, to economic, and now to informational resources,[43] so that control over knowledge, beliefs, and ideas is increasingly regarded as a complement to control over tangible resources such as military forces, raw materials, and economic productive capability. Much of this thinking can also be found in that part of the information warfare literature that believes in a significant change in the nature of warfare due to the expansion of the battlefield to the infosphere.[44]

The most popular and most frequently used tag to emerge from this debate is 'soft power', defined as the ability to achieve goals through attraction rather than coercion.[45] It refers to communications, entertainment, and ideas, and has a strong cultural and psychological component. Because soft power works by convincing others to follow or getting them to agree to norms and institutions that produce the desired behaviour, the persuasiveness of the concept of soft power and the idea of *structural power* are closely connected.[46] It has been said that international actors are more interested in exercising structural power, a power that is less visible, since the possessor of power is able to change the range of choices open to others without the apparent use of pressure.[47]

---

43 Jeffrey Hart and Sangbae A. Kim, 'Power in the Information Age', in Jose V. Ciprut (ed.), *Of Fears and Foes, International Relations in an Evolving Global Political Economy* (Westport, 2000); David J. Rothkopf, 'Cyberpolitik, The Changing Nature of Power in the Information Age', *Journal of International Affairs*, 51/2 (Spring 1998): 325–60.

44 Michael Vlahos, 'Entering the Infosphere', *Journal of International Affairs*, 2 (Spring 1998): 497–525; Gebhard Geiger, *Offensive Informationskriegsführung. Die 'Joint Doctrine for Information Operations' der US-Streitkräfte, Sicherheitspolitische Perspektiven*, SWP Studie (Berlin, 2002).

45 Joseph Nye, 'Soft Power', *Foreign Policy*, 80 (Fall 1990): 153–71; Joseph Nye, *Power in the Global Information Age, From Realism to Globalization* (London, 2004); Robert O. Keohane and Joseph S. Nye, 'Power and Interdependence in the Information Age', *Foreign Affairs*, 77/5 (September/October 1998): 81–94.

46 Jeffrey Hart, 'Three Approaches to the Measurement of Power in International Relations', *International Organization*, 30/2 (1976): 289–305; Susan Strange, *The Retreat of the State: The Diffusion of Power in the World Economy* (Cambridge, 1996); Hart and Kim, 'Power in the Information Age'.

47 Thomas J. Volgy, Kristin Kanthak, Derrick Frazier, and Robert Stewart Ingersoll, 'Structural versus Relational Strength, The Cohesion of the G7 and the Development of the Post-Cold War International System', paper presented at the Fifth Annual Pan European International Relations Conference, 9–11 September 2004, The Hague.

Of course, the reality and importance of soft power is a matter of much controversy, and realists are naturally among the most virulent critics of that concept. Even though they accept economic factors as being important to the extent that they reflect or affect national power or capabilities, they hold that the mightiest of all forms of power remains the military pillar. In addition, even though the information revolution has put ICT in the hands of non-state actors, it is still the state that has the information advantage most of the time: strategic information is not widely available, and actors other than states mostly lack the abilities and resources to collect and edit specific information.[48]

Liberalists, on the other hand, claim that there are two interlinked factors leading to a redistribution of power due to the information revolution. They purport that on the one hand, the information revolution enables an ever-widening range of actors, giving them access to more or less powerful information tools for the rapid collection, production, and dissemination of information on a worldwide scale. This development leads to the *skill revolution*,[49] signifying the strengthened position of individuals due to the expansion of their diagnostic capabilities, which make citizens more competent and sharpens their analytical skills. Since many of these thinkers view information as a central power resource, on the other hand, the argument runs that the individual gains considerable influence, and, as a consequence, demands more authority in various issue areas, which then again leads to a rearrangement of global power relationships, and is likely to result in a skewed, complex, and volatile pattern of power distribution.[50]

The problem with these observations is that, although a lot of the claims about changes in power structures ring true, it is very hard to produce any stringent empirically-grounded research either for or against the anecdotal evidence that is frequently offered in support of this view, the main reason being that the underlying concepts are very hard to operationalise; even for realists, for whom power is the key concept, there is no clear consensus on how to define the term or how to measure it.[51]

In addition, most of these claims are based on the premise that an increase in information and communication technologies automatically means a qualitative difference, and are therefore implicitly using the traditional *power as resource* approach, which measures power as the sum of military, economic, technological,

---

48 Dunn, *Information Age Conflicts*.

49 James Rosenau, 'Global Affairs in an Epochal Transformation', in C. Ryan Henry and Edward C. Peartree (eds), *Information Revolution and International Security* (Washington D.C., 1998), pp. 33–57.

50 Daniel S. Papp and David S. Alberts, 'The Impacts of the Information Age on International Actors and the International System', in David S. Alberts, and Daniel S. Papp (eds), *The Information Age, An Anthology of Its Impacts and Consequences* (Washington D.C., 1997); Rosenau, *Turbulence in World Politics, A Theory of Change and Continuity*; Joseph S. Nye, 'U.S. Security Policy, Challenges for the 21st Century', *USIA Electronic Journal*, 3/3 (July 1998).

51 Hart and Kim, 'Power in the Information Age'; Paul R. Viotti and Mark V. Kauppi, *International Relations Theory, Realism, Pluralism, Globalism, and Beyond* (Needham Heights, 1999, 3rd edition).

diplomatic, and other capabilities at the disposal of the state, which are a function of control over specific types of resources, such as territory, population, energy, etc.[52] However, even if we were to count the numbers of computers connected to the internet, the use of mobile phones as a percentage of the overall population of a country, or the whole extent of the information that is available on the World Wide Web, no convincing conclusion is possible as to the *impact* of these factors.[53]

Even though it is obvious that quantities are important, only our attribution of a *meaning* to them will allow us to theorise reliably about the information age. Meaning is the link connecting quantitative changes (causes) to qualitative changes (consequences). In fact, without a discussion of how we attribute meaning to quantities, we have no way of knowing when change becomes significant, or when it is or becomes truly transformational.[54] In addition, we must also be aware that change is inherently a matter of perceptions. Not only is change an evolutionary process rather than a single event with clearly discernible beginning or end, change is also not universally given; it is rather a question of scales, and of arbitrarily chosen reference points. In a short-term or micro perspective, last year was fundamentally different from this year – in a macro or long-term perspective, truly fundamental alterations of the deeper dynamics and patterns of power, authority, status, and nature of social institutions are lacking.[55]

In this context, the puzzle of discovery and innovation is fundamental: How can we notice a 'pattern' we have never seen before?[56] In fact, there is always an ad-hoc quality to the recognition of something new. While such patterns may merit consideration in their own right, the ontological validity of a perceived novelty remains unclear. Because patterns must be 'recognised' by the observer, any observed structure or patterns may be an artefact of the research question; other patterns may go unnoticed for the same reasons.[57]

We see the solution to this dilemma in the acknowledgement that the perception of issues – such as change – by key actors will have a considerable impact on their beliefs and actions. It makes little sense to focus on the question of 'change or no

---

52 A.F.K. Organski, *World Politics* (New York, 1968).; David J. Singer, Stuart Bremer and John Stuckey, 'Capability Distribution, Uncertainty, and Major Power War, 1820–1965', in Bruce Russett (ed.), *Peace, War, and Numbers* (Beverly Hills, 1972), pp. 21–27; Hart, 'Three Approaches to the Measurement of Power in International Relations'.

53 K. J. Holsti, 'The Problem of Change in International Relations Theory', Institute of International Relations, The University of British Columbia, Working Paper No. 26, December 1998.

54 Ibid., p. 5.

55 Ibid., p. 4.

56 James P. Crutchfield, 'Is Anything Ever New? Considering Emergence', in G. Cowan, D. Pines, and D. Melzner (eds), *Complexity, Metaphors, Models, and Reality*, SFI Series in the Sciences of Complexity XIX (Addison-Wesley, 1994), pp. 479–97; James P. Crutchfield, 'What Lies Between Order and Chaos?', in John L. Casti and A. Karlqvist, *Art and Complexity* (Oxford, 2002).

57 Kevin Mihata, 'The Persistence of 'Emergence'', in Raymond A. Eve, Sara Horsfall, and Mary E. Lee (eds), *Chaos, Complexity, and Sociology, Myths, Models, and Theories* (Thousand Oaks, 1997), p. 32.

change' as a matter of objective truth, but it is better to concentrate on the implications of this development, the main one being the growing number of actors in the policy domain: According to the observations made above, there are more actors on the international stage today, with more influence due to the skill revolution and more knowledge at their hands, suggesting both a quantitative and a qualitative change in power structures. Ultimately, however, it does not matter whether this change is objectively 'true' or not, but what matters is that states are willing to include non-state actors in the policy process, for various reasons, and the implications of this development for security and governance should be the focus of our attention.

More Stakeholders in the Security Process

Today, the states' monopoly on authority seems to have become fragmented, as a plethora of non-governmental organisations, social movements, and other transnational non-state networks compete with states for influence in a variety of issue areas.[58] The result of this is the emergence of a range of often ad-hoc public and private governance structures that undermine the state both from above and from below, resulting in splintered states and fragmented authority.[59] This development fosters the multiplication of unclear boundaries between the responsibilities and capacities of the state and of the private sector, respectively,[60] and we can observe a increase in the number of private regimes, or regimes in which the balance of authority between public and private actors has been swinging in favour of the latter and increased their sway over decision-making.[61]

Because of the expanding partnership between the public and private sectors to provide services, the distinction in jurisdiction, authority, duties, and, above all, risks that used to apply to different segments of societies have become blurred. Governments can no longer 'go it alone', and the process of policy-making is changing from a single-entity phenomenon to a multi-entity one, as it has become both customary and necessary to involve representatives of major stakeholders in the policy preparation process.[62]

When aiming to secure the information age, governments are therefore challenged to operate in unfamiliar ways. They will need to share influence with experts in the IT community, with businesses, and with non-profit organisations, because the

---

58 Alberts, Papp, and Kemp, 'The Technologies of the Information Revolution'; Brian Nichiporuk and Carl H. Builder, 'Societal Implications', in John Arquilla and David Ronfeldt (eds), *In Athena's Camp, Preparing for Conflict in the Information Age* (Santa Monica, 1997), pp. 295–314; Jean-Marie Guéhenno, *The End of the Nation-State* (Minneapolis, 1995).

59 Rosenau, 'Global Affairs in an Epochal Transformation'.

60 Philip G. Cerny, 'Globalization and the Erosion of Democracy', *European Journal of Political Research*, 36/1 (1999), p. 14.

61 Virginia Haufler, 'Crossing the Boundary between Public and Private, International Regimes and Non-State Actors', in Volker Rittberger (ed.), *Regime Theory and International Relations* (Oxford, 1993), pp. 94–110.

62 Kevin A. O'Brien, Andreas Ligtvoet, Andrew Rathmell, and Douglas MacKenzie, *Using Scenarios to Support Critical Infrastructure Analysis and Assessment Work*. ACIP, Package 3 Deliverable D3.4, 2003.

critical systems are owned, operated, and supplied by a largely private industry that is diverse, intermixed, and relatively unregulated.[63] Collectively, this industry has far more technical resources and operational access to the infrastructures than a government does, so that ultimately, the private sector will have to do most of the work and bear most of the burden to make infrastructures more secure.[64]

The mixed character of protection policies intended to secure the information infrastructure is a clear indication of this development. In the realm of cyber-threats, the maintenance of 'business continuity' for an individual, corporate or local actor, and security efforts aimed at national or even international security often are the same.[65] Because the technology generating the risk makes it very difficult to fight potential attackers in advance, protective measures focus on preventive strategies and on trying to minimize the impact of an attack when it occurs. Apart from a basic understanding of what to protect and how to protect it, the variations in conceptions and viewpoints held by these various stakeholders logically also have an impact on protection measures: Depending on their influence or on the resources at hand, various key players shape the issue in accordance with their view of the problem. Different groups, whether they be private, public, or a mixture of both, do not usually agree on the exact nature of the problem, or on what assets need to be protected with which measures. The character of the threat itself exacerbates this situation.

The Unsubstantiated Nature of Cyber-threats

Experts do not agree on the gravity of the cyber-threat and grapple with the answer to the question of how soon an incident with truly society-threatening impact might occur. The question is notoriously hard to answer, especially because there are too many unknowns. For one thing, the degree of vulnerability of any nation's critical infrastructures to deliberate attacks is currently a matter of some controversy.[66] Lewis in particular has argued that the assumption of vulnerability is wrong, because automatically linking computer network vulnerability to critical infrastructure vulnerability is misleading, since critical infrastructures, especially in large market

---

63 Baird, 'Governing the Internet, Engaging Government, Business, and Nonprofits'.

64 Seymour E. Goodman, Pamela B. Hassebroek, Daving Kind, and Andy Azment, 'International Coordination to Increase the Security of Critical Network Infrastructures', Document CNI/04, paper presented at the ITU Workshop on Creating Trust in Critical Network Infrastructures, Seoul, 20–22 May 2002; Olivia Bosch, 'Cyber Terrorism and Private Sector Efforts for Information Infrastructure Protection', paper presented at the ITU Workshop on Creating Trust in Critical Network Infrastructures (Seoul, 20–22 May 2002).

65 Chris C. Demchak, (1999), '"New Security" in Cyberspace, Emerging Intersection between Military and Civilian Contingencies', *Journal of Contingencies and Crisis Management*, 7/ 4 (1999): 181–98.

66 Cf. James A. Lewis, *Assessing the Risks of Cyber-terrorism, Cyber War and Other Cyber Threats* (Washington, 2002); George Smith, 'How Vulnerable Is Our Interlinked Infrastructure?', in David S. Alberts and Daniel S. Papp (eds), *The Information Age, An Anthology of Its Impacts and Consequences, Vol. II* (Washington, 2000), pp. 507–23.

economies, are more distributed, diverse, redundant, and self-healing than a cursory assessment may suggest, rendering them less vulnerable to attack.[67]

To truly know how vulnerable critical infrastructures are to cyber-attack, however, we would need a much more detailed assessment of redundancy for each target infrastructure, as well as the normal rates of failure and response, the degree to which critical functions are accessible from public networks, and the level of human control, monitoring, and intervention in critical operations.[68] There are two main reasons why this is difficult or even impossible: First, there are no public or even readily available data on how vulnerable critical systems might be. The computers of the defence establishment are buried under layers of secrecy and classification, and private companies are not likely to volunteer such information.[69] Second, such an assessment is difficult not only because the data is not available, but also because this data alone would not be sufficient to establish criticality. On the one hand, what is considered critical is constantly changing,[70] and on the other, the criticality of an infrastructure or service can never be identified preventively based on empirical data alone, but only *ex post facto*, after a crisis has occurred and as the result of a normative process.[71]

Even if we are willing to believe that infrastructures are vulnerable due to the cyber-factor, the essential question then is whether there are actors with the capability and motivation to carry out such operations. Only some of the more cautious estimates on the level of threat take into account the *capabilities* of potential adversaries, a factor that has been part of traditional threat assessment for years.[72] In this, they counterbalance a whole series of reports and publications that follow the same analytically flawed approach:[73] They catalogue the dependency that comes with interconnectivity, and take it as given that the means to carry out a cyber-attack will be easily available. These analyses have identified the plethora of vulnerabilities in automated information systems and assumed that terrorist organisations or other malicious actors are willing to exploit these vulnerabilities, and therefore conclude

---

67 Lewis, *Assessing the Risks of Cyber-terrorism, Cyber War and Other Cyber Threats*.

68 Ibid., p. 10; Yacov Y. Haimes and Pu Jiang, 'Leontief-Based Model of Risk in Complex Interconnected Infrastructures', *Journal of Infrastructure Systems*, 7/1 (2001): 1–12; Barry C. Ezell, John V. Farr, and Ian Wiese, 'Infrastructure Risk Analysis of Municipal Water Distribution System', *Journal of Infrastructure Systems*, 6/3 (2000): pp. 118–22.

69 Chapman, 'National Security and the Internet'.

70 John D. Moteff, *Critical Infrastructures, Background, Policy, and Implementation*, Congressional Research Report for Congress, RL30153, 10 February 2003 (Washington, D.C., 2003).

71 Daniel Sarewitz, Roger Pielke, and Mojdeh Kaykhah, 'Vulnerability and Risk, Some Thoughts from a Political and Policy Perspective', *Risk Analysis, An International Journal*, 23/4 (2003): 805–10; Jan Metzger, 'The Concept of Critical Infrastructure Protection (CIP)', in A. J. K. Bailes and Isabelle Frommelt (eds), *Business and Security, Public-Private Sector Relationships in a New Security Environment* (Oxford, 2004), pp. 197–209.

72 David J. Singer, 'Threat-Perception and the Armament-Tension Dilemma', *Journal of Conflict Resolution*, Vol. II (March 1958): 90–105.

73 Cf. President's Commission on Critical Infrastructure Protection, *Critical Foundations, Protecting America's Infrastructures*.

that cyber-attacks are inevitable because this course of action provides enemies with a potentially strategic advantage over the US.[74]

In general, cyber-threats show features also associated with other 'new' and often non-military threats that were moved onto the security political agendas of many countries following the disintegration of the Soviet Union.[75] Even though the label new is not justified in most cases, many of these threats are distinctly different from Cold War security threats. The main difference is a quality of uncertainty about them, which is largely new and unprecedented.[76] Uncertainty surrounds the identity and goals of potential adversaries, the timeframe within which threats are likely to arise, and the contingencies that might be imposed on the state by others.[77] Further, there is uncertainty concerning the capabilities against which one must prepare, and also about what type of conflict to prepare for.

This leads to the fact that any attempt to objectively define the level of risk arising from cyber-threats is inherently futile. In addition, the indeterminate nature of the issue means that the perception of the risk will be contested between different social groups. In absence of any real-world occurrences, different scenarios provide the grounds on which decisions have to be made. The different actors involved in the policy process are thus competing with each other by means of constructed versions of the future.[78] That national security has always been a combination of both real and imagined threats and assets is nothing new; but the nature of information and information technologies makes perceptions even more important, because there are almost no tangible facts. Because we can expect that the dearth of information as described above will continue, and as long as no actual incidents occur, the controversy about the nature and scope of the threat will no doubt extend far into the future.

This has concrete implications for the question of how best to approach the issue analytically: The elusive and unsubstantiated nature of cyber-threats means that only an approach rooted in the constructivist mindset with a subjective ontology is suitable for its analysis. Instead of conceiving threats as something given and objectively measurable, these approaches focus on the process by which a shared understanding of what is to be considered and collectively responded to as a threat to security is inter-subjectively constructed among key actors. We therefore believe that the key to understanding the information revolution's implications for international

---

74 Center for the Study of Terrorism and Irregular Warfare, *Cyberterror, Prospects and Implications*, White Paper (Monterey, 1999), p. vii.

75 Barry Buzan, Ole Wæver, and Jaap de Wilde, *Security: A New Framework for Analysis* (Boulder, 1998).

76 Jef Huysmans, 'Security! What Do You Mean? From Concept to Thick Signifier', *European Journal of International Relations*, 4/2 (1998): 226–55.

77 Emily O. Goldman, 'New Threats, New Identities and New Ways of War, The Sources of Change in National Security Doctrine', *Journal of Strategic Studies*, 24/3 (2001): 12–42.

78 Ralf Bendrath, 'The American Cyber-Angst and the Real World – Any Link?', in Robert Latham (ed.), *Bombs and Bandwidth, The Emerging Relationship between IT and Security* (New York, 2003), pp. 49–73; Myriam Dunn (2005), 'The Socio-Political Dimensions of Critical Information Infrastructure Protection (CIIP)', *International Journal for Critical Infrastructure Protection*, 1/2–3 (2005): 58–68.

relations and security is to look at how features of the technological environment and their implications for national security are perceived by experts and key players in the policy domain.

Conclusion

The aim of this chapter was to identify what sets security in the information age apart from security in other ages. There is one simple answer to the question 'is anything ever new?' It is: 'Yes, if we see it as such'. We have taken this constructivist reasoning into account by pointing to the importance of the perceptions of key decision-makers. This is not just an intellectual exercise, because we believe that these perceptions have a direct bearing on the policy formulation process, which leads to authoritative decisions. These authoritative decisions can take a variety of forms, for example, statutes, official government regulations, executive orders, court decisions, or formal written agreements reached between political or administrative elites and other public or private actors. Understood in this way, laws (national, regional, and international), protocols, and norms of behaviour are shaped by policy-makers' (threat) perceptions, so that they have a concrete impact on the issue area of security in the information age.

The answer is slightly less 'simple' if we venture to identify qualitative changes brought on by the sheer mass of information technology. This, of course, is our specific perception of the issue. Foremost, we are convinced that the forces of the information revolution have not necessarily changed the conditions of security, defined in an objective sense as the absence of threat to a society's core values and in a subjective sense as the absence of the fear that these values will be attacked.[79] In other words, the information revolution has not changed the core values of society; they have remained more or less constant over the years. What has changed significantly in our view, however, are some of the conditions for *securing*. This distinction between 'security' and 'securing' is slight but pivotal: while 'security' is a momentary static condition, 'securing' has a somewhat differing connotation: it involves the act of making something safe or secure and thus of actively thwarting possible threats to any given referent object of security, implying actors, politics, and policies. According to this reasoning, we can observe a qualitatively significant change in some of the means of achieving the goal of security today, which mainly affects the various obstacles along the way.

First, the 'threat' against which the referent object must be secured is qualitatively different. Cyber-threats are pictured as being disconnected from a territorially-based state entity. Due to the global nature of information networks, attacks can be launched from anywhere in the world, and discovering their origin, if they are detected in time at all, remains a major difficulty. Cyber-attacks can be carried out in innumerable ways by anyone with a computer connected to the internet, and for purposes ranging from juvenile hacking, organised crime, and political activism to strategic warfare.

---

79 Arnold Wolfers, 'National Security as an Ambiguous Symbol', in Arnold Wolfers, *Discord and Collaboration, Essays on International Politics* (Baltimore, 1962), pp. 147–65.

Hacking tools are easily downloaded from the internet, and have become both more sophisticated and user-friendly. This aspect is seen to be particularly daunting because the 'enemy' becomes a faceless and remote entity, a great unknown who is almost impossible to track, and who opposes established security institutions and laws that are ill-suited to counter or retaliate against such a threat. In connection with the dependency of modern societies on the reliable functioning of information and communication technologies, this creates a very specific (and unprecedented) starting position for the drafting of protection policies.

Second, the relative loss of power of state actors vis-à-vis non-state actors as a reason for the proliferation of information technology – or at least the perception thereof – leads to specific obstacles for securing efforts, as it leads to the inclusion of various non-state actors into the securing process. In the area of critical information infrastructure protection, governments all over the world actively seek cooperation with the private sector. Different types of such partnerships are emerging, including government-led partnerships, business-led partnerships, and joint public-private initiatives. Rather than indicating a loss of state power, these developments show that having come under pressure from the conditions of a rapidly changing international environment, the state is willing to adapt some of its functions to new circumstances.

While the second point mainly reveals that any conception of security that is to be capable of dealing with the current world order needs to be linked to a much broader notion of governance than the one that characterized the Cold War, the first issue, concerning the (new) characteristics of threats connected to the information age, has additional implications for security and also for security studies. Very importantly, the unsubstantiated nature of cyber-threats opens the floodgates for all kinds of exaggerations. Even though many years have passed since the threat first appeared on the political agenda, there is still a fair amount of hype surrounding the topic, in part fuelled by careless fear-mongering on the part of government officials. The reason for this is relatively simple to determine: Producers of information security technology may benefit financially if they can scare more people into purchasing security products. Similarly, academics competing for the latest homeland security grants may be tempted to overstate the problem. 'Professionals of security' also play a considerable role: National security institutions are bureaucratic outgrowths of the state; deprived of their exterior enemy after the end of the Cold War, these bureaucracies had to redefine their role as protectors of society, and did so partly by adding new threats to the political agenda when the old ones disappeared.

Most observers agree that unnecessary 'cyber-angst' is not particularly helpful when it comes to finding solutions. However, when 'information-age security' is seen through the lens of national security, exaggeration of the scope of the threat is unavoidable. For this reason, it can be argued that one solution to the problem is to focus on economic and market aspects of the issue instead.[80] On the one hand,

---

80 Ross Andersson, 'Why Information Security is Hard, An Economic Perspective', in IEEE Computer Society (ed.), *Proceedings of the 17th Annual Computer Security Applications Conference*, New Orleans, 10–14 December 2001, <http//www.ftp.cl.cam.ac.uk/ftp/users/rja14/econ.pdf>.

looking at cyber-security as an economic problem helps to 'de-securitise' the issue. Desecuritisation as the 'unmaking of security' has been considered a technique for defining down threats, in other words, a 'normalisation' of threats that were previously constructed as extraordinary because they were regarded as a national-security issue. This normalisation is a process by which security issues lose their security aspect, making it possible to interpret them in multiple ways. Desecuritisation, therefore, allows more freedom both at the level of interpretation and in actual politics or social interaction. On the other hand, to focus on market aspects of the issue will help create a market for cyber-security, which could reduce much of the insecurity of the information infrastructure, and thus also diminish the vulnerability of society.

References

Abele-Wigert, Isabelle and Myriam Dunn, *The International CIIP Handbook 2006: An Inventory of Protection Policies in 20 Countries and 6 International Organizations* (Vol. I) (Zurich: Center for Security Studies, 2006).

Akdeniz, Yaman, 'The Regulation of Internet Content in Europe: Governance Control versus Self-Responsibility', *Swiss Political Science Review*, 5/2 (1999): 123–31.

Alberts, David S., Daniel S. Papp, and W. Thomas Kemp III, 'The Technologies of the Information Revolution', in: Alberts, David S. and Daniel S. Papp (eds), *The Information Age: An Anthology of Its Impacts and Consequences* (Washington D.C.: National Defense University, 1997).

Arquilla, John and David F. Ronfeldt, *The Advent of Netwar* (Santa Monica: RAND, 1996).

Arquilla, John and David Ronfeldt (eds), *Networks and Netwars: The Future of Terror, Crime, and Militancy* (Santa Monica: RAND, 2001).

Baird, Zoë, 'Governing the internet: Engaging Government, Business, and Nonprofits', *Foreign Affairs*, 81/6 (2002): 15–20.

Batelle, The Business of Innovation, 'Technology Forecast – Strategic Technologies for 2020', <http://www.battelle.org/forecasts/technology2020.stm>, accessed 18 April 2007.

Bendrath, Ralf, 'The American Cyber-Angst and the Real World – Any Link?', in Robert Latham (ed.), *Bombs and Bandwidth: The Emerging Relationship between IT and Security* (New York: The New Press, 2003), pp. 49–73.

Berkowitz, Bruce D., 'Warfare in the Information Age', in John Arquilla and David Ronfeldt (eds), *In Athena's Camp: Preparing for Conflict in the Information Age* (Santa Monica: RAND, 1997).

Berkowitz, Bruce D., *The New Face of War: How War Will Be Fought in the 21st Century* (New York: Simon & Schuster International, 2002).

Berners-Lee, Tim, *Weaving the Web: The Original Design and Ultimate Destiny of the World Wide Web* (New York: Harper Collins, 1999).

Beus, J.G. de, *Shall we Make the Year 2000?* (London: Sidgwick & Jackson, 1985).

Blank, Stephen J., *Rethinking Asymmetric Threats* (Carlisle: Strategic Studies Institute, 2003).

Borgmann, Albert, *Holding on to Reality: The Nature of Information at the Turn of the Millennium* (Chicago: University of Chicago Press, 1999).

Bosch, Olivia, 'Cyber Terrorism and Private Sector Efforts for Information Infrastructure Protection', paper presented at the ITU Workshop on Creating Trust in Critical Network Infrastructures (Seoul, 20–22 May 2002).

Buzan, Barry, Ole Wæver, and Jaap de Wilde, *Security: A New Framework for Analysis* (Boulder: Rienner, 1998).

Campen, Alan, *The First Information Warfare* (Fairfax, AFCEA International Press, 1992).

Campen, Alan and Douglas H. Dearth (eds), *Cyberwar 2.0: Myths, Mysteries and Reality* (Fairfax, AFCEA International Press: 1998).

Castells, Manuel, *The Rise of the Network Society* (Oxford: Blackwell, 1996).

Cerny, Philip G., 'Globalization and the Erosion of Democracy', *European Journal of Political Research*, 36/1 (1999): 1–26.

Chapman, Gary, 'National Security and the Internet', paper presented at the Annual Convention of the Internet Society (Geneva, July 1998).

Crutchfield, James P., 'Is Anything Ever New? Considering Emergence', in G. Cowan, D. Pines, and D. Melzner (eds), *Complexity: Metaphors, Models, and Reality*, SFI Series in the Sciences of Complexity XIX (Addison-Wesley: Redwood City, 1994), pp. 479–97.

Crutchfield, James P., 'What Lies Between Order and Chaos?', in John L. Casti, and A. Karlqvist, *Art and Complexity* (Oxford: Oxford University Press, 2002).

Center for Strategic and International Studies, *The Information Revolution and International Security: Robert F. McMormich Tribune Foundation Report* (Washington D.C., Center for Strategic and International Studies, 1996).

Center for the Study of Terrorism and Irregular Warfare, *Cyberterror: Prospects and Implications*, White Paper (Monterey: Center on Terrorism and Irregular Warfare, 1999).

Cukier, Kenneth Neil, 'Internet Governance and the Ancient Regime', *Swiss Political Science Review*, 5/1 (1999): 127–33.

Deibert, Ronald J., 'Exorcismus Theoriae: Pragmatism, Metaphors and the Return of the Medieval in IR Theory,' *European Journal of International Relations*, 3/2 (June 1997): 167–92.

Dekker, Marcel, 'Security of the Internet', in *The Froehlich/Kent Encyclopedia of Telecommunications*, Vol. 15 (New York, 1997), pp. 231–55.

Demchak, Chris C., '"New Security" in Cyberspace: Emerging Intersection between Military and Civilian Contingencies', *Journal of Contingencies and Crisis Management*, 7/4 (1999): 181–98.

Deutsch, Karl W., 'Mass Communications and the Loss of Freedom in National Decision-Making: A Possible Research Approach to Interstate Conflicts', *Journal of Conflict Resolution*, 1/2 (1957): 200–11.

Drucker, Peter F., *The New Realities: In Government and Politics, in Economics and Business, in Society and World View* (New York: Harper Collins Publishers, 1989).

Dunn, Myriam, *Information Age Conflicts: A Study on the Information Revolution and a Changing Operating Environment*, Zürcher Beiträge zur Sicherheitspolitik und Konfliktforschung, No. 64 (Zurich: Center for Security Studies, 2002).

Dunn, Myriam, 'The Socio-Political Dimensions of Critical Information Infrastructure Protection (CIIP)', *International Journal for Critical Infrastructure Protection*, 1/2–3 (2005): 58–68.

Dunn, Myriam and Isabelle Wigert, *The International CIIP Handbook 2004: An Inventory of Protection Policies in Fourteen Countries* (Zurich: Center for Security Studies, 2004).

Ellison, R. J., D. A. Fisher, R. C. Linger, H. F. Lipson, T. Longstaff, and N. R. Mead, 'Survivable Network Systems: An Emerging Discipline', Technical Report, CMU/SEI-97-TR-013. ESC-TR-97-013, November 1997, <http://www.cert.org/research/97tr013.pdf>, accessed 18 April 2007.

Eriksson, Johan (ed.), *Threat Politics: New Perspectives on Security, Risk and Crisis Management* (Ashgate: Aldershot, 2001).

Fisher, Uri, 'Information Age State Security: New Threats to Old Boundaries', *Journal for Homeland Security*, November 2001, <http://www.homelandsecurity.org/journal/articles/fisher.htm>, accessed 18 April 2007.

French, Geoffrey S., 'Shunning the Frumious Bandersnatch, Current Literature on Information Warfare and Deterrence', TRC Analysis (The Terrorism Research Center, 2000), <http://www.terrorism.com/modules.php?op=modload&name=News&file=article&sid=5648&mode=thread&order=0&thold=0>, accessed 18 April 2007.

Geiger, Gebhard, *Offensive Informationskriegsführung. Die 'Joint Doctrine for Information Operations' der US-Streitkräfte: Sicherheitspolitische Perspektiven*, SWP Studie (Berlin: Stiftung Wissenschaft und Politik, 2002).

General Accounting Office, *Computer Security: Hackers Penetrate DOD Computer Systems*, GAO/T-IMTEC-92-5, 20 November 1991 (Washington, D.C,: Congressional Research Service, 1991).

Giacomello, Giampiero, 'Taming the Net? The Issue of Government Control on the internet', *Swiss Political Science Review*, 5/2 (1999): 116–22.

Goldman, Emily O., 'New Threats, New Identities and New Ways of War: The Sources of Change in National Security Doctrine', *Journal of Strategic Studies*, 24/3 (2001): 12–42.

Goodman, Seymour E., Pamela B. Hassebroek, Daving Kind, and Andy Azment, *International Coordination to Increase the Security of Critical Network Infrastructures*, Document CNI/04, paper presented at the ITU Workshop on Creating Trust in Critical Network Infrastructures (Seoul, 20–22 May 2002).

Guéhenno, Jean-Marie, *The End of the Nation-State* (Minneapolis: University of Minnesota Press, 1995).

Haimes, Yacov Y. and Pu Jiang, 'Leontief-Based Model of Risk in Complex Interconnected Infrastructures', *Journal of Infrastructure Systems*, 7/1 (2001): 1–12.

Halperin, David, 'The Internet and National Security: Emerging Issues', in David S. Alberts and Daniel S. Papp (eds), *The Information Age: An Anthology of Its*

Impacts and Consequences, Vol. II (Washington: National Defense University Press, 2000): pp. 137–73.

Hart, Jeffrey, 'Three Approaches to the Measurement of Power in International Relations', *International Organization*, 30/2 (1976): 289–305.

Hart, Jeffrey, and Sangbae A. Kim, 'Power in the Information Age', in Jose V. Ciprut, (ed.), *Of Fears and Foes: International Relations in an Evolving Global Political Economy* (Westport CT: Praeger, 2000).

Haufler, Virginia, 'Crossing the Boundary between Public and Private: International Regimes and Non-State Actors', in Volker Rittberger (ed.), *Regime Theory and International Relations* (Oxford: Clarendon Press, 1993): pp. 94–110.

Herrera, Geoffrey, 'Technology and International Systems', *Millennium*, 32/3 (2003): 559–94.

Hobart, Michael E. and Zachary S. Schiffman, *Information Ages: Literacy, Numeracy, and the Computer Revolution* (Baltimore: Johns Hopkins University Press, 2000).

Holsti, K.J., 'The Problem of Change in International Relations Theory', Institute of International Relations, The University of British Columbia, Working Paper No. 26, December 1998.

Hundley, Richard O. and Robert H. Anderson, 'Emerging Challenge: Security and Safety in Cyberspace', in John Arquilla and David Ronfeldt (eds), *In Athena's Camp: Preparing for Conflict in the Information Age* (Santa Monica: RAND, 1997), pp. 231–52.

Huysmans, Jef, 'Security! What Do You Mean? From Concept to Thick Signifier', *European Journal of International Relations*, 4/2 (1998): 226–55.

Keohane, Robert O. and Joseph S. Nye, 'Power and Interdependence in the Information Age', *Foreign Affairs*, 77/5 (September/October 1998): 81–94.

Kolet, Kristin S., 'Asymmetric Threats to the United States', *Comparative Strategy*, 20 (2001): 277–92.

Kushnick, Bruce, *The Unauthorized Biography of the Baby Bells & Info-Scandal* (New York: New Networks Institute, 1999).

LaPorte, Todd R. (ed.), *Organized Social Complexity: Challenge to Politics and Policy* (Princeton: Princeton University Press, 1975).

Lewis, James A., *Assessing the Risks of Cyber-terrorism, Cyber War and Other Cyber Threats* (Washington: Center for Strategic and International Studies, 2002).

Loon, Joost van, *Risk and Technological Culture: Towards a Sociology of Virulence* (London: Routledge, 2002).

Luiijf, Eric A.M., Helen H. Burger, and Marieke H.A. Klaver, 'Critical Infrastructure Protection in The Netherlands: A Quick-scan', in Urs E. Gattiker, Pia Pedersen and Karsten Petersen (eds), *EICAR Conference Best Paper Proceedings 2003*, <http://www.tno.nl/instit/fel/refs/pub2003/BPP-13-CIP-Luiijf&Burger&Klaver.pdf>, accessed 18 April 2007.

Metzger, Jan, 'The Concept of Critical Infrastructure Protection (CIP)', in A.J.K. Bailes and Isabelle Frommelt (eds), *Business and Security, Public-Private Sector Relationships in a New Security Environment* (Oxford: Oxford University Press, 2004), pp. 197–209.

Mihata, Kevin 'The Persistence of 'Emergence', in Raymond A. Eve, Sara Horsfall, and Mary E. Lee (eds), *Chaos, Complexity, and Sociology, Myths, Models, and Theories* (Thousand Oaks: Sage Publications), pp. 30–8.

Moteff, John D., *Critical Infrastructures: Background, Policy, and Implementation*, CRS (Congressional Research Service) Report for Congress, RL30153, 10 February 2003 (Washington, D.C.: Congressional Research Service, 2003).

Moteff, John, Claudia Copeland, and John Fischer, *Critical Infrastructures: What Makes an Infrastructure Critical?* CRS (Congressional Research Service) Report for Congress, RL31556, 30 August 2002 (Washington, D.C.: Congressional Research Service, 2002).

Näf, Michael, 'Ubiquitous Insecurity? How to "Hack" IT Systems', *Information & Security: An International Journal, Volume 7* (2001): 104–18.

Naisbitt, John, *Megatrends: Ten New Directions Transforming Our Lives* (New York: Warner Books, 1982).

Negroponte, Nicholas, *Being Digital* (New York; Alfred A. Knopf, 1995).

Nichiporuk, Brian and Carl H. Builder, 'Societal Implications', in John Arquilla and David Ronfeldt (eds), *In Athena's Camp, Preparing for Conflict in the Information Age* (Santa Monica: RAND, 1997): pp. 295–314.

Nye, Joseph S. Jr., *Power in the Global Information Age: From Realism to Globalization* (London: Routledge, 2004).

Nye, Joseph S. Jr, 'Soft Power', *Foreign Policy*, 80 (Fall 1990): 153–71.

Nye, Joseph S. Jr., 'US Security Policy: Challenges for the 21st Century', *USIA Electronic Journal*, 3/3 (July 1998), <http://usinfo.state.gov/journals/itps/0798/ijpe/pj38nye.htm>, accessed 18 April 2007.

O'Brien, Kevin A., Andreas Ligtvoet, Andrew Rathmell, and Douglas MacKenzie, *Using Scenarios to Support Critical Infrastructure Analysis and Assessment Work*, ACIP, Package 3 Deliverable D3.4 (Brussels 2003).

Office of Critical Infrastructure Protection and Emergency Preparedness, 'Threat Analysis', Number, TbA03-001, 12 March 2003, <http,//www.ocipep-bpiepc.gc.ca/opsprods/other/TA03-001_e.pdf>, accessed 18 April 2007.

Organski, A.F.K., *World Politics* (New York: Alfred A. Knopf, 1968).

Papp, Daniel S and David S. Alberts, 'The Impacts of the Information Age on International Actors and the International System', in David S. Alberts, and Daniel S. Papp (eds), *The Information Age, An Anthology of Its Impacts and Consequence* (Washington D.C.: National Defense University, 1997).

Papp, Daniel S. David S. Alberts, and Alissa Tuyahov, 'Historical Impacts of Information Technologies, An Overview', in David S. Alberts and Daniel S. Papp (eds), *The Information Age, An Anthology of Its Impacts and Consequences* (Washington D.C.: National Defense University, 1997).

President's Commission on Critical Infrastructure Protection, *Critical Foundations: Protecting America's Infrastructures* (Washington, D.C.: Government Printing Office, October 1997).

Rosenau, James, 'Global Affairs in an Epochal Transformation', in C. Ryan Henry and Edward C. Peartree (eds), *Information Revolution and International Security* (Washington D.C.: Center for Strategic and International Studies Press, 1998): pp. 33–57.

Rosenau, James N., *Turbulence in World Politics: A Theory of Change and Continuity* (Princeton: Princeton University Press, 1990).

Rosenau, James N., 'Governance, Order, and Change in World Politics', in James N. Rosenau and Ernst-Otto Czempiel (eds), *Governance Without Government: Order and Change in World Politics*, Cambridge Studies in International Relations Nr. 20. (Cambridge: Cambridge University Press, 1992): pp. 1–29.

Rothkopf, David J., 'Cyberpolitik: The Changing Nature of Power in the Information Age', *Journal of International Affairs*, 51/2 (Spring 1998): 325–60.

Sarewitz, Daniel, Pielke, Roger and Kaykhah, Mojdeh, 'Vulnerability and Risk: Some Thoughts from a Political and Policy Perspective', *Risk Analysis: An International Journal*, 23/4 (2003): 805–10.

Singer, David J., Stuart Bremer and John Stuckey, 'Capability Distribution, Uncertainty, and Major Power War, 1820–1965', in Bruce Russett (ed.), *Peace, War, and Numbers* (Beverly Hills, Sage Publications, 1972): pp. 21–7.

Singer, David J., 'Threat-Perception and the Armament-Tension Dilemma', *Journal of Conflict Resolution, Vol. II* (March 1958): 90–105.

Smith, George, 'How Vulnerable Is Our Interlinked Infrastructure?', in David S. Alberts and Daniel S. Papp (eds), *The Information Age, An Anthology of Its Impacts and Consequences, Volume II* (Washington, D.C.: National Defense University Press, 2000), pp. 507–23.

Smith, Merritt Roe and Leo Marx (eds), *Does Technology Drive History? The Dilemma of Technological Determinism* (Cambridge: MIT Press, 1994).

Strange, Susan, *The Retreat of the State: The Diffusion of Power in the World Economy* (Cambridge: Cambridge University Press, 1996).

Strogatz, Steven H., 'Exploring Complex Networks', *Nature*, 410 (8 March 2001): 268–76.

The White House, *A National Security Strategy for a New Century* (Washington, D.C.: Government Printing Office, 1997).

Toffler, Alvin, *Future Shock* (New York: Bantam Books, 1970).

Toffler, Alvin, *Third Wave* (New York: Bantam Books, 1980).

Toffler, Alvin, *Power Shift* (New York: Bantam Books, 1981).

Department of the United States Air Force, *Cornerstones of Information Warfare* (Washington D.C.: Department of the United States Air Force, 1995).

United States Joint Forces Command (2004), *United States Joint Forces Command Glossary*, <http://www.jfcom.mil/about/glossary.htm>, accessed 18 April 2007.

Viotti, Paul R. and Mark V. Kauppi, *International Relations Theory, Realism, Pluralism, Globalism, and Beyond* (Needham Heights: Prentice Hall, 1999, 3rd edition).

Vlahos, Michael, 'Entering the Infosphere', *Journal of International Affairs*, 2 (Spring 1998): 497–525.

Volgy, Thomas J., Kristin Kanthak, Derrick Frazier, and Robert Stewart Ingersoll, 'Structural versus Relational Strength, The Cohesion of the G7 and the Development of the Post-Cold War International System', paper presented at the Fifth Annual Pan European International Relations Conference (The Hague, 9–11 September 2004).

Winner, Langdon, *Autonomous Technology: Technics-out-of-control as a Theme in Political Thought* (Cambridge: MIT Press, 1977).

Wolfers, Arnold, 'National Security as an Ambiguous Symbol', in Arnold Wolfers, *Discord and Collaboration, Essays on International Politics* (Baltimore: Johns Hopkins, 1962): pp. 147–65.

Zacher, Mark W., 'The Decaying Pillars of the Westphalian Temple: Implications for International Order and Governance', in James N. Rosenau and Ernst-Otto Czempiel (eds), *Governance Without Government, Order and Change in World Politics*, Cambridge Studies in International Relations Nr. 20 (Cambridge: Cambridge University Press): pp. 58–101.

Chapter 3

Meta-power, Networks, Security and Commerce

J.P. Singh[1]

Introduction

We need a theory of interaction in global politics to understand global transformations. So far, we have lacked one because in a world ordered by nation-states and their interactions, global transformations were fairly regularized, with the status quo-interests usually trumping attempts at transformation. Most current theories, therefore, take actors' identities and preferences for granted and then proceed to analyze outcomes that result from them. That successive interactions might affect the identity and preferences of an individual will come as no surprise to a child psychologist. In international relations, a discipline ossified by its paradigms, such a statement ruffles all feathers except for those of the constructivist faction. However, if identity is constituted and preferences come about as a result of this identity, then it is time not just to re-specify outcomes, but to reconceptualise one of the basic understandings of political science, namely that of power. This paper attempts such conceptualization by advancing the concept of meta-power, and then examines its implications for governance in issue-areas of security and commerce. The conceptualization of meta-power is offered after reviewing the relevant social science literature in the context of a proliferation of information technologies. The discussion of the two issue-areas is suggestive rather than exhaustive of meta-power.

The bold statement about needing a theory of interaction is, hopefully, tempered by the simplicity of the argument in this essay: if interaction changes identity, then information networks – as the sine qua non of globalised interactions in our times – enhance the velocity and scope of these identity changes.[2] For global security and

---

1 Previous versions of this paper were presented at the International Studies Annual Convention, San Diego, 22–25 March 2006, and at the 1st International Conference on 'The Information Revolution and the Changing Face of International Relations and Security' at the Center for Security Studies, Swiss Federal Institute of Technology (ETH Zurich) and the Comparative Interdisciplinary Studies Section (CISS) of the International Studies Association, 23–25 May 2005, in Lucerne, Switzerland. I thank the participants at these events for their feedback, especially Myriam Dunn and Daniel S. Papp. Thanks to Marcus Holmes for research assistance.

2 For the purposes of this paper, the term 'information networks' refers narrowly to all inter-linked human beings and technologies that help to produce, gather, distribute, consume, and store information. These may include, but are not limited to, print and broadcast media, telecommunications (telephone, fax, the internet, the world wide web, etc.), channels of

commerce, this implies that as actors identities' are reconstituted and they pursue new preferences, the challenges lie not just in dealing with the old identities and preferences, but also in trying to shape new habits of governance that do indeed bring security, prosperity, and democracy.

The argument modifies one of the tenets of liberal political theory that celebrates all forms of exchanges; individual interactions make democracies grow and national commercial exchanges thwart war. 'When goods do not cross borders, armies do,' said president Franklin Delano Roosevelt's secretary of state, Cordell Hull. Exchanges can still result in these global 'goods' being provided. However, this assumes an enlightened and educated view of human nature. That all interactions in an age of information networks will validate such a view of human nature is empirically questionable. The same argument applies to the melancholic or pessimistic Hobbesian view of nature. It may not be empirically verifiable.

The Rise of Meta Power[3]

Global politics are inherently relational and interactive. Equations of power can be simplified to 'who does what to whom'. This may entail an analysis of who is empowered, as opposed to those that are disempowered (instrumental power); who is constrained in a given situation as opposed to those who get to write the rules (structural power); and, finally, how basic identities, interests, and issues themselves are reconstituted or transformed in particular historical contexts, in turn redefining other relations of power (called 'meta-power' here). International relations research has concentrated on instrumental and structural variants of power. This essay contends that constructivists implicitly employ a different understanding of power in noting the construction of actors' identities and interests that is termed 'meta-power' here.

Technologies not only have an impact on existing actors and issues, but as an increasing number of authors note, networked interaction itself is a constituting element of the identities of actors and issues in global politics. If we merely focus on actors' capabilities and take their identities and interests as given, as most instrumental and structural power versions do, the transformation being brought about by information networks is missed. Networking is highly interactive. 'Meta-power' thus refers to how networks reconfigure, constitute, or reconstitute identities, interests, and institutions. Here, the transformation brought about does not affect how X leads to Y, but the nature of X and Y is changed. Thus, instead of speaking of the impact of a particular resource in an issue-area, meta-power speaks to how we must now speak of the issue-area itself in a different way because of the changes in underlying 'resources'.

---

communication (satellites, different types of cables including fibre optics), computers, and storage devices (DVDs, CD-ROMs).

3   This sub-section is adapted and updated from J.P. Singh, 'Introduction: Information Technologies and the Changing Scope of Power and Governance', in James N. Rosenau and J.P. Singh (eds), *Information Technologies and Global Politics: The Changing Scope of Power and Governance* (Albany, 2002), pp. 1–38.

The need to advance beyond instrumental or structural power to understand global transformations is increasingly recognized in international relations theorizing. Interestingly enough, even neo-realists implicitly recognized the notion of meta-power early on. Gilpin, for example, distinguishes between regular interstate interactions and changes in systemic governance versus fundamental changes of the system dealing with 'the nature of the actors or diverse entities that compose an international system'.[4] He notes that the latter change is understudied but that it is 'particularly relevant in the present era, in which new types of transnational and international actors are regarded as taking roles that supplant the traditional dominant role of the nation-state, and the nation-state itself is held to be an increasingly anachronistic institution'.[5] However, while recognizing these transformations, Gilpin does not deviate much from the instrumental notions of power.

Krasner refers directly to meta-power when noting post-colonial Third World advocacy.[6] Meta-power would allow these states to steer the structure and rules of the market-based liberal international economy toward rules favoring them through authoritative redistributions. Krasner views calls in developing countries for the creation of UNCTAD, a New International Economic Order (NIEO), and a New World/Information Communication Order (NWICO) as strategies for power maximization. He then returns to a familiar conclusion: meta-power itself depends on capabilities; the Third World must suffer what it must. It cannot reconstitute the system. Nevertheless, implicitly he makes a fundamental point in the context of this essay: a change of the system must be understood in meta-power terms.

Nye and Keohane and Nye point out the ascendancy of 'soft power', or power through persuasion and attraction rather than force, as a new salient feature of global politics when information networks proliferate.[7] Soft power, though, is again conceived as a resource that changes the actors' identities and the nature of the issue-area. The only difference is that persuasion and diplomacy are used as resources instead of the force of hard power that comes from military and economic resources.

Nye comes close to a notion of 'meta-power' in his writing on soft power, but backs away from it in favour of explaining outcomes by taking actor identities and interests as constant. He goes beyond an instrumental understanding in explaining soft power in noting, for example, that cultural exchanges can change people's preferences.[8] Here Nye is not merely outlining choices within a given preference ordering, as assumed in most rational choice analyses, but he is noting a change in preferences themselves. The conceptual leap that Nye has made to co-opt

---

4   Robert Gilpin, *War and Change in World Politics* (Cambridge, 1981), p. 39.

5   Ibid., p. 41.

6   Stephen Krasner, *Structural Conflict: The Third World Against Global Liberalism* (Berkeley, 1985) pp. 14–18.

7   Joseph S. Nye Jr., *The Paradox of American Power: Why the World's Only Superpower Can't Go It Alone* (Oxford, 2002); Joseph S. Nye Jr., *Bound to Lead: The Changing Nature of American Power* (New York, 1990); Robert Keohane and Joseph S. Nye Jr., 'Power and Interdependence in the Information Age', *Foreign Affairs*, 77/5 (1998): 81–94.

8   Joseph S. Nye Jr., *Soft Power: The Means to Succeed in World Politics* (New York, 2004), pp. 5, 6, 14.

constructivist concepts here is quite clear. What is unclear is how the instrumentality of soft power can accommodate the notion of changing preferences, or that of identities underlying preferences. If X incorporates Y's cultural values through the workings of soft power, X moves toward cultural hybridity– that changes not just her preferences but perhaps also her identity and the choices she makes with it. It also cannot be assumed that such cultural hybridity will not engender conflict or that it will always lead to good outcomes.

The cognitive and interpretative insights offered by a few other neo-liberal scholars also address issues of how interests and preferences are formed.[9] Nonetheless, most neo-liberals and neo-realists, with few exceptions, take their cues from rational-choice analyses, in which the identities and interests of actors, mostly nation-states, are posited ex-ante. Gilpin's concern is not how identity is constituted, but how new types of actors (be they empires, nation-states, or transnational enterprises) influence the international system. Krasner's meta-power theory is about weak nation-states clamouring for power in the world system. Keohane and Nye's soft power is related to actor interests that are taken as given. These static notions are under scrutiny by analysts situating their arguments in historical sociology, a growing tradition in international relations, now called 'the constructivist turn'.[10] The challenge is best summarized by one of the chief proponents of constructivism, Alexander Wendt: 'Despite important differences, cognitivists, poststructuralists, standpoint and postmodern feminists, rule theorists, and structurationists share a concern with the basic 'sociological' issue bracketed by rationalists – namely, the issue of identity- and interest-formation. [...] They share a cognitive, intersubjective conception of process in which identities and interests are endogenous to interaction, rather than a rationalist-behavioural one in which they are exogenous.'[11] Wendt recognizes that there are scholars, especially in the neo-liberal tradition, who have craved such

---

9   Ernst Hass, *When Knowledge is Power* (Berkeley, 1989); Susan Sell, *Power and Ideas: North-South Politics of Intellectual Property and Antitrust* (Albany, 1998); John Odell, *Negotiating the Global Economy* (Ithaca, 2000).

10 Well-known works include Martha Finnemore, *National Interest in International Society* (Ithaca, 1996); Margaret E. Keck and Kathryn Sikkink, *Activists Beyond Borders: Advocacy Networks in International Politics* (Ithaca, 1998); Peter J. Katzenstein (ed.), *The Culture of National Security: Norms and Identity in World Politics* (Ithaca, 1996); Thomas J. Biersteker and Cynthia Weber, *State Sovereignty as Social Construct* (Cambridge, 1996); John Gerard Ruggie, 'Territoriality and Beyond: Problematizing Modernity in International Relations', *International Organization*, 17 (1993): 139–74; Alexander Wendt, *Social Theory of International Politics* (Cambridge, 1999); Alexander Wendt, 'Anarchy is What States Make of It: The Social Construction of Power Politics', *International Organization*, 46/2 (Spring 1992): 391–425; Nicholas Onuf, *A World of Our Making: Rules and Rule in Social Theory and International Relations* (Columbia, 1989). Postmodernists and gender theorists, whose work overlaps with this tradition, include Cynthia Weber, *Faking It: U.S. Hegemony in a 'Post-Phallic' Era* (Minneapolis, 1999); Spike V. Peterson, 'Whose Crisis? Early and Post-Modern Masculinism', in Stephen Gill and James H. Mittelman (eds), *Innovation and Transformation in International Studies* (Cambridge, 1997), pp. 185–201; Cynthia Enloe, *The Morning After* (Berkeley,1993); James Der Derian and Michael J. Shapiro (eds), *International/Intertextual Relations* (Lexington, 1989).

11 Alexander Wendt, 'Anarchy is What States Make of It', 393–94.

analysis, and he is answering the critics of constructivism as well as trying to bring about a gestalt shift in them. Keohane, years earlier, had called these traditions 'reflectivist'.[12] While appreciating the historical contextuality of intersubjective interest and identity formation, Keohane noted that 'the sociological approach has recently been in some disarray, at least in international relations: its adherents have neither the coherence nor the self-confidence of the rationalists.'[13] Keohane's critique notwithstanding, other disciplines have long offered the kind of empirical insights that he demands. Within social sciences, anthropology and sociology provide early examples. Halbwach's early work on collective memory showed how images and symbols that societal groups hold can be traced historically and shape the preferences of group members.[14] Halbwach concludes that 'all social thought is essentially a memory and its entire content consists only of collective recollections or remembrances. But it also follows that, among them, only those recollections subsist that in every period society, working within its present-day frameworks, can reconstruct.'[15] Berger and Luckmann call attention to primary and secondary socializations to argue that reality is a social construction: 'Identity is formed by social processes. Once crystallized, it is maintained, modified, or even reshaped by social relations.'[16] Anthropologist Geertz was a forceful early advocate: 'To set forth symmetrical crystals of significance, purified of the material complexity in which they are located, and then attribute their existence to autogenous principles of order, universal properties of the human mind, or vast a priori weltanschauungen, is to pretend a science that does not exist and imagine a reality that cannot be found.'[17] Putting it bluntly, 'there is no such thing as a human nature independent of culture'.[18] Sociologist Castells would agree: 'It is easy to agree on the fact that, from the sociological perspective, all identities are constructed. The real issue is how, from what, by whom, and for what.'[19]

The Contribution of Cultural Studies

Meta-power goes beyond changes in preferences to examine changes in the underlying identities of international actors as well as changes in the identities of the issue-areas. Adherents of the meta-power theory thus benefit from insights in cultural studies that identity issues need to be examined from the perspective of everyday life or culture

---

12 Robert Keohane, 'International Institutions: Two Approaches', *International Studies Quarterly*, 32/4 (1988): 379–96.

13 Ibid.: 381.

14 Maurice Halbwach, *On Collective Memory* (Chicago, 1992/1941).

15 Ibid., p. 189.

16 Peter Berger and Thomas Luckmann, *The Social Construction of Reality: A Treatise in the Sociology of Knowledge* (New York, 1967), p. 173.

17 Clifford Geertz, *The Interpretation of Cultures* (New York, 1973), p. 20.

18 Ibid., p. 49.

19 Manuel Castells, *The Information Age: Economy Society and Culture: The Power of Identity* (Oxford, 1997), vol. 2, p. 7.

and the way it is influenced by power holders. Meta-power here would then refer to the changing epistemes of everyday life as a result of information networks.

Foucault's analyses painstakingly reconstruct the social circumstances that privilege particular knowledge.[20] All forms of knowledge then reveal micro-power relations carrying subtle means of co-opting or marginalizing individuals. Said, acknowledging an intellectual debt to Foucault, shows how colonizing Europe in fact created the Orient as a location, idea, and homogenous culture: 'Knowledge of the Orient, because generated out of strength, in a sense creates the Orient, the Oriental, and his world. [...] Orientalism, then, is knowledge of the Orient that places things Oriental in class, court, prison, or manual for scrutiny, study, judgment, discipline, or governing.'[21] The construction and domination of the Orient are inextricably linked.

In gender studies, the realist worldview is posited as androcentric and posited as stuck in an 'us' versus 'them' binary/dichotomy. In the words of Spike Peterson, the observations are not 'out there,' but 'in here.'[22] In her example, patriarchy cannot be observed out there; it is in people's heads. 'Hence, knowers cannot stand 'outside of' the reality they observe because their participation in that reality is a necessary condition for the object observed to have any meaning; both subject and object gain their meaning and intelligibility by reference to their location in a system of meaning (language and thought) that encompasses both.'[23] Second, even when we may be able to observe particular phenomena, they may not help to clarify the real underlying causes of phenomena. To merely observe consumption choices reveal to us neither the origins nor the outcomes of these choices. Adorno and Horkheimer's thesis on cultural industries asserts that the latter beguile the workers into supporting capitalism.[24] If we then merely see workers as consumers, we miss the ideology of consumerism that enslaves the consumers and the effects of capitalism on human behaviour.

Things 'as they are' mean very little in a cultural studies methodology. Things 'as they came into being' mean a whole lot more. Furthermore, this is not a simple question of making valid inferences. In semiotics, the relationship between the signifier and signified can only be laid bare by problematising the process that links the two phenomena. We must have historical and contextual knowledge prior to making the inference, not after it. Arriving at the inference, it seems, is far more important than making further inferences from it. In introducing a body of work that deals with the semiotics of visual images, Evans and Hall write that they 'are not concerned with the 'meaning' of any image or corpus of images, but with a culture in which reproducibility provides the conditions of existence of any particular meaning.'[25]

---

20 Michel Foucault, *The Order of Things: An Archaeology of the Human Sciences* (New York, 1970).

21 Edward Said, *Orientalism* (New York, 1978), p. 40f.

22 Peterson, 'Whose Crisis?'.

23 Spike Peterson and Anne Runyan, *Global Gender Issues* (Boulder, 1998), p. 24.

24 Theodor Adorno and Max Horkheimer, 'The Culture Industry: Enlightenment as Mass Deception', in *Dialectic of Enlightenment,* trans. John Cumming (New York, 1972).

25 Jessica Evans and Stuart Hall (eds), *Visual Culture: A Reader* (London, 1999), p. 3.

In international relations terms, cultural studies scholars are asking us to problematise the world orders we study rather than study particular relationships within these world orders. In fact, were we to do this, we would not ask the kinds of questions we do at present, which seem to cultural studies to be vacuous and meaningless. To them, studying the rise of consumption institutions is far more important than the preference orderings of individual consumers.[26] At the very least, cultural studies scholars ask us to question why we ask the questions we do. In a broad sense, they are asking us to study the how and why of institutions and world orders more before we turn to the behaviour of actors (atomistic or not) within them.

Indeed, while the 'constructivist turn' is somewhat new in international relations scholarship, conceptually scholarship stands to benefit from the claims/insights of historical sociology and cultural studies. This is a valuable exercise in refining the concept of meta-power. Other social theorists may relate the constitution of identities and interests in global politics to similar conceptualizations.

Linking Constructivism with Information Networks

The link between information networks and constructivism can now be made explicit. The collective meanings that actors hold about themselves, or the meanings imposed upon them, are shaped by networks and in turn influence networks. But the constitution and effects of such identity formation remain contested among scholars. A few theorists see technology as merely playing a catalytic role in accelerating or reinforcing extant or incipient processes. Others see technologies as allowing for new types of identity and collective meanings. A quote from Said is illustrative: 'One aspect of the electronic, postmodern world is that there has been a reinforcement of the stereotypes by which the Orient is viewed. Television, the films, and all the media's resources have forced information into more and more standardized molds.'[27] Here technology remains neutral, reinforcing existing stereotypes.

Litfin offers a nuanced empirical case of the complicated, and somewhat serendipitous, processes governing network effects.[28] Building on Foucault and on Jeremy Bentham's plans for the Panoptican prison, where a 'disciplinary gaze' monitors and conditions the human behaviour, Litfin notes that the diffusion of networks also leads to the decentralization of this gaze and to the proliferation of 'public eyes.' In understanding such shifts, therefore, we must move beyond analyses that view technology only in an instrumental fashion. Litfin shows that information networks are in fact facilitating a new social episteme that not only changes the definition of issues in question (security, environment and human rights), but also allows for new actors (NGOs, in Litfin's example) to start playing key roles in global

---

26 Edward Comor, 'New Technologies and Consumption: Contradictions in the Emergent World Order', in Rosenau and Singh, pp. 169–88.

27 Said, *Orientalism*, pp. 40f.

28 Karen Litfin, 'Public Eyes: Satellite Imagery, the Globalization of Transparency, and New Networks of Surveillance', in Rosenau and Singh, pp. 65–90.

politics.[29] Her analysis, therefore, illustrates 'both of the ways in which technological change can alter international reality: instrumentally and constitutively.'

Litfin's assessment makes us question the assumption of technological neutrality, according to which technology merely facilitates preexisting actors and issues and does not propose new identities or action. This, however, is not technological determinism. Vattimo's notes on technology and post-modernity are instructive: '[W]hat concerns us in the postmodern age is a transformation of (the notion of) Being as such – and technology, properly conceived, is the key to that transformation.'[30]

Medium theorists have long argued that technological media privilege particular social epistemes and identities while weakening others. In a famous phrase in *Empire and Communication*, Harold Innis pointed out that written media extend administrative control through time, while oral traditions extend it temporally.[31] Media thus propose conditions of organization that are realized through societal interactions. Marshall McLuhan's medium theory focuses on how media shape individual and societal experiences. At an individual level, 'hot' media like radio and print are authoritative and do not allow for much audience participation, but 'cool' media like television and telephone do allow for interaction and participation. McLuhan would probably argue that information networks are 'cool' interactive media, although they offer endless possibilities for conflict and cooperation as we come together into a 'global village.'[32] Consider the following statement by McLuhan: 'The alphabet (and its extension into typography) made possible the spread of power that is knowledge and shattered the bonds of tribal man, thus exploding him into an agglomeration of individuals. Electric writing and speed pour upon him instantaneously and continuously the concerns of all other men. He becomes tribal once more. The human family becomes one tribe again.'[33]

Benedict Anderson, while not a medium theorist, is appreciative of the transformative features of media. The spread of printed vernacular languages, as opposed to Latin, when printing began helped to form notions of nationalism and the 'imagined community' of a nation-state: 'These print-languages laid the basis for a national consciousness in three distinct ways. First and foremost, they created unified fields of exchange and communication below Latin and above the spoken vernaculars. [...] Second, print-capitalism gave a new fixity to language, which in the long run helped to build that image of antiquity so central to the subjective idea of the nation. [...] Third, print-capitalism created languages-of-power of a kind different from the older administrative vernaculars.'[34] Technology does not determine politics, but in the context of capitalism and of what Anderson calls 'fatality' or 'pre-existing

---

29 Litfin, 'Public Eyes: Satellite Imagery, the Globalization of Transparency, and New Networks of Surveillance'.

30 Gianni Vattimo, 'Postmodernity, Technology, Ontology', in Arthur M. Meltzer, Jerry Weinberger, and M. Richard Zinman (eds), *Technology in the Western Political Tradition* (Ithaca, 1993), pp. 214–28.

31 Harold Innis, *Empire and Communications* (Oxford, 1950).

32 Marshall McLuhan and Bruce Powers, *The Global Village* (New York, 1989).

33 Marshall McLuhan, *Understanding Media: The Extensions of Man* (Cambridge, 1964/1997).

34 Benedict Anderson, *Imagined Communities* (London, 1983/1991), pp. 44–5.

conditions,' technology shapes the rise of nation-states and nationalism. Technology helps a modernizing Europe to organize territory and time.

Deibert extends medium theory and Anderson's analysis to argue that the kind of collective images that information networks or hypermedia privilege differ from authoritative nation-state oriented images of the past.[35] Ideas of security centred on nations or states are unlikely to endure in interconnected information networks. He notes the rise of 'network security' in which 'the primary 'threat' of the Internet is the potential for systems 'crash,' loss, theft or corruption of data, and interruption of information flows. The primary object of security is the network.'[36]

Gilpin had argued that developments in military technology allowed states to think of territorial expansion as the only means and end of power.[37] However, physical territory itself, as epitomized geographically in nation-states, continued to be of importance. Deibert and others now posit constitutive contexts where territoriality no longer governs human interaction. The world of 'hyper-space' challenges the idea of 'territorial space' especially as defined by nation-states, as the only kind of space, especially defined by nation-states. Ruggie and Castells advocate looking at 'space of flows' in information networks along with 'spaces-of-places' that existed earlier.

The preceding analysis postulates that each epoch's interactions are in part proposed and molded by its technologies. Information technology networks in particular show how the collective social epistemes are shifting away from hierarchical authoritative contexts privileging nation-states. Interconnected networks may flatten hierarchies, or transform them altogether, into new types of spaces where territoriality itself becomes extinct.

Luke offers an alternative view. While discarding the linear perspectivism offered by 'modernity,' he is less sanguine about empowerment of marginal actors. For him, 'informational modes of production' lead to 'completely commodified communication'.[38] Combining cultural theory (Horkheimer and Adorno), semiotics (Barthes, Baudrillard) and Marxist theory, he notes: 'The power exercised in nonlinear, screenal space, however, is more puzzling. It seems to require continuous coproduction by those with access to 'behind the screens' and those without access 'before the screens.' Power here is essentially seductive, motivating its subjects with images to collaborate in reproducing or completing the codes' logic or sequence at their screens. Individuals recreate themselves continuously in the permissive coding of individual self-management. The institutional leadership of informational society recognizes that 'rebelling' within such screenal spaces is not necessarily a serious threat to the social order.'[39]

---

35 Ronald Deibert, 'Black Code: Censorship, Surveillance, and the Militarization of Cyberspace', *Millennium*, 30/3 (2003): 501–30; Ronald Deibert, *Parchment, Printing, and Hypermedia: Communication and World Order Transformation* (New York, 1997).

36 Ronald Deibert, 'Circuits of Power: Security in the Internet Environment', in Rosenau and Singh, pp. 115–42.

37 Gilpin, *War and Change in World Politics*.

38 Timothy Luke, *Screens of Power: Ideology, Domination and Resistance in Information Society* (Urbana, 1989), p. 24.

39 Ibid., p. 48.

Constructivism in international relations scholarship and cultural studies in general support the basis for what this essay terms meta-power. A caveat is nonetheless necessary. Taken to an extreme, meta-power does not merely supplement, but also replaces traditional notions of power and authority. The constitution of ideas, interests, and institutions is important, but that should not limit us from not noticing actors' capabilities within particular contexts. For Wendt, while state interests may change, they can also be taken as given in the short-run.[40] Similarly, this essay argues for noticing the changing scope of power in all its variants above. However, it emphasizes conceptualizations of meta-power for transformational contexts.

To summarize, information networks in an instrumental sense can be seen as only enhancing or diminishing the capabilities of actors. In a meta-power sense, information networks change the very context – understood here as the identities of issues and actors – within which interactions take place. Thus, meta-power is antecedent to instrumental power and supplements our understanding of the context within which instrumental power works. It is argued here that meta-power is to constructivism what instrumental power was to liberal theory. Meta-power then refers to the information base or the episteme of actors and issues; it does not or cannot explain how this episteme will change. For that, the constructivist paradigm itself or the propositions derived from it must be taken into account. Similarly, instrumental power is not a worldview by itself; liberal theory is the ontology that is derived from it.

Information networks → Transformation of context (via change in information base or episteme) → capabilities of actors (instrumental power) → international outcomes

Applications to Issue-Areas

Transformations overlap with the status quo rather than replacing it altogether. Nation-states have in the past overlapped with empires, the church, and the city-states. Transformations also propose several institutional outcomes and it can be hard to predict which one of the institutional solutions will win.[41] The first task, nonetheless, is to take stock of the old and the new identities of actors, as well as of global issues of security and commerce.

Security

It is no coincidence that issues of culture have come to the fore in thinking of security.[42] 'Security' in a cultural sense means the absence of any threat to identity,

---

40 Wendt, 'Anarchy is What States Make of It'.

41 Social scientists are not afraid to try. Hendrik Spruyt, *The Sovereign State and its Competitors* (Princeton, 1996) analyzes how the nation-state arose from among a variety of institutional forms that existed in the modern era. Deibert (2002) proposes that networks are better privileged than other institutional forms such as states or nations as a result of information technologies.

42 See, for example, Katzenstein, *The Culture of National Security*.

or a way of life, and to the territorial or extra-territorial boundaries that contain this identity.[43] Meta-power calculations can inform us about the relevant epistemes here, by outlining identity, boundaries, and the actors involved. For example, the threats that realist international relations scholars have most readily recognized are those to national identity. In networked environments, such threats may not be reducible to national contexts.

Huntington's realist thesis is the most well known in linking culture and security.[44] But networks do not feature in his analysis, and identity is far from being understood in an anthropological micro-level sense relating to everyday life. Instead, identity is conceived in the context of the 'broader reaches of human history' at the civilizational level of Christianity versus Islam and Confucianism. Nation-states arbitrate this conflict: 'Nation-states will remain the most powerful actors in world affairs, but the principal conflicts will occur between nations and groups of different civilizations.'[45] For many pundits, the events of 9/11 and the invasions of Afghanistan and Iraq lend credence to Huntington's prognosis.

The question of information networks is seldom brought up in realist theory except perhaps in an instrumental sense. Nye's states use persuasion or soft power to enhance their objectives.[46] Rosecrance's 'virtual states' can realize their interests only by networking with other states.[47] This leaves open the question of the derivation of interests itself. Realists get around the problem of constructing national interests by deducing them from influences at the systemic or structural levels. Thus, a nation-state derives its interests from its position in the hierarchy of power or by the power posturing of other states in the system.[48]

Historical sociologists move beyond the 'us' versus 'them' binary that traditional realists pose to acknowledge that culture is a social fact such that the meaning of security can only be understood by understanding how national interests are constructed and not just deduced from a given hierarchy.[49] Here, state identities are constructed, but not the states themselves, thus leaving open the question of the mutations of state identities and the threats to the centrality of states from emergent institutional forms. However, Boulding's early essay can be seen as prodding us to do so.[50] National images are formed during childhood and not just imposed by the

---

43 Understood in a networked sense, this definition tries not to reduce security threats to a particular actor or the act that it finds threatening. Nevertheless, it tries to build upon the idea of 'securitization' offered by Barry Buzan, 'The Security Dynamics of a 1+4 World', in Ersel Aydinli and James N. Rosenau (eds), *Paradigms in Transition: Globalization, Security and the Nation-State* (Albany, 2005), pp. 177–98: 'a security issue is posited (by a securitizing actor) as a threat to the survival of some referent object (nation, state, the liberal international economic order, the rain forest), which is claimed to have a right to survive'.

44 Samuel Huntington, 'The Clash of Civilizations?', *Foreign Affairs*, 73 (1993): 22–49.

45 Ibid.: 22.

46 Nye, *The Paradox of American Power*; and Nye, *Bound to Lead*.

47 Richard Rosecrance, 'The Rise of the Virtual State', *Foreign Affairs*, 75 (1996): 45–61.

48 Kenneth Waltz, *Theories of International Politics* (New York, 1979).

49 See, for example, Katzenstein, *The Culture of National Security*.

50 Kenneth Boulding, 'National Images and International Systems', *Journal of Conflict Resolution*, 3/2 (1959): 120–31.

elite. Collective memories sustain the images. He calculates systemic level security through a matrix of each state's friendliness or hostility toward other states that is contingent upon the national images it holds. This leads to a simple but telling conclusion: 'It is hard for an ardent patriot to realize that his country is a mental, rather than a physical phenomenon, but such indeed is the truth!'.[51]

An understanding of meta-power and information networks supplements rather than replaces traditional notions of security. The relevant question is, what is security? Whose security? And who provides it? The answers are networks, networks, and networks. The idea of networked security is important in that it does not turn everything into a security issue, but does link important past conceptions of security with emerging ones. Ole Wæver, detailing various constructs of security in Europe, writes: 'While not wanting any power external to themselves to dominate, Europeans increasingly accept the idea that Europe should be organized in some mixed form combining independent states and a center.'[52] Later he notes: 'A concept and vision of Europe has become critical to each nation's 'vision of itself' and therefore since it is very hard, notably in Germany and France, to construct convincing narratives of 'where we are heading' without presenting or drawing upon a project of European integration.'[53]

The following table contrasts the major differences between national and networked security scenarios:

Neither the actors nor the issues look the same in a networked security environment. The only way to understand the new context is through cultural meta-power lenses. Like the concept of instrumental power, meta-power is not a variable, but a conceptual category. If instrumental power is about enhancing the capabilities

Dimensions	**National Security**	**Networked Security**
Actors	Nation-states	Nation-states and non-state actors
Authority structures	Hierarchical	Networked
Security threats	Understood territorially	Understood territorially and extra-territorially
Absence of threats	Balance of power	Stabilized or secure identities of issues and actors
Containing threats	Arms races, military alliances	Effective networking
Linkages with other issues	Military threats dominate over others	Issue-structures contain complex linkages among issues

of actors, meta-power is about redefining the identity of the actors as well as the issues.

---

51 Boulding, 'National Images and International Systems': 122.

52 Ole Wæver, 'The Constellation of Securities in Europe', in Aydinli and Rosenau, *Paradigms in Transition*, pp. 151–74.

53 Wæver, 'The Constellation of Securities in Europe'.

Two illustrations drawn from the European and US contexts can be illustrative. The war on terror, an abstraction, when conceptualized in national security terms, calls for transforming 'terror' into a national category and then waging a war on a nation-state. Such thinking, often critiqued in the opinion pages of papers, does not reduce the security threat, but produces some comfort for those who see threats as being best met through military force.[54] A Pew Research Center survey, the fourth in a series since 1987, found that those who favour military responses as appropriate for dealing with terrorism outnumber those who believe such responses only create more insecurity.[55] It is in this context of two contrasting worldviews that one can understand the resignation statement offered by John Brady Kiesling, a career foreign service officer, to Secretary of State Colin Powell: 'We have begun to dismantle the largest and most effective web of international relationships the world has ever known. Our current course will bring instability and danger, not security.'

It is unclear whether European power capitals are responding to perceived security threats any differently than the US. This in spite of the media reports that posit the Europeans as less unilateralist and more peace loving than the pro-Bush Americans. The response to perceived threats from its migrant communities, especially Muslim migrants, is harsh. The rise of right-wing extremism, violence, and political support are key indicators. There are other indicators of which the most ominous at an everyday level is the denial of basic citizenship rights to communities that migrated generations ago. At work again is an imaginary that favours the nation-state.[56]

Meta-power issues in security, which were in turn brought to fore by the proliferation of information networks, highlight the varied cultural contexts in which security must be understood. Here, the meaning of the issues area, namely security, or that of the actors involved (the 'enemy', for example), must be re-understood. Security understood in a territorial sense and with the enemy being a particular nation-state takes the world 'as-is,' not how it has been transformed by technology. Not only do we then have a faulty theoretical model of the world, but more importantly, the resultant policy prescriptions are ineffective.

The cultural context of security means that information networks cannot be understood in territorial terms. Security must be understood at the epistemic level at which people experience the world with respect to their identity. Take two recent

---

54 However, cases do exist where the war on terror in not reduced to national security terms; these include surveillance or restrictions on the movements of individuals, information, finance, and military armaments. For example, following 9/11, the bank accounts of several charities suspected of funnelling money to terrorists in the Arab and Muslim worlds were monitored or closed down. I thank Dan Papp for pointing this out to me.

55 *Financial Times*, 13 May 2005, p. 1.

56 Several essays in Mabel Berezain and Martin Schain (eds), *Europe Without Borders: Remapping Territoriality, Citizenship, and Identity in a Transnational Age* (Baltimore, 2003) point out the imprint, but ultimately also the limited ability, of the nation-state in dealing with issues of migration within European borders. 'An important number of networks – some formal, some informal; some based on identity, some on interest, some often on both – cross national borders and form a spiderweb that covers Europe.' (Riva Kastorvano, 'Transnational Networks and Political Participation: The Place of Immigrants in the European Union', in Berezin and Schain, pp. 64–85).

cases involving information networks and the circulation of images: photographs taken by US soldiers of inmates at the Abu Ghraib prison outside of Baghdad and circulated over media channels starting April 2004; and, the publication of cartoons caricaturing Prophet Mohammed by the Danish newspaper *Jyllands-Posten* on 30 September 2005. In instrumental terms, the impact of both of these images can be examined within the context of nation-states (US-Iraq war on terror; protests against Denmark). In meta-power terms, the very definition of security and the actors involved must be questioned. First, why were the images so important? How did they relate to identity issues? How can we understand the meaning of security with respect to these images?[57] In meta-power terms, our answers to these questions will bring to fore issues listed in the third column of the table above: nation-states and other actors; networked interactions; territoriality and extra-territoriality; identity of actors and issues; and complex linkages among issue-structures.

In an instrumental sense, our answers to these questions will involve nation-states understood in hierarchical and territorial terms. Security is conceived territorially and is enforced primarily through military means. Deibert notes the following dimensions in the responses by nation-states and powerful commercial sectors to the proliferation of cyberspace: increasing censorship, surveillance, and militarization.[58] To this can be added the continuing perception of cyberspace in territorial terms. All these notions are best understood as internalizations of instrumental power frames among the powerful. Security, in the meantime, continues to be re-defined by the meta-power of information networks.

The Global Information Economy (GIE)

The rise of the global information economy is directly attributable to information technologies, and varies from one-half to two-thirds of the world's total output. Meta-power calls attention to the rise of the GIE and the way commercial exchanges are both transformed and facilitated in this changed context. By focusing on the global information economy, we are also focusing on cases that are often taken to be the sine qua non of globalization. GIE presents us several cases in which the old and the new world are colliding and which are thus ideal for analyzing the working of instrumental power, and also for the rise of new identities and issues via the workings of meta-power.

I focus here on international negotiations underlying the global information economy, theoretically interesting for two reasons: first, negotiations are highly interactive and thus in themselves a microcosm for observing the workings of meta-power; second, the rise of the global information economy is itself making salient the issues of meta-power.

Examples of interest alteration through increased interaction abound. Perhaps, the example of cultural industry export – as in the case of security, involving circulation

---

57 I have deliberately shied away from answering these questions myself. Meta-power only calls these issues to question. Ontological schools of thought such as constructivism then must be used to answer them.

58 Deibert, 'Black Code'.

of images – is theoretically useful for us. The entire argument centred on the so-called 'cultural exception' – entailing protecting cultural industries from free trade because they are intimately connected with the identity of peoples – comes about due to the preponderance of exports generated by the cultural industry, especially those emanating from Hollywood. That these services can now be delivered over the internet points to both the importance of networks and, perhaps, also to the increasing contentious attempts by institutions to try to stem identity change. International negotiations where cultural industry issues are raised arouse heated debates and coalitional passions. It is not hard to argue that issues related to the cultural industry, which often touch on people's identities, reflect the challenges of globalization in the ordinary lives of people everywhere.

Negotiation theory, rooted in the practice of several interactive tactics, is well situated to explain the failure of many of the negotiations involving the trade in cultural goods. Negotiation analysis also helps to explain how particular national or other identities are created or reinforced in international debates involving cultural issues. Meta-power analysis can help to explain the process by which cultural identities evolve and are involved in negotiations. In particular, the evolution of Western Europe's preferences as they relate to cultural goods, with special reference to France, is interesting because it allows us to see how the French idea of a cultural exception has evolved over time and how it is linked with evolving European identity. The issue almost broke apart the Uruguay Round of trade talks (1986–1994) in the end game of negotiations during the latter half of 1993, when EC insisted on the now-famous MFN exemption on audio-visual goods and services, otherwise known as the cultural exception. Canada and France have since then taken the issue to UNESCO, where a Convention on Cultural Diversity is being sought that will make it possible, among other things, for countries to regulate their cultural industries and override any related WTO provisions. A global network of cultural industry organizations and professionals also backs the convention.

To understand the evolving shape of the global information economy, theoretical models that privilege only nation-states and the deduction of their interests from hierarchical power distributions are insufficient. In the case above, the interplay of France, EU, WTO, UNESCO, Hollywood, and international networks reveals to us the many forces at play here. Nevertheless, the state-centric security-dominated world is reflected well in international relations theory. To some extent, the following famous appraisal of the field of 'International Relations,' dating a quarter of a century back, may still be valid. Stanley Hoffmann tells us that the state-centric security-dominant model reflected in practice in what he calls 'the relays between the kitchens of power and the academic salon.'[59] He notes that 'what the scholars offered, the policy-makers wanted. [...] Realism, however critical of specific policies, however (and thus self-contradictorily) diverse in its recommendations, precisely provided what was necessary.'[60] Instead of *explaining* state interests, realism here *forms* state interests. As a theoretical model, a self-fulfilling prophecy!

---

59 Stanley Hoffmann, 'An American Social Science: International Relations', *Daedalus*, 106/3 (1977): 41–60.
60 Hoffmann, 'An American Social Science': 47–8.

Theories in international economic negotiations that still hearken to such analyses usually only feature state actors. Other actors, if allowed, are subservient to state interests. In such cases, state interests are guided by maximization of power politically even when negotiating on economic matters. Economic negotiations between the US and the Europeans or the Japanese in the immediate post-war period are frequently cited as examples. Given its superior capabilities (potential power) and the predominance of authority, the salience of military-political relations in the world, a powerful state can easily convert its capabilities into action (actual power/fungibility of power) because there is great deal of fungibility of power where military-political relations are concerned. Instrumental power, therefore, extends across many issue-areas. Strong states can also discipline or socialize weaker states into following their dictates. For example, it was only in the Uruguay Round of trade talks (1986–94) that developing countries were effectively included in economic negotiations. Until then, great powers used their authority to exclude them, discipline them (President Reagan in Cancun in 1983 telling the countries from the southern hemisphere to allow international investments or expect nothing), or to make them conform (unilaterally imposed quantitative restrictions to exports from the developing world). The weak, on their part, protest or use confrontational strategies, but to little avail. At best, they manage to play off great powers against each other in order to squeeze concessions for themselves, or try to find loopholes in the odds against them to improve their own position.[61]

The alternatives to weaker powers in such a distributions of power are limited and posit a sort of Catch-22. In a take-it-or-leave-it situation, the option of 'taking it' is often only slightly better than 'leaving it.' For stronger powers, however, the alternative to a negotiated agreement may not be that bad. They may make a few marginal gains from making weak powers acquiesce to a negotiation, but they might gain even more by following a unilateral strategy. Krasner is right in noting that in a few issues areas (such as broadcasting, espionage), strong states did not negotiate in earnest in the 20th century because they had nothing much to gain.[62]

Negotiations no longer take place in a context defined solely by states and their 'instrumental' power maximization prerogatives, but in a 'diffusion of power' consisting of many actors in pursuit of many goals and issues and exercising different forms of power.[63] The power of dominant state actors is overlapped by the multiple influences of international organizations, market-oriented actors, transnational or domestic interest groups, and other societal actors. These groups may not pursue their interests through the state, or they may operate in situations where the state's authority to enforce its prerogatives is increasingly limited. Here, instead of power across many issue areas exercised by an omnipotent actor (state), power structures in particular issue areas become important.

---

61 For an example of the former strategy, see Wriggins (1976). For the latter see David B. Yoffie, *Power and Protectionism: Strategies of the Newly Industrializing Countries* (New York, 1983).

62 Stephen Krasner, 'Global Telecommunications and National Power', *International Organization*, 43 (1991): 336–66.

63 J.P. Singh, *Negotiating the Global Information Economy* (forthcoming).

International relations theorizing takes interests deduced from power structures as given, and then proceeds to analyze outcomes with fixed interests. However, as indicated above, interest calculations are an inherently social act, even when an individual makes them alone, for example with recourse to a framing device. They are also cognitive processes. We need to take note of the processes that allow actors to make sense of information. Information networks and negotiation processes can thus be seen as the production, dissemination, and disposal of information to actors involved. That they then result in changing the interests of actors should come as no surprise. In taking interests as given, international relations theory, therefore, partly annuls the very interactions that it tries to explain.

Conclusion

The convergence of issues of culture, information networks, and globalization is not unusual. The concept of meta-power – the changes in identity of actors and issues under highly interactive circumstances – helps to specify the rationale of such co-incidence. Meta-power theorizing supplements, rather than replaces, instrumental notions of power. States, for example, remain important actors, but must now operate in a vastly changed cultural context in which neither security nor commerce may be understood in territorial and hierarchical terms.

Transformational technologies lead to unforeseen change. Globalization led by information networks cannot be fully explained by traditional theories dealing with instrumental power where technology enhances or limits the capability of actors, and where issue-areas are already well defined. As seen in the case of security and commerce above, the multiplicity of issue-definitions and the identities of actors involved continue to evolve as information networks proliferate. This essay shies away from positing the direction of this change, but does note the conflict between the status quo and change. It also notes that conceptualizations used to explain the status quo are insufficient to explain change.

The idea of meta-power is suggestive here. To note that meta-power is the power of technology to change our understanding of actors and issues is a mere start. Further work is needed to specify the particular conditions under which particular types of identity changes take place. Nonetheless, meta-power must be understood as altering the informational base of identities and thereafter preceding the exercise of other types of power. To maintain in an instrumental sense that X leads to Y assumes that we know the identities of X and Y. Only meta-power analysis can help us determine how to unravel the identities of X and Y. I end with Dido's lament from Henry Purcell's Dido and Aeneas:

> When I am laid on earth
> May my wrongs create no trouble, no trouble in thy breast.
> Remember me, but ah, forget my fate.

From Virgil to Purcell to Samuel Huntington, Dido is remembered. Centuries after Roman Senator Cato habitually ended his speeches with the recurring statement 'Carthago delenda est,' or 'Carthage must be destroyed,' Rome remains Rome and

Carthage the Arab world, and ne'er the twain shall meet. Alas, we remember her but because of her fate. The rising commercial prominence of Carthage threatened Rome leading to the Punic Wars and the eventual destruction of Carthage. What would Virgil's lovers make of the Huntington's civilizational clash that affixes them on either side of a wide gaping sea? What would they make of commercial and other networks that now cross the Mediterranean as they did then? Nothing, if human nature and the cultures it fosters are never transformed. But what if there is change?

References

Adorno, Theodor W. and Max Horkheimer, 'The Culture Industry: Enlightenment as Mass Deception', in *Dialectic of Enlightenment*, trans. John Cumming (New York: The Seabury Press, 1972).

Adorno, Theodor W., *The Culture Industry: Selected Essays on Mass Culture* (London: Routledge, 1991).

Anderson, Benedict, *Imagined Communities* (London: Verso, 1983/1991).

Berezain, Mabel and Martin Schain (eds), *Europe without Borders: Remapping Territoriality, Citizenship, and Identity in a Transnational Age* (Baltimore: The Johns Hopkins University Press, 2003).

Berger, Peter L. and Thomas Luckmann, *The Social Construction of Reality: A Treatise in the Sociology of Knowledge* (New York: Anchor Books, 1967).

Biersteker, Thomas J. and Cynthia Weber, *State Sovereignty as Social Construct* (Cambridge: Cambridge University Press, 1996).

Boulding, Kenneth, 'National Images and International Systems', *Journal of Conflict Resolution*, 3/2 (June 1959): 120–31.

Buzan, Barry, 'The Security Dynamics of a 1+4 World', in Ersel Aydinli and James N. Rosenau (eds), *Paradigms in Transition: Globalization, Security and the Nation-State* (Albany: State University of New York Press, 2005).

Castells, Manuel, *The Information Age: Economy Society and Culture: The Power of Identity* (Oxford: Blackwell, 1997), Vol. 2.

Comor, Edward, 'New Technologies and Consumption: Contradictions in the Emergent World Order', in James N. Rosenau and J.P. Singh (eds), *Information Technologies and Global Politics: The Changing Scope of Power and Governance* (Albany: SUNY Press, 2002), pp. 169–88.

Deibert, Ronald, 'Black Code: Censorship, Surveillance, and the Militarization of Cyberspace', *Millennium*, 30/3 (2003): 501–30.

Deibert, Ronald, 'Circuits of Power: Security in the Internet Environment,' in James N. Rosenau and J.P. Singh (eds), *Information Technologies and Global Politics: The Changing Scope of Power and Governance* (Albany: SUNY Press, 2002), pp. 115–42.

Deibert, Ronald, *Parchment, Printing, and Hypermedia: Communication and World Order Transformation* (New York: Columbia University Press, 1997).

Der Derian, James and Michael J. Shapiro (eds), *International/Intertextual Relations* (Lexington: Lexington Books, 1989).

Der Derian, James, 'The (S)pace of International Relations: Simulation, Surveillance, and Speed', *International Studies Quarterly*, 44 (1990): 295–310.

Enloe, Cynthia, *The Morning After: Sexual Politics at the End of the Cold War*. (Berkeley: University of California Press, 1993).

Evans, Jessica and Stuart Hall (eds), *Visual Culture: A Reader* (London: Sage Publications, 1999).

Finnemore, Martha, *National Interests in International Society* (Ithaca: Cornell University Press, 1996).

Foucault, Michel, *The Order of Things: An Archaeology of the Human Sciences* (New York: Vintage, 1970).

Geertz, Clifford, *The Interpretation of Cultures* (New York: Basic Books, 1973).

Gilpin, Robert, *War and Change in World Politics* (Cambridge: Cambridge University Press, 1981).

Haas, Ernst, *When Knowledge is Power* (Berkeley: University of California Press, 1989).

Halbwachs, Maurice, *On Collective Memory* (Chicago: University of Chicago Press, 1992/1941).

Hoffmann, Stanley, 'An American Social Science: International Relations', *Daedalus*, 106/3 (1977): 41–60.

Innis, Harold, *Empire and Communications* (Oxford: The Clarendon Press, 1950).

Kastorvano, Riva, 'Transnational Networks and Political Participation: The Place of Immigrants in the European Union', in Mabel Berezain and Martin Schain (eds), *Europe without Borders: Remapping Territoriality, Citizenship, and Identity in a Transnational Age* (Baltimore: The Johns Hopkins University Press, 2003) pp. 64–85.

Katzenstein, Peter J. (ed.), *The Culture of National Security: Norms and Identity in World Politics* (Ithaca: Cornell University Press, 1996).

Keck, Margaret E. and Kathryn Sikkink, *Activists Beyond Borders: Advocacy Networks in International Politics* (Ithaca: Cornell University Press, 1998).

Keohane, Robert and Joseph S. Nye, Jr., 'Power and Interdependence in the Information Age', *Foreign Affairs*, 77/5 (1998): 81–94.

Keohane, Robert, 'International Institutions: Two Approaches', *International Studies Quarterly*, 32/4 (1988): 379–96.

Keohane, Robert, *After Hegemony: Cooperation and Discord in the World Political Economy* (Princeton: Princeton University Press, 1984).

Krasner, Stephen D., 'Global Telecommunications and National Power', *International Organization*, 43 (1991): 336–66.

Krasner, Stephen D., *Structural Conflict: The Third World Against Global Liberalism* (Berkeley: University of California Press, 1985).

Litfin, Karen, 'Public Eyes: Satellite Imagery, the Globalization if Transparency, and New Networks of Surveillance.' in James N. Rosenau and J.P. Singh (eds), *Information Technologies and Global Politics: The Changing Scope of Power and Governance* (Albany: SUNY Press, 2002), pp. 65–90.

Luke, Timothy, *Screens of Power: Ideology, Domination and Resistance in Information Society* (Urbana: University of Illinois Press, 1989).

McLuhan, Marshall and Bruce R. Powers, *The Global Village* (New York: Oxford University Press, 1989).
McLuhan, Marshall, *Understanding Media: The Extensions of Man* (Cambridge: The MIT Press, 1964/1997).
Nye, Joseph S., Jr., *Bound to Lead: The Changing Nature of American Power* (New York: Basic Books, 1990).
Nye, Joseph S., Jr., *Soft Power: The Means to Succeed in World Politics* (New York: Public Affairs, 2004).
Nye, Joseph S., Jr., *The Paradox of American Power: Why the World's Only Superpower Can't Go It Alone* (Oxford: Oxford University Press, 2002).
Odell, John, *Negotiating the Global Economy* (Ithaca: Cornell University Press, 2000).
Onuf, Nicholas, *A World of Our Making: Rules and Rule in Social Theory and International Relations* (Columbia: University of South Carolina Press, 1989).
Peterson, Spike V., 'Whose Crisis? Early and Post-Modern Masculinism', in Stephen Gill and James H. Mittelman (eds), *Innovation and Transformation in International Studies* (Cambridge: Cambridge University Press, 1997), pp. 185–201.
Rosecrance, Richard, 'The Rise of the Virtual State', *Foreign Affairs*, 75 (Fall 1996): 45–61.
Rosecrance, Richard, *The Rise of the Trading State: Commerce and Conquest in the Modern World* (New York: Basic Books, 1986).
Ruggie, John Gerard, 'Territoriality and Beyond: Problematizing Modernity in International Relations', *International Organization*, 17 (1993): 139–74.
Said, Edward, *Orientalism* (New York: Vintage, 1978).
Sell, Susan, *Power and Ideas: North-South Politics of Intellectual Property and Antitrust* (Albany: SUNY, 1998).
Singh, J.P., 'Introduction: Information Technologies and the Changing Scope of Power and Governance', in James N. Rosenau and J.P. Singh (eds), *Information Technologies and Global Politics: The Changing Scope of Power and Governance* (Albany: State University of New York Press, 2002), pp. 1–38.
Singh, J.P., *Negotiating the Global Information Economy* (forthcoming).
Spruyt, Hendrik, *The Sovereign State and its Competitors* (Princeton: Princeton University Press, 1996).
Vattimo, Gianni, 'Postmodernity, Technology, Ontology', in Arthur M. Meltzer, Jerry Weinberger, and M. Richard Zinman (eds), *Technology in the Western Political Tradition* (Ithaca: Cornell University Press, 1993), pp. 214–28.
Wæver, Ole, 'The Constellation of Securities in Europe', in Ersel Aydinli and James N. Rosenau, *Paradigms in Transition: Globalization, Security and the Nation-State* (Albany: State University of New York Press, 2005), pp. 151–74.
Waltz, Kenneth, *Theories of International Politics* (New York: McGraw Hill, 1979).
Weber, Cynthia, *Faking It: U.S. Hegemony in a 'Post-Phallic' Era* (Minneapolis: University of Minnesota Press, 1999).
Wendt, Alexander, 'Anarchy is What States Make of It: The Social Construction of Power Politics', *International Organization*, 46/2 (1992): 391–425.

Wendt, Alexander, *Social Theory of International Politics* (Cambridge: Cambridge University Press, 1999).

Wriggins, Howard, 'Up for Auction: Malta Bargains with Great Britain', in I. William Zartman (ed.), *The 50% Solution: How to Bargain Successfully with Hijackers, Strikers, Bosses, Oil Magnates, Arabs, Russians, and Other Worthy Opponents in the Modern World* (New Haven: Yale University Press, 1976).

Yoffie, David B., *Power and Protectionism: Strategies of the Newly Industrializing Countries* (New York: Columbia University Press, 1983).

Chapter 4

Cyberspace and Sovereignty: Thoughts on Physical Space and Digital Space

Geoffrey L. Herrera

Introduction

The commonplace assumption is that cyberspace[1] is a great 'no place'. This means that the digital realm transcends physical space. Information and the beings manipulating it are like electrons – everywhere and nowhere at once. John Perry Barlow put it more flamboyantly, 'Governments of the Industrial World, you weary giants of flesh and steel, I come from Cyberspace, the new home of Mind ... I ask you of the past to leave us alone ... You have no sovereignty where we gather'.[2] Buried in this quote are two assertions relevant to international security. First, cyberspace conceived as 'no place' is very different from ordinary international political space and is subject to different rules, different potentialities, and different threats. Second, there is not much the traditional geographic world can do about it. Now, more than a decade after Barlow's Garbo-esque request to be left alone – after experiencing mountains of spam, the 11 September 2001 attacks, tales of terrorist chat-rooms, identity theft, denial of service attacks, and worms and viruses – students of international politics have concluded that global digital networks represent a very serious threat to international security as traditionally understood, and to the very foundations of the nation-state system.[3]

---

1 I will use 'cyberspace', 'the digital realm', 'ICT' (or information and communications technologies), 'digital information networks', and similar phrases more or less interchangeably in this essay. Increasingly, this includes traditional information technology such as telephony, radio, and television, as all signs point towards the eventual convergence of all these forms of digital carriage over a common network. I understand there are differences. But I use these terms as a convenient shorthand for the sum total of connected digital information networks, and to avoid using the same term over and over again.

2 John Perry Barlow, 'A Declaration of the Independence of Cyberspace', in Ludlow (ed.), *Crypto Anarchy, Cyberstates, and Pirate Utopias* (Cambridge, Massachusetts, 2001), pp. 27–30.

3 Ryan Henry and C. Edward Peartree, *The Information Revolution and International Security* (Washington, 1998); Ronald J. Deibert, 'Circuits of Power: Security in the Internet Environment', in Rosenau and Singh (eds), *Information Technologies and Global Politics: The Changing Scope of Power and Governance* (New York, 2002), pp. 115–42; Robert Latham, *Bombs and Bandwidth: The Emerging Relationship Between IT and Security* (New York, 2003); Yale H. Ferguson and Richard W. Mansbach, *Remapping Global Politics: History's Revenge and Future Shock* (Cambridge, 2004).

Activities in the realm of the great 'no place' have impinged deeply on traditional political space. A territorially bound political authority would find it very difficult to control a non-territorial realm, as Rachel Yould writes: 'Despite the persistence of geographically defined jurisdictions, information technology unmistakably mitigates the primacy and impermeability of national borders'.[4]

In this essay, I argue that we can observe in international politics today a simultaneous double move: the territorialisation of cyberspace and the deterritorialisation of state security. In other words, assertions about the placeless-ness of cyberspace are overstated. This double move is neither inevitable, nor necessarily desirable. But it is clearly in evidence in contemporary world politics, and its existence exposes the fallacies of traditional ways of thinking about technology and its relationship to international politics.

The notions of 'cyberspace' and of the 'territorial state' are based on ideal types that verge on caricature. Cyberspace is sometimes compared to an ocean where information flows to-and-fro freely and the shortest distance between any two points isn't a straight line at all – the points are instantly connected by the flows. Yet each node on the internet has always been linked with a specific Internet protocol (IP) address, which in turn corresponds to a specific computer in a particular location. These IP addresses have long been organised into national domains. The state, on the other hand, is strictly a territorial entity, imposing uniform authority within its borders and confronting anarchy (and other uniform authorities) without. But the territorial system has always allowed for certain ambiguities, paradoxes, and twists of the paradigm that served the purposes of international actors – examples are Antarctica, agreements governing global communications, and conventions that establish embassies as extraterritorial territory.

My argument exploits the space between the two ideal types. In the first section of the paper, I present the arguments for the placeless-ness of cyberspace. The second section explores the assumptions that this hypothesis makes about technology and its relation to international politics, exposes the flaws in these assumptions, and shows how they distort our ability to understand developments at the intersection of cyberspace and international politics. In the final section, I offer evidence for the double move and the plasticity of cyberspace. Choosing examples is a tricky business. The global digital information infrastructure is a single case, making it resistant to traditional comparative case-study analysis. My strategy in case selection was to select two classes of 'cases', or components of a digital information infrastructure. The first set is in cyberspace itself – in the digital realm. I evaluate the three socio-technical components of cyberspace that are most critical to the placeless-ness hypothesis (in other words, hard cases) and show how we can see evidence of the double move in each: anonymity; frictionless, borderless commerce; and censorship-resistance. The second set shows the migration of digital technologies to geographic space. I selected a handful of information technologies – satellite imaging, global positioning systems

---

4 Rachel Yould, 'Beyond the American Fortress: Understanding Homeland Security in the Information Age', in Latham (ed.) *Bombs and Bandwidth: The Emerging Relationship Between IT and Security* (New York, 2003), pp. 74–98.

(GPS), and radio-frequency identification (RFID) – that empower territorial entities to render physical space in digital terms and so expose it to greater control.

At first glance, this discussion might appear to be of idiosyncratic interest. I claim that the placeless-ness hypothesis deserves the attention not just of students of the information revolution and international politics, but of international relations scholars more broadly. In the end, the hypothesis is a strong version of the globalisation argument – that technological and economic processes are fundamentally undermining state sovereignty. The double move, despite some rather enormous normative tensions, provides a strong rebuttal, and I hope it will contribute to a more meaningful discussion of *how* states are being transformed by globalisation (and transforming themselves), and a move away from the rather tired discussion of whether there is more or less territoriality and sovereignty.

Articulating and Assessing the Placeless-ness Hypothesis

This section offers an analysis of the placeless-ness hypothesis. In the end, this essay offers a refutation of it, but here the goal will be to present it as fully and fairly as possible. The hypothesis is composed of two distinct parts: an analysis of the physical qualities of information networks, and an argument about the relations of those networks with transnational political activity. It begins with a specific conception of information and on technical characteristics of digital networks – their layout and design, and the protocols that govern them.[5] We are living through an information revolution, one that touches all aspects of economy, society, and politics. Fewer and fewer people work in agriculture and industry, and more and more are knowledge workers. Greater value (and profit) is added by mixing knowledge with a commodity than by adding strength or effort. More and more commodities are themselves information – media of all kinds, books, television, films, games, and music. Managing information plays an ever-greater role in the lives of citizens of the developed (and, though more slowly, the developing) world. Yet, information itself has no physicality, and having none, has no borders.

Cyberspace is the right medium for this new world. It is a global conduit for all of this information, and like information itself, transcends physical space. This is because of its ubiquity and its speed, and because it is open (borderless). By design, information is free to travel anywhere it is requested regardless of national borders – provided, of course, that the controllers of the information have released it into the networks. These characteristics are strengthened by three elements of networks: they are networks, they are digital, and, increasingly, they are packet-switched.

---

5 Manuel Castells, *The Rise of the Network Society* (Cambridge, Massachusetts, 1996); Deibert, 'Circuits of Power'; Stephen J. Kobrin, 'Economic Governance in an Electronically Networked Global Economy', in Hall and Biersteker (eds), *The Emergence of Private Authority in Global Governance* (Cambridge, 2002), pp. 43–75; Yould, 'Beyond the American Fortress'.

Research on networks and networked organisations is very much in vogue in economics, sociology, and political science.[6] Their principles are drawn from physical networks. Instead of rigid hierarchies, where nodes (physical or social) have connections only to those nodes above and below them in the chain of command, nodes in a network can be connected to every other node. There is no discrimination, and communication between nodes occurs on an as-needed basis. There is still organisation and structure, but it has a degree of fluidity, flexibility, and speed that a hierarchical organisation lacks.[7] This attribute of global information networks is enhanced by the digital nature of the information. Binary language is like a common currency, in which every form of information – text, sound, image, video – can be converted, transported, and expressed digitally. Medium and data are in harmony. The final piece in the 'boundary-less sea of information' metaphor for the networks is packet-switching. The internet is the most important example of a packet-switched network, though increasingly the technology is spreading to other networks such as the telephone.[8] Packet-switched networks split information into small chunks or packets, address each packet, and send them. The packets pass through routing stations that collect them if they belong there, or pass them on to the next node if they don't. No preset path is chosen for the message, and there is no need for the packets to travel, or arrive, in order. From among all the packets that pass through its router, the recipient node collects only those intended for it, assembles the complete message, and delivers it. This is true whether the information is a text e-mail, an image, a web page, streaming video, or even a telephone conversation. All the intelligence is in the packets. The routers don't need to know the destination of each packet for the network to function. Packet-switching enhances the ocean-like character of the internet. Not only is there no hierarchy of information, but it is not even possible to identify a single stream of information as coming from a given source or being sent to another.

These three factors in combination lift the transmittal of information out of the realm of the geographic or territorial and to another realm where (conceptually at least) all information exists everywhere all the time. Three-dimensional space does not order relations between nodes on the network. Distance and borders have no relevance. And what is true for the nodes on the network is also true of social actors on the network. This is the materialist core of the placeless-ness hypothesis.

---

6 Mark S. Granovetter, 'The Strength of Weak Ties', *American Journal of Sociology*, 78/6 (1973): 1360–80; Walter W. Powell, 'Neither Market nor Hierarchy: Network Forms of Organization', *Research in Organizational Behavior*, 12 (1990): 295–336; Albert-László Barabási, *Linked: The New Science of Networks*, 2002); Margaret E. Keck and Kathryn Sikkink, *Activists Beyond Borders: Advocacy Networks in International Politics* (Ithaca, New York, 1998); David Ronfeldt and John Arquilla, 'Networks, Netwars, and the Fight for the Future', *First Monday*, 6/10 (2001).

7 A group of computers could be organised in a hierarchical, or pyramidal fashion. A computer network need not be a 'network'.

8 Increasingly, SCADA systems for controlling power plants, water treatment facilities, and the like are also moving to packet-switched networks. The phenomenon of digitalisation is larger than just the Internet.

These factors, the hypothesis asserts, have certain determinative social effects. They include time-space distanciation – which Giddens called the characteristic feature of modernity – carried to its logical extreme. He describes distanciation as 'the 'lifting out' of social relations from local contexts of interaction and their restructuring across indefinite spans of time-space'.[9] Digital information networks allow for easy and instantaneous communication, organisation, identity-formation, and action without regard for space. For purposes of international security, the most important consequences of this are anonymity, hidden or secret action unbounded by space, and the ease and low cost of such action. These can generate a number of significant international threats.

The growth of information and communications technologies (ICT) and globalisation are interdependent. The intersection of ICT and international security depends on the expanded trade, financial, and information flows generated by globalisation. This synergistic relationship could certainly bring forth threats to regime stability, threats from terrorism, vandalism, and crime. The survival of political regimes, especially the authoritarian variety, depends on control over the flow of information. Opposition groups can undermine this control by using the open flow and high quality of information and the organisational capacities of digital communications technologies. Such regimes typically own outright or manage through official and unofficial censorship the print media, television, and even film and popular culture generally. They stifle dissent, inhibit opposition organisation, and prevent news from circulating that might undermine the regime. The borderlessness of global media, its decentralisation, and its resistance to tracing and tapping means that repressive regimes are finding it increasingly harder to control the news and information their citizens receive.[10]

The threats from terrorists, vandals, and other criminals arise from actions that are similar to those taken by political dissidents, though the motivations of the actors differ. In these cases, the relationship between the action and the digital environment has two facets: the organisation of the actors, and the target. The organisational costs of illicit activity – including recruitment, fund-raising, record-keeping, planning, operations, etc. – are low in cyberspace. The actors can conceal their activities efficiently and cheaply irrespective of their geographic location. Moreover, the communications network facilitates the formation of social networks.[11] What is true for the group also applies to the individual. The digital environment is an important

---

9 Anthony Giddens, *The Consequences of Modernity* (Stanford, California, 1990).

10 Shanthi Kalathil and Taylor C. Boas, *Open Networks, Closed Regimes: The Impact of the Internet on Authoritarian Rule* (Washington, D.C., 2003); Marc Lynch, *Voices of the New Arab Public: Iraq, Al-Jazeera, and Middle East Politics Today* (New York, 2006).

11 Ronald J. Deibert and Janice Gross Stein, 'Social and Electronic Networks in the War on Terror', in Latham (ed.) *Bombs and Bandwidth: The Emerging Relationship Between IT and Security* (New York, 2003), pp. 157–74; Gabriel Weimann, *Terror on the Internet: The New Arena, the New Challenges* (Washington, D.C., 2006); Shaul Mishal and Maoz Rosenthal, 'Al Qaeda as a Dune Organization: Toward a Typology of Islamic Terrorist Organizations', *Studies in Conflict and Terrorism*, 28/4 (2005): 275–93; Chris Dishman, 'The Leaderless Nexus: When Crime and Terror Converge', *Studies in Conflict and Terrorism*, 28/3 (2005): 237–52.

new target for terrorists and criminals. Digital ICT has spread throughout modern society's social and economic infrastructure – commerce, transportation systems, power generation and transmission, medicine, even government. As the networking of socio-technological systems increases (the same effects that benefit networked terrorist groups also benefit traditional organisations), so do its vulnerabilities. The list of vulnerable targets is familiar: air-traffic control systems, nuclear power plants, electronic commerce sites, financial institutions, political organisations, and personal identity. Internet security expert Bruce Schneier suspects that the August 2003 blackout in the northeastern US was caused by the Blaster computer worm.[12] In spring 2005, a string of large-scale financial data thefts from large banks, data collection firms, and even a significant US defense contractor highlighted the vulnerability of personal information on data networks. And the 2001 US-China spy plane incident led to hundreds of reported hacks and website defacements by Chinese and US hackers.[13] There are widespread reports of extremist groups using e-mail, encrypted chat rooms, and recruitment videos, and even hiding secret messages in image files. There is suspicion, and some evidence of plans for cyber-attacks by these same groups.[14] The placeless-ness hypothesis supports the notion that these vulnerabilities will be very hard for territorial political authority to combat. The technology allows terrorists to be geographically dispersed, yet just as potent as if they operated in shared space, and very well hidden. The possible consequences of an attack range from the inconsequential, such as website defacements, to serious economic disruption from an attack on financial markets or the transportation system, to the catastrophic, such as a nuclear accident.[15]

Hacking, or cracking, as some prefer to call it,[16] is the cyberspace equivalent of vandalism, though it can easily slide into theft. Hacking refers narrowly to breaking into secure systems, though it has come to refer to a broader range of actions, including writing and releasing worms and viruses and denial-of-service (DOS) attacks. Some of the more spectacular internet outages have been the work of individuals, typically

---

12 Bruce Schneier, 'Blaster and the August 14th Blackout', *Crypto-Gram Newsletter*, 15 December 2003.

13 Thomas C. Greene, 'ID Theft is Inescapable', *The Register*, 23 March 2005; Michelle Delio, 'Al Qaeda Website Refuses to Die', *Wired News*, 7 April 2003. Zone-H tracks website defacements and counts between 2,000 and 3,000 per day around the world <http://www.zone-h.org>.

14 Daniel Benjamin and Steven Simon, *The Next Attack: The Failure of the War on Terror and a Strategy for Getting It Right* (New York, 2005); Gabriel Weimann, 'www.terror.net: How Modern Terrorism Uses the Internet' (Washington, DC, March 2004); Andrew Higgins, Karby Leggett and Alan Cullison, 'How al Qaeda Put Internet in Service of Global Jihad', *Wall Street Journal*, 11 November 2002.

15 Jonathan Zittrain, 'Without a Net', *Legal Affairs* (2006).

16 Hackers, correctly, insist that poking around secure computer systems for vulnerabilities is a serious, important, and socially responsible task. They differentiate themselves from crackers who seek to crack into systems merely to cause mischief. Despite a book by that name by Steven Levy, one of the most prominent journalists covering the US information technology industry and culture, the term has never caught on outside a small subculture. Steven Levy, *Hackers: Heroes of the Computer Revolution* (Garden City, New York, 1984).

adolescent males, for no other apparent reasons than the sport of it and bragging rights in the hacker community. While some hackers live in physical proximity to one another and are friends in the conventional sense, the community is a virtual and global one. Two recent high-profile arrests were of a young male from a Toronto suburb, and another from the small Swedish university town of Uppsala.

The motivations notwithstanding, hacking poses a fairly serious international security threat. Severe economic dislocation and even damage to physical infrastructure are some of the more obvious possible consequences. Less significant examples are pilfering of trade secrets, exposing political or business leaders' private financial or medical information, and even release of secret national security information. One hacker claims to have taken the blueprints for the F-18 jet fighter from a computer system at a naval air station in Maryland, US.[17] If Schneier's supposition about the Blaster worm (see above) is correct, national security planners have to worry greatly about unintended consequences of cyberspace mischief directed at poorly defended critical systems. Such attacks are notoriously hard to prevent or stop. Investigators have had some success finding perpetrators after the fact, but the global, anonymous nature of the internet makes detection and blocking very difficult.

There is a fine line between vandalism and crime. The tools are much the same, though the targets are usually more narrowly focused. Mounting law enforcement evidence suggests that hackers and criminals are morphing into each other, or that the latter are actively recruiting and employing the hackers.[18] They use DOS attacks and identity theft to blackmail victims – demanding compensation, for example, before turning off an attack or for the return of stolen information. In 2001, the FBI arrested two hackers in Russia who had been extorting money from US businesses for several years.[19] Despite a few successes such as this, law enforcement is up against a serious global threat from criminals whose operations are unconstrained by distance and whose anonymity is hard to crack. In brief, several forces and processes that pose threats to international security are converging. Technological innovation and the diffusion of ICT spurs greater global interdependence. Globalisation pushes this process as well (and pushes innovation too). Both encourage the conversion of more and more information into digital form. The feedback loops linking technological and economic forces feed off each other to create a bigger and more ubiquitous, homogeneous, deterritorialised sphere for information and communications. All nodes in cyberspace are potentially vulnerable, and territorial political entities are relatively helpless to do anything about it. This circumstance is due to the very nature of the network itself.

---

17 John Markoff and Lowell Bergman, 'Internet Attack Called Broad and Long Lasting by Investigators', *New York Times*, 10 May 2005.

18 Evan Ratliff, 'The Zombie Hunters', *The New Yorker*, 10 October 2005.

19 Ariana Eunjung Cha, 'Despite U.S. Efforts, Web Crimes Thrive', *Washington Post*, 20 May 2003.

The Politics of Technology

The placeless-ness hypothesis has very weak theoretical underpinnings. Is placeless-ness the true 'nature' of ICT networks – can they not be reterritorialised? To answer this question in the negative is to accept an idea of technology that is completely at odds with decades of work in the history of science and technology. The idea that technology has some fixed, immutable form (and with it fixed social and political effects) is a form of essentialism or determinism vastly at odds with theoretical reflection and the historical record. There is nothing natural or inherent about technologies. They are human creations, and as such subject to conscious and unconscious shaping by social actors and institutions. In other words, technology is political.

It is political in at least two ways. First, the construction of technological systems is subject to political contestation. Political actors disagree about the direction the development of a certain technology should take, or whether one or another of competing technologies should be chosen for a given purpose. These differences have substantive effects. For example, opposition to nuclear power in the US – driven by concerns about waste disposal and plant safety – has hindered development of the technology. Second, more philosophically, technology is not really a 'thing' (or an assembly of 'things'), but practical knowledge embedded in material artifacts, in institutions built to manage the artifacts, and in their interface with other social institutions. This larger bundle of institutions and artifacts, which theorists of technology call complex socio-technical systems, is what constitutes technology.[20]

This argument has several consequences for the relationship between cyberspace and geopolitical space. The first is that the very nature of cyberspace (as a political phenomenon) has been shaped by geopolitics. Global digital networks exhibit certain features– placeless-ness, anonymity, and ubiquity – because of politics, not in spite of them. Looking at the present and future, then, this means that ICT can be shaped and reshaped going forward. The social shaping of the technical is not absolute; the physical world is not endlessly malleable, nor is 'the 'interpretive flexibility' of an artifact' infinite.[21] But there is no intrinsic reason why cyberspace cannot be made more territorial.

The placeless-ness argument's persuasiveness suggests that the current conception of cyberspace is quite entrenched. Technological systems have much in common with social institutions. Studies of path dependency argue that institutions are more open to change at their founding (when they are undeveloped and immature), and at conjunctural moments after crises when there is sufficient political momentum

---

20 Thomas P. Hughes, 'The Evolution of Large Technological Systems', in Bijker, Hughes, and Pinch (eds), *Social Construction of Technological Systems: New Directions in the Sociology and History of Technology* (Cambridge, Massachusetts, 1987), pp. 51–82; Paul N. Edwards, 'Infrastructure and Modernity: Force, Time, and Social Organization in the History of Sociotechnical Systems', in Misa, Brey and Feenberg (eds), *Modernity and Technology* (Cambridge, Massachusetts, 2003), pp. 185–225.

21 Ronald Kline and Trevor Pinch, 'The Social Construction of Technology', in MacKenzie and Wajcman (eds), *The Social Shaping of Technology* (Buckingham, 1999), pp. 113–15.

to overcome entrenched institutional inertia.[22] The accumulation of cyberspace vulnerabilities detailed above, in combination with the 11 September 2001 terror attacks in the US, are providing just such a moment. As I see it, recent developments in the digital realm are generating a double move: the reterritorialisation of cyberspace and the deterritorialisation of national security. Reterritorialisation does not mean that the infrastructure of the internet, for example, is being ripped up and interconnections are being dismantled. Rather it means that modifications and controls are being placed on cyberspace (the potential for which has always existed) that allow for greater control by territorial entities. Cyberspace is proving to be a flexible environment. Deterritorialisation of national security is an adaptation by states to the digital revolution – a reconfiguring of state practices along nonterritorial lines. The goal here is not to valorise these developments, and in fact several recent works have observed these trends with considerable alarm.[23] Rather, the point is to document the trend lines and to provide a theoretical foundation for why and how it might be occurring. This enterprise, within the context of social science, is a difficult business. I am taking current developments and trying to project them out into the future rather than explain developments in the past. Predicting the future has a greater chance of error than explaining the past. Yet it is the position of the essay, and the larger book, that the effort is worth the inherent risks.

The Territorialisation of Cyberspace/The Deterritorialisation of Security

The best way to explore the double move is through an in-depth examination of critical socio-technical components at the interface of cyberspace and territorial states. Digging deeply into the details of information technology may seem an odd strategy for a paper on international security. But I believe that technology and politics are inseparable, and the best way to root out their interdependence is at the roots. The best way to make my argument for the connection between territorial and non-territorial space is to show there is geopolitics in the deep structure of our built environment. I have chosen two sets of components of the digital information infrastructure: the first set is taken from the digital environment, and the second is derived by applying digital information technologies to physical space.

---

22 Stephen Skowronek, *Building a New American State: The Expansion of National Administrative Capacities, 1877–1920* (New York, 1981); Paul Pierson, *Politics in Time: History, Institutions, and Social Analysis* (Princeton, New Jersey, 2004).

23 Lawrence Lessig, *Free Culture: The Nature and Future of Creativity* (New York, 2004); International Campaign Against Mass Surveillance, 'The Emergence of a Global Infrastructure for Mass Registration and Surveillance', *ICAMS*, April 2005; Goldsmith and Wu, *Who Controls the Internet? Illusions of a Borderless World* (Oxford and New York, 2006).

The Double Move in Cyberspace: Anonymity, Frictionless Commerce, Censorship Resistance

The three examples here are not 'technologies' in the standard sense of the word. That is, they are not bundles of physical material or lines of computer code. Hopefully, the prior section has showed the limitations of such a truncated view of technology. Instead, all three, the placeless-ness hypothesis argues, are essential socio-political implications of the underlying physical infrastructure of cyberspace. In the following, we will highlight each of these alleged links between physical structures and politics, show its limitations, and provide some evidence of contrary moves by states.

Cyberspace and Anonymity Anonymity is a key feature of the placeless-ness hypothesis. If actors in cyberspace can be readily identified, then the speed and ubiquity of the networks will actually work against the hypothesis. Anonymity is maintained both by the massive volume of information flowing through the networks, and by features that allow users to cloak their identity and activities. With anonymity gone, centralised authorities would be able to use the power of computer information processing to track activity on the networks to a degree not available in the terrestrial world.[24] The hypothesis holds that there is little the state can do about anonymity. It is literally written into the structure of cyberspace itself and cannot be dislodged without destroying the networks. But the features exploited by extremists, hackers, and criminals can also, in modified form, strengthen state surveillance and law enforcement capability. This process is akin to an arms race. Illicit actors continually amaze those in global law enforcement with the speed at which they stay one step ahead in the technology race.[25] But territorial states have the advantage of law and the ability to modify the technological environment by fiat. If non-territorial actors make use of ICT to plan and carry out illicit activities, then territorial authorities can modify the architectures of these networks to make detection and capture easier.

Anonymity is a 'feature' of the internet because of the way information moves through it, and the way it is governed. The underlying architecture was intended to be robust and survivable. The solution to this problem was a packet-switched network more or less immune to disruption.[26] The internet was also designed 'stupid', in that the intelligence resided at the ends of the network, not in the network itself.[27] Routing tools, software applications, and information requests come from

---

24 This poses an interesting paradox: cyberspace is (potentially) both more and less anonymous than terrestrial space.

25 Douglas Farah, 'Colombian Drug Cartels Exploit Tech Advantage', *Washington Post*, 15 November 1999.

26 Janet Abbate, *Inventing the Internet* (Cambridge, Massachusetts, 1999); Paul Baran, 'On Distributed Communications: IX. Security, Secrecy, and Tamper-Free Considerations', *RAND Corporation*, 1964; Michael T. Zimmer, 'The Tensions of Securing Cyberspace: The Internet, State Power and the National Strategy to Secure Cyberspace', *First Monday*, 9/3 (2004).

27 David Isenberg, 'Rise of the Stupid Network', <http://www.hyperorg.com/misc/stupidnet.html>, accessed 26 April 2006.

the ends, in contrast to a traditional telephone network, in which the switches, routing protocols, etc. are contained in the network itself. The difference makes the internet simpler, and makes it much harder to trace individual bits of information once they are in the network. The internet's governance structure reflects its design. The Internet Engineering Task Force (or IETF) is open and democratic. Decision-making is carried out via electronic request-for-comments (RFCs). IETF members (who could be any interested person) read, comment on, and criticize the RFCs, and a collaborative decision is made.[28] Because of packet-switching, 'stupid' design, and the governance structure, it is very hard to control who moves what information over the internet.

Two different efforts at control may change this. The first emanates from governments, the second from the private sector. The security of the 'national information infrastructure' has concerned government policy-makers in the US and elsewhere since the 1990s, but the attacks on New York and Washington of 2001 focused attention on the problem to a greater degree. The vulnerability of the US information infrastructure to terrorist attacks generated an extensive 2003 report. The report acknowledges that, as the internet is almost completely in private hands, a public-private partnership is necessary to secure the infrastructure.[29] Nevertheless, federal initiative is necessary for 'forensics and attack attribution, protection of networks and systems critical to national security, indications and warnings, and protection against organised attacks capable of inflicting debilitating damage to the economy'.[30] The report recommends a number of proposals – attack detection, coordinated response planning, and changing the routers and protocols of the internet itself – to make it more secure.[31] Finally, the report recommends supporting private-sector initiatives to construct trusted digital control systems (discussed below).

In the wake of 11 September 2001 and the USA PATRIOT Act, the US government has moved even further towards securing the internet and removing some of its anonymity. The Department of Justice has increased its wiretap capacities in the law and its technical capabilities in relations with ISPs. The USA PATRIOT Act has made it easier to establish digital wiretaps, and has expanded their scope.[32] The FBI is also seeking to expand its telephone wiretap capacity to include Voice over Internet Protocol (VoIP).[33] The EU and individual countries (most notably the UK) have taken similar steps, and a recent critical report charges that the EU has increased

---

28 Abbate, *Inventing the Internet*; Paulina Borsook, 'How Anarchy Works', *Wired*, October 1995.

29 This is Yould's point as well. Yould, 'Beyond the American Fortress'.

30 Department of Homeland Security, 'The National Strategy to Secure Cyberspace', March 2003.

31 Ibid.

32 <http://www.epic.org/privacy/terrorism/usapatriot/>.

33 Stephen Labaton, 'Easing of Internet Regulations Challenges Surveillance Efforts', *New York Times*, 22 January 2004; Declan McCullagh, 'FBI Pushes for Broadband Wiretap Powers', *CNET News.com*, 12 March 2004; Federal Communications Commission, 'FCC Adopts Notice of Proposed Rulemaking and Declaratory Ruling Regarding Communications Assistance for Law Enforcement Act', *Federal Communications Commission*, 4 August 2004.

cooperation with the US to bring more of the internet under a comprehensive surveillance regime.[34]

Any one or combination of these initiatives would erode the distributed and 'stupid' character of the internet and embed physical controls within the network itself. Such efforts could fail, however, because the global character of the internet makes national-level initiatives insufficient.[35] Cooperative regimes between the US and the EU may change that somewhat, as the bulk of internet traffic passes through the national jurisdictions of these two regions. Changes in the US alone may have similar global effect as well, because of the US's dominant role as a 'price maker'

The private-sector initiative, trusted computing architecture, offers the possibility of changing the nature of the networked computing experience at the ends, rather than in the middle. It holds the promise of achieving states' objectives to a far greater degree than increased surveillance technology and authority. Trusted computing, along with firewalls, digital certificates, and digital rights management, can turn the internet into a tightly controlled and monitored space *not* by altering the physical characteristics of the internet or by changing the legal environment in which it is embedded, but by altering the ends of the network and turning every piece of information traversing the network into a self-monitoring entity. Trusted computing platforms are intended to solve multiple security problems found on the internet – including unwanted e-mail (spam), intellectual property theft, and identity fraud – by requiring authentication for activities such as sending e-mail, distributing files, and engaging in e-commerce. Documents, images, audio and video files, and software would be coded to report who created them, who has rights to use them, and where they have been.[36] This information, for the state's purposes, could be obtained by subpoena.[37]

Microsoft's long-delayed update to its system software Windows XP, now named Vista, is crucial for advancing trusted computing. Windows software is installed on the vast majority of machines connected to the internet, so if Vista were to develop along the lines suggested by the company's press releases, it would become the *de facto* experience of the internet for most users and would create a very different kind of digital world.[38] Anonymity would end; the internet would turn into a controlled and monitored space where none of the illegal activities that bedevil the networks

---

34 International Campaign Against Mass Surveillance, 'The Emergence of a Global Infrastructure'.

35 Stephen J. Lukasik, Seymour E. Goodman, and David W. Longhurst, 'Protecting Critical Infrastructures Against Cyber-Attack', *Adelphi Papers*, 359 (2003); Zimmer, 'The Tensions of Securing Cyberspace'.

36 For a jeremiad against trusted computing see John Walker, 'The Digital Imprimatur', <http://www.fourmilab.ch/documents/digital-imprimatur>, accessed 7 May 2004. For a critique of the complaint, see Jeroen Meijer, 'Lights Going Out on the Internet? Not Just Yet', <http://www.circleid.com/posts/lights_going_out_on_the_internet_not_just_yet/>, accessed 21 May 2004.

37 The US government's legal demand for Internet search records from Yahoo!, Google, and MSN in the winter of 2006 shows how state authority might work here.

38 Richard Forno, 'MS to Micro-Manage Your Computer', *The Register*, 24 June 2002.

today could exist. This would cripple the activities of placeless actors that depend upon the cloaking power of the internet to mask their activities.

There are reasons for skepticism. Vista is much delayed, and some of the more robust trusted computing features have been dropped for the time being.[39] But trusted computing will remain a goal because it promises solutions to so many of the security problems that afflict the industry. Critics of Microsoft's plans are probably right: the version of Vista that finally gets released will be a compromise version of that first sketched out by Microsoft, gaps in the trusted infrastructure will exist, and some of the original, 'anarchic' nature of the internet will remain. But the most important thing for this analysis is that increased control of cyberspace either through legal and technical changes to the middle of the network, or changes to the end, make possible, maybe even probable, substantial alterations to cyberspace. Anonymity is not an inherent characteristic of computer networks. It is questionable whether the status of cyberspace as an uncontrolled space free from formal political authorities can continue for much longer. In spite of its history, and the resistance – open and covert – that will accompany efforts to 'tame' it, states have legal authority and therefore power over the architecture of the digital realm, and therefore possess the ability to reduce the scope of anonymity. This analysis also points to a tension between the interests of the state in controlling this version of the security threat posed by information technology, and the interests of private capital.

Cyberspace and transaction cost-free commerce Global electronic commerce is an ideal example of the placeless-ness hypothesis. Transactions costs are a principle barrier to trade over distance. When national boundaries are added to the equation, international trade in the geopolitical space becomes even more costly. Moving transactions to the digital realm overcomes these obstacles. Transaction costs fall to the barest minimum. The increased efficiency of digital markets, however, is a fiscal security problem for territorial entities. Tracking transactions, collecting the appropriate taxes, making the traded goods conform to local and national design regulations, safety, content, and so forth, are increasingly difficult undertakings. The task is hard enough with physical products, but as more and more of the global economy is made up of knowledge work, its products increasingly lack physical form, and are produced, transmitted, and consumed digitally instead. Controlling media commerce in the digital realm should be nearly impossible – a perfect example of the inability of territorial entities to cope with a placeless, digital world.[40] Deterritorialised commerce, like anonymity, is seen as an inherent consequence of the physical properties of cyberspace: it is digital, it is global, it is instantaneous, it resists monitoring and regulation, and the costs of transport are negligible.

Yet the e-commerce revolution hasn't quite played out the way the placeless-ness hypothesis suggests. Two examples help make this case. First, the iTunes music store

---

39 Andrew Orlowski, 'MS Trusted Computing Back to Drawing Board', *The Register*, 6 May 2004; Mike Ricciuti and Martin LaMonica, 'Longhorn Goes to Pieces', *CNET News. com*, 13 May 2004.

40 For an argument along these lines where the example is digital currencies, see: Kobrin, 'Electronic Cash and the End of National Markets', *Foreign Policy*, 107 (1997): 65–77.

is a small slice of the e-commerce world, but it illustrates the ability of the territorial world to make the digital world conform to its requirements. The second, e-cash or digital cash, is a much more significant example of the failure of the initial promise of borderless e-commerce and the success of digital versions of older territorial financial instruments.

The global music industry has spent the past half-decade of so in a state of anxiety over the diffusion of global file sharing of compressed music files. The introduction of Napster, and the subsequent ascendancy of a host of other peer-to-peer file-swapping technologies, is a perfect example of how the internet undermines a social practice in the physical space (in this case, the selling of prerecorded music on compact disks and magnetic tape cassettes). Digitally stored music (and any other information product) is where we would expect to feel the effects of the placeless-ness hypothesis most strongly, and could therefore be expected to serve as a case in point for my argument. However, the most successful licit source of digital music files, Apple Computer's iTunes Music Store (iTMS), is designed to carefully conform to the rules set out by existing national legal jurisdictions and international copyright law. Music files on iTMS are protected by digital rights management (DRM) encryption to prevent illegal distribution. Each national jurisdiction has a separate iTMS, and not for national cultural reasons, but because Apple must negotiate separate music licensing arrangements for each country as well as make the appropriate arrangements for paying taxes. Individual iTMSs are being unveiled slowly, as it takes time to complete negotiations with all the rights holders and governments.

The iTunes DRM has been successfully hacked, and it is likely that there are workarounds for the e-commerce sites as well (basically convincing iTMS that users are connecting from a certain national jurisdiction when they are not). But they key here is relative cost and ease. Illicit peer-to-peer file trading was initially successful because it was easy and fast. The successful prosecutions by the music industry of Napster and others led to innovations in peer-to-peer software to shield the authors from Napster-like liability (the recent Grokster case in the US shows that courts have found even these modifications illegal). But the innovations also made the software harder to use, left searches incomplete, and made downloading less reliable. The success of iTMS shows that for most people, there is a tipping point where the price of the free source cannot compensate for the trouble. Law and terrestrial authority can in fact increase the transaction costs even in frictionless cyberspace.

For my purposes, these two examples show how national boundaries and national and international law can change the technology of e-commerce (and by extrapolation, that of cyberspace as a whole) to make it conform to the dictates of the territorial world. The placeless-ness of cyberspace remains. Illicit sharing of music files still goes on, even across international borders. But there has always been illicit activity in and across every organised political authority. Smuggling emerged the moment the first frontier was established. The important issue is the pervasiveness of the illegal activity. The file-sharing evidence suggests that it is not pervasive enough to seriously undermine territorial authority. On the contrary, traditional legal authority appears to have adapted rather well to the file-sharing phenomenon.

The second e-commerce example, E-cash, was predicted to have a more profound transformation than music-file swapping. When purely digital money emerged as a possibility in the mid-1990s, Kobrin argued that electronic cash represented a fundamental challenge to the territorial state.[41] Private-sector cash was the future because currency could now be digital, authenticated by non-state entities, anonymous, and swappable in an infinite number of ways. In the mid-1990s, there was a rush of enthusiasm in the internet community and a popular press for e-cash. Several competing systems undertook trial runs. The most prominent system for completely secure (encrypted), totally anonymous, privately issued e-cash was developed by the mathematician, cryptographer, and ardent libertarian David Chaum.[42] Chaum argued that methods for conducting transactions at a distance were either ill-suited to the digital medium, such as bank drafts, or too expensive, such as credit cards and bank transfers, and that all lacked a key feature of traditional cash transactions – anonymity. He regarded his system as a technological and historical necessity.

The results were disappointing. All of the initial projects are now bankrupt, and the underlying systems have not been integrated into existing digital financial tools. These technologies have, for the time being anyway, failed. Instead, credit cards are the overwhelming choice for online transactions, and credit card companies are encouraging their customers to use (and strong-arming merchants to accept) their cards for increasingly smaller transactions.[43] Credit card transactions over the internet are no different from those in territorial space. They offer all the advantages of boundary-free, placeless commerce, but with all of the legal requirements and traceability that territorial political authorities require (more, in fact, as credit card transactions can be tracked and analyzed in ways that cash and even checks cannot). Merchants must have accounts with the credit card companies in order to accept the cards, as do consumers. The result is a vast e-commerce system that is global and digital, but is also rooted in traditional geopolitical space and capable of surveillance and analysis by states.

Some quasi-cash modes have emerged for smaller transactions or for vendors who lack the infrastructure to accept credit cards, most notably PayPal. But PayPal is not anonymous and, as it cooperates extensively with regulatory authorities, operates more like a traditional bank moored in geographic space. There are also a number of micro-transactions vendors on the internet – such as Peppercoin in the US and Firstgate in Germany – that facilitate compensation for artists, writers and the like in amounts too small to be attractive for credit-card companies (in the thousandths of currency units). Neither is very widespread. Both depend in the end on the credit card system for settlement and conform to territorial banking regulations.[44] One vendor, Paystone,[45] supports accounts in 15 national jurisdictions

---

41 Ibid.

42 David Chaum, 'Achieving Electronic Privacy', *Scientific American*, August 1992; Steven Levy, 'E-Money (That's What I Want)', *Wired*, December 1994.

43 Dina ElBoghdady, 'For Some, No Purchase Is Too Small For Plastic', *Washington Post*, 23 February 2005.

44 Gregory T. Huang, 'The Web's New Currency', *Technology Review*, December-January 2004; Peter Wayner, 'Cybercash on Vacation', *Technology Review*, March 2005.

45 <http://paystone.com>.

and even facilitates remittances to the Philippines. But all accounts are held in dollars except the Philippine's where pesos are necessary for remittances. The promise of anonymous, deterritorialized e-cash has faded into something of a compromise. E-cash in its current manifestation takes advantage of the speed and borderless character of cyberspace, but it also conforms to terrestrial laws and regulations. This outcome conforms far more to the double move hypothesis than the placeless-ness theory does.

The example of al-Qaida's finances provides a fascinating coda. Money-laundering experts agree that efforts at disrupting the group's financial networks since 11 September 2001 have been successful, but they have not succeeded in stopping the flow of money from supporters to organisers and operatives.[46] Al-Qaida has largely abandoned conventional methods of storing and moving money, and instead is depending more and more on cash, diamonds, drug smuggling, and other illicit business, and the hawala method for money transfer.[47] In order to escape detection from territorial financial surveillance mechanisms, al-Qaida has gone low-tech, not high-tech.

Both iTMS and e-cash suggest that territorial authority has adapted well to the challenge posed by e-commerce – not by reasserting its authority in traditional ways, but by adapting its monetary regime to a changed environment. One recent development makes the point in another way. The EU has begun experimenting with RFID tags in bank notes.[48] The measure is supposed to help prevent counterfeiting, but it also enables tracking of cash transactions in some settings. States have long wished to have more control over the cash economy; now perhaps information technology will give them the necessary tools. This is a perfect illustration of the double-edged nature of digital information technologies; they give unprecedented power to private citizens, but they also empower states.

There probably always will be a clandestine digital economy, but avoiding state surveillance will be difficult. Available methods will not leverage the power of ICT to the degree expected by the placeless-ness hypothesis. Those methods remain – as clandestine methods for skirting state authority have for centuries – expensive, time-consuming, and burdensome. They only appeal to a small minority with a great interest in secrecy. By adapting and by insisting on changes in technology – the heart of the double move – territorial authorities will retain considerable control over electronic commerce.

Cyberspace, infrastructure, and censorship Perhaps the most pervasive myth about the internet is that it is censorship-resistant. In fact, given the layout of the infrastructure, the metaphor of the ocean of data where all information can travel on any of an almost infinite number of routes to get to its destination is a bit deceptive. Several ambitious plans to build global geosynchronous satellite networks in the

---

46 Don Van Natta, 'Terrorists Blaze a New Money Trail', *New York Times*, 28 September 2003; Mark Basile, 'Going to the Source: Why Al Qaeda's Financial Network Is Likely to Withstand the Current War on Terrorist Financing', *Studies in Conflict and Terrorism*, 27/3 (2004): 169–85.

47 Douglas Farah, *Blood From Stones: The Secret Financial Network of Terror* (New York, 2004).

48 Janis Mara, 'Euro Scheme Makes Money Talk', *Wired News*, 9 July 2003.

1990s failed, leaving land-based copper wire and fiber-optic cable as the physical media of choice for the vast majority of information traffic.[49] This means that in many territorial jurisdictions, there is at least one fat information pipe running across their borders – a convenient spot to place surveillance technologies to monitor incoming and outgoing traffic. For example, Brazil has four international cable lines,[50] and China has five national backbones through which all traffic flows.

Authoritarian regimes have noticed this and are actively using surveillance techniques against their own citizens in an effort to safeguard the regimes. The surprising thing, given the placeless-ness hypothesis, is that the efforts seem to be working. Kalathil and Boal's book surveys digital censorship efforts in Burma, China, Cuba, Egypt, Saudi Arabia, Singapore, the United Arab Emirates, and Vietnam. The work and the global surveys conducted by the OpenNet Initiative[51] show that authoritarian regimes have had fair success in blocking the internet.

The important question is whether these efforts will sufficiently transform the internet itself to make it compatible with the needs of territorial authorities. If the internet remains relatively open,[52] then authoritarian regimes will be overpowered in the battle for information supremacy. They will be unable to control the domestic flow of information between their societies and the outside world. If, on the other hand, the internet evolves so as to allow more centralised control, then their task will be much easier and the threat to traditional territoriality will not be as great. Business interests and consumer inertia keep the internet relatively open now, but nothing inherent in the software and hardware architecture of the internet mandates that this be so. Any of several developments could push the architecture of the internet in a less open direction: consumer discontent with spam and crime could push popular opinion in favor of a more centralised internet and give policy-makers the leverage they need to overcome business opposition.

Individual initiatives to block internet access are less interesting from the perspective of the placeless-ness hypothesis than the question of whether those initiatives are modifying the technical nature of the internet itself. The most telling evidence of this is the merging of public and private power. States make use of tools provided by multinational computer software and hardware manufacturers who are pursuing their own vision of a closed, controlled internet.[53]

---

49 Geoffrey Herrera, 'The Politics of Bandwidth: International Political Implications of a Digital Information Infrastructure', *Review of International Studies*, 28/1 (2002): 93–122.

50 <http://www.rnp.br/backbone/>.

51 Kalathil and Boas, *Open Networks, Closed Regimes*; <http://www.opennetinitiative.net>.

52 By 'open', I mean network topology that is relatively decentralised; the network itself is 'dumb' (information processing happens at the network ends, not in the middle – the telephone network, with its centralised switches, is a 'smart' network), and the software protocols that route Internet traffic allow anonymity. Isenberg, 'Rise of the Stupid Network'. The Internet is not really an open network. Virtual private networks (VPNs), digital rights management (DRM), network address translation (NAT) firewalls, and other developments have served to introduce some measure of centralisation and control over the Internet.

53 The network hardware manufacturer Cisco came under criticism in early 2006 for helping the Chinese government censor the Internet for Chinese users.

The internet is not a global computer network, but a network of networks. The topology of the internet reflects the Westphalian order it was built on. Local Internet service providers (ISPs) as well as corporate and public-sector networks are connected to national network backbones. The backbones are connected globally via international gateways. This mode of organisation is not a necessary consequence of the technology of computer networks. Private actors could lay fibre-optic lines across international borders (though such activity is doubtless illegal under current legislation, unless coordinated with the states in question). But the internet as a socio-technical system has developed along state-centric lines, and due to the sunk costs associated with its development trajectory, it is unlikely that its topology will be undone. It is a simple matter for states to control the flow of information in and out of their territories, especially if, as in most of the developing world, the government owns the backbone.

States control internet-based information by blocking requests for foreign websites; because so much of the internet's content is concentrated in the US and Western Europe, this is sufficient to regulate the flow of potentially threatening information. States are thus able to filter content at the backbone or gateway level. This is brute force filtering – blocking access to entire sites or domains based on packet address.[54] China, for instance, has only a few national backbones (CHINANet, CERNet, CSTNet, CHINAGBN, and UNINet). Some are private ISPs; others are government-controlled networks. Content on subjects such as the Falun Gong, Taiwan, Tiananmen Square, Tibet, and human rights are effectively blocked across the networks.

As with the e-commerce example, where territorial and non-territorial actors adjust their actions and strategies to take into account the actions of the other, efforts by individuals to circumvent filtering and blocking have tried to keep pace with state capacity. The OpenNet Initiative is busy developing a proxy server tool called Psiphon to allow users to temporarily borrow another user's internet connection in their country. This would in principle avoid all efforts at censorship, as the connection would be to an obscure address, and would change frequently. Other similar initiatives have been developed both by NGOs and private individuals. But they suffer from the same limitations as illegal file trading. While technically feasible, territorial authorities will be able to raise the costs (in time and money) of using these tools and the level of technical expertise required so high as to limit their ability to meaningfully scale.

From the perspective of national security, these efforts at controlling national internet space to keep out ideas, arguments, and information considered subversive or dangerous have the effect of creating virtual borders as states expand their territoriality beyond the constraints of their physical territory.[55] The placeless-ness

---

54 Nart Villeneuve, 'Project C: Tracking Internet Censorship in China', <http://www.chass.utoronto.ca/~citizenl/assets/articles/ProjectC-r1.pdf>, accessed 24 May, 2004; Jonathan Zittrain and Benjamin Edelman, 'Empirical Analysis of Internet Filtering in China', <http://cyber.law.harvard.edu/filtering/china>, accessed 24 May, 2004.

55 Peter Andreas, 'Redrawing the Line: Borders and Security in the Twenty-First Century', *International Security*, 28/2 (2003): 78–111.

hypothesis – that territorial states will be unable to cope with non-territorial threats – would predict that censorship on the internet, or walling off part of the internet, is impossible. While this is not the case, the situation is far from constituting an easy triumph for the forces of state power. To maintain information security, states have had to transform their border control regimes and harness the success of their efforts to another global, stateless force – the international computer industry. The threat to territoriality, from the perspective of states that censor the internet, is real. States have recourse, however, to powerful tools to combat these information flows, provided they are willing to transform state practices and enter into new, and potentially troubling, relations of external dependence with private firms.

The Double Move in Physical Space: The Digitalisation of Terrestrial Surveillance

The second set of socio-technical components contains digital solutions to the problem of tracking physical objects in three-dimensional space: satellite imaging, global positioning, and radio frequency identification systems. The examples of anonymity, e-commerce, and censorship show states trying to bring territorial order to a borderless space generated by information technology. Here, the reverse is the case: Information technology is being imposed on territory. Satellites, GPS, and RFID operate in an intriguing mix of cyberspace and territorial space. But do these systems favor territorial or non-territorial actors? If the latter, do they pose a threat to international security, and if so, what kind of threat? The placeless-ness hypothesis makes no direct predictions about territorial space, of course, but these three technologies have evolved to link cyberspace and physical space, so we should expect the hypothesis to hold.

At first glance, it does. Trends over the past decade or more have been towards a relinquishing of state control. The US and the USSR developed satellite-imaging systems during the Cold War to monitor each other's military capabilities. Photographs taken by orbiting satellites were beamed back to earth for analysis. Privatisation in the 1990s established a trend that promised greater civilian use and eventual deterritorialisation of terrestrial surveillance.[56] A recent spectacular example is Google Earth.[57] Computer-generated maps of the world and address information are combined with satellite imagery that Google acquired in 2004 when they purchased Keyhole to produce a seamless blend of computer-based mapping and actual images (Google Earth is also an excellent example of the merging of virtual and terrestrial technologies).

The US GPS is an example of a global navigation satellite system (GNSS). The Russian government operates a second system, GLONASS, and the EU plans to deploy its own Galileo system in 2008. Most civilians use GPS.[58] GNSS combine

---

56 Susan Landau, 'The Transformation of Global Surveillance', in Latham (ed.), *Bombs and Bandwidth: The Emerging Relationship Between Information Technology and Security* (The New Press, 2003): 117–30.

57 <http://earth.google.com/>.

58 The Chinese military uses GPS, though to distribute the risk, it also relies on GLONASS.

terrestrial handheld receivers and signals from satellites to pinpoint the location of the receiver within 15 meters. A shift to private uses, similar to that which occurred with satellites, happened with GNSS. GPS receivers have come into widespread civilian use since the end of the Cold War. They are installed in many automobiles and are crucial components of navigation and tracking systems in the trucking and maritime industries. More than a decade ago, Lachow worried that privatisation would weaken the military utility of GPS.[59] But in 2000, the US government turned off selective availability anyway, raising the accuracy of the system for civilians almost to the military level. Though the armed forces retain the authority to introduce an intentional error into the signal in a national emergency, many civilian GPS experts think the error signal can be hacked and overcome. Moreover, if Galileo comes online in 2008 as planned, this competing (and, according to European commentators, more accurate) system will make the US military's efforts to protect GPS irrelevant.[60] Commentators on the privatisation of satellite imaging argue that NGOs and other non-state, non-territorial actors are empowered by these developments. They can use the imagery to challenge government efforts at control, and they can 'watch the watchers', in David Brin's phrase.[61] Others reiterate Lachow's fear that this development is a significant threat to national security.[62]

RFID are systems of small radio transmitters with unique signatures and larger receiver or detection units. The transmitters are imbedded in products, pets, and humans to track the movements of the objects within a relatively limited range. Only a handful of pilot RFID projects exist, but the giant US retailer Wal-Mart intends to place RFID tags in its entire inventory, and there have been pilot projects to 'chip' schoolchildren, club-goers, and law enforcement personnel. As a new, relatively untested technology, RFID has not followed a trajectory similar to that of satellite imaging and GNSS. But as a private-sector technology with far-reaching implications, it represents another significant shift from public to private power.

The September 2001 attacks have impeded that shift. Since then, in the name of national security, states have proposed and begun to implement a wide variety of new controls using location-identification information technologies. In the words of one critical report:

Under the radar screen of the public, a global registration and surveillance infrastructure is quietly being constructed. It consists of numerous initiatives, most of which have been agreed to by governments without any democratic debate through international forums,

---

59 Irving Lachow, 'The GPS Dilemma: Balancing Military Risks and Economic Benefits', *International Security*, 20/1 (1995): 126–48.

60 Galileo's World, 'Galileo Progress: New Alliances, ITTs', *GPS World*, 1 November 2003.

61 Karen Litfin, 'Public Eyes: Satellite Imagery, The Globalization of Transparency, and New Networks of Surveillance', in Rosenau and Singh (eds), *Information Technologies and Global Politics: The Changing Scope of Power and Governance* (New York, 2002), pp. 65–89; David Brin, *The Transparent Society: Will Technology Force Us to Choose Between Privacy and Freedom?* (Reading, Massachusetts, 1998).

62 Steve Livingston and Lucas Robinson, 'Mapping Fears: The Use of Commercial High-Resolution Satellite Imagery in International Affairs', *Astropolitics*, 1/2 (2003): 3–25.

treaties and arrangements [...] The object of the infrastructure that is being constructed is not ordinary police or intelligence work but, rather, mass surveillance of entire populations [...T]he system that is currently being constructed is unlike anything that has come before [...] its technological capacity dwarfs any previous system and makes Orwell's book Nineteen Eighty-Four look quaint.[63]

Hyperbole, perhaps, but satellite, GPS, and RFID systems are undoubtedly critical parts of an emerging global surveillance security system. Both the US and the EU are considering RFID passports. The chips would be checked at embassies and customs around the world. They would serve to rapidly match passports against a database from about three meters away. The EU passport would also include biometric data (face and fingerprints are planned at the moment) to confirm identity via irrefutable biological characteristics.[64] The US is also considering the use of RFID tags to track imported goods in truck containers via the Customs and Border Protection Agency's Container Security Initiative. The private sector and private citizens are pushing wider use of RFID too. The parents of a school district in Texas voted to insert RFID transmitters in badges worn by their children so their passage onto and off school buses and into and out of school can be tracked; and potential kidnap targets in Mexico are voluntarily 'chipping' themselves so they can be tracked after a kidnapping (though given the short range of RFID chips, it's not clear how the tracking is supposed to take place).[65]

Private firms are expanding development of GPS tracking technologies – often for 'public' purposes. GPS receivers on school buses soothe anxious parents, chips in mandatory phones allow employers to track their employees, and GPS tracking devices supplied by IBM and built into cars will allow the government of the United Arab Emirates to monitor all of the kingdom's drivers for speeding and other traffic violations.[66] Extrapolating from the way governments treat Internet Service Providers and e-mail wiretaps, it is likely that the collected information can and will be made available to state authorities.

Each of these initiatives, public and private, is expanding the scope of digitally monitored physical space. They suggest that digital information technologies can successfully be applied to traditional territorial tasks and do them better and more comprehensively than older technologies. GPS, RFID, and satellite reconnaissance are becoming critical national security tools. This is not surprising, but it does run counter to the placeless-ness hypothesis, which argues that digital information

---

63 International Campaign Against Mass Surveillance, 'The Emergence of a Global Infrastructure'.

64 Kim Zetter, 'Feds Rethinking RFID Passport', *Wired News*, 26 April 2005; John Lettice, 'EU Biometric RFID Scheme Unworkable, Says EU Tech Report', *Wired News*, 23 December 2004.

65 Matt Richtel, 'In Texas, 28,000 Students Test an Electronic Eye', *New York Times*, 17 November 2004; Lester Haines, 'Kidnap-Wary Mexicans Get Chipped', *The Register*, 14 July 2004.

66 Ariana Eunjung Cha, 'To Protect and Intrude', *Washington Post*, 15 January 2005; Ben Charny, 'Big Boss Is Watching', *CNET News.com*, 24 September 2004; Martin LaMonica, 'IBM Car Tech to Nab Speeders', *CNET News.com*, 14 April 2005.

technology undermines territorial authority. But this is not an unmitigated triumph for traditional authorities. The same theme of compromise and transformation found in the first set of examples accompanies state behavior with regard to location-identification technologies. Public-private partnerships and rivalries pervade this arena, requiring states to be adaptive. Satellite navigation, to pick one example, is more than just a national security tool. It is just as vital a part of the global economy as telephone lines and national highway networks are. The US could not shut off GPS (or stop the development of Galileo) even if it wanted to. The open global economy depends on it. But it can alter it to better suit its needs.

Conclusion: The Deterritorialisation of National Security

Cyberspace is non-territorial. Because of its physical nature, design, and operation, it does have different organisational imperatives than traditional territorial space. But the political meaning of technologies never rests on hard technical facts alone. This is why the claim that territorial authority cannot control cyberspace – the placelessness hypothesis – is overstated. Cyberspace is composed of information in the form of electrons whizzing around a network of wires, but this is only the first (and largely irrelevant) fact. The political implications emerge when physical objects fuse with human rules and institutions. Cyberspace does not exist without those rules. The question is, how flexible is the socio-technical system? How much can political actors bend and shape it to fit their wishes and needs? In the case of cyberspace, on the evidence of the two sets of examples provided here, the answer seems to be: quite a lot. While the 'nature' of cyberspace may be non-territorial, its implications for international security are not.

States have responded to the threats posed by cyberspace with a double move: they have partially deterritorialised themselves, and they have partially territorialised cyberspace. They have also deployed cyberspace and other information technologies to better control people and territory. States, principally the US and the EU members, have altered their borders by conducting visa checks and cargo inspections in other territories or at sea. They monitor global information networks at all levels: keystroke logging at the user end, wiretapping at the level of the Internet service provider, and in the case of states such as Saudi Arabia and China, at the level of the backbone and at key international nodes. States have imposed territorial order on cyberspace by insisting that respect for national borders be built into internet protocols and e-commerce, and by empowering international organisations to aggressively pursue their intellectual property rights. Furthermore, states have deployed information technology to increase their surveillance capabilities in remarkable ways. Cyberspace may, in principle, be 'no place', but territorial authorities are proving that they have the capability to make it 'someplace'.

I claim that the double move is under way. But this should not be taken as endorsement. I am very attuned to the possibility of overreaching by states, and I am as concerned as anyone about the potential reduction in privacy and personal freedom posed by these developments, and bemused (and a little confused) at the thought of billions of objects and millions of people being tracked globally, in real-time. Yet my argument, which stresses the flexibility of socio-technical systems and the importance of conjunctural events (like 11 September 2001) for shaping the development trajectory of these systems, offers the possibility of a re-reshaping along less statist lines.

Lastly, my argument can contribute to a larger discussion on globalisation and the transformation of the state system. Much of the debate in recent decades has been binary – either the sovereign state is disappearing, or it is not. We would be wiser to move beyond that sterile dichotomy and instead explore the ways in which sovereignty and territoriality are changing, as well as the ways in which they are staying the same. My analysis strongly suggests that the diffusion of ICT is transforming the environment in which states have to act and changing the threats that states need to be secure from. In response, states are transforming themselves, and in the process are changing conceptions of sovereignty, territory, and national security. The next step for research is to determine just what these conceptions are.

References

Abbate, Janet, *Inventing the Internet* (Cambridge, Massachusetts: MIT Press, 1999).

Andreas, Peter, 'Redrawing the Line: Borders and Security in the Twenty-First Century', *International Security*, 28/2 (2003): 78–111.

Barabási, Albert-László, *Linked: The New Science of Networks* (New York: Plume, 2002).

Baran, Paul, 'On Distributed Communications: IX. Security, Secrecy, and Tamper-Free Considerations', Memoranda RM-3765-PR (Santa Monica: RAND, 1964).

Barlow, John Perry, 'A Declaration of the Independence of Cyberspace', in Peter Ludlow (ed.), *Crypto Anarchy, Cyberstates, and Pirate Utopias* (Cambridge, MA: MIT Press, 2001).

Basile, Mark, 'Going to the Source: Why Al Qaeda's Financial Network Is Likely to Withstand the Current War on Terrorist Financing', *Studies in Conflict and Terrorism*, 27/3 (2004): 169–85.

Benjamin, Daniel and Steven Simon, *The Next Attack: The Failure of the War on Terror and a Strategy for Getting It Right* (New York: Times Books, 2005).

Borsook, Paulina, 'How Anarchy Works', *Wired*, Issue 3.10, October 1995, < http://www.wired.com/wired/archive/3.10/ietf.html>, accessed 18 April 2007.

Brin, David, *The Transparent Society: Will Technology Force Us to Choose Between Privacy and Freedom?* (Reading: Addison-Wesley, 1998).

Castells, Manuel, *The Rise of the Network Society* (Cambridge: Blackwell Publishers, 1996).

Cha, Ariana Eunjung, 'Despite U.S. Efforts, Web Crimes Thrive', *Washington Post*, 20 May 2003.

Cha, Ariana Eunjung, 'To Protect and Intrude', *Washington Post*, 15 January 2005.

Charny, Ben, 'Big Boss Is Watching', *CNET News.com*, 24 September 2004.

Chaum, David, 'Achieving Electronic Privacy', *Scientific American* (August 1992), p. 96–101.

Deibert, Ronald J., 'Circuits of Power: Security in the Internet Environment', in James N. Rosenau and J. P. Singh (eds), *Information Technologies and Global Politics: The Changing Scope of Power and Governance* (Albany, NY: State University of New York Press, 2002).

Deibert, Ronald J. and Janice Gross Stein, 'Social and Electronic Networks in the War on Terror', in Robert Latham (ed.), *Bombs and Bandwidth: The Emerging Relationship Between Information Technology and Security* (New York: The New Press, 2003).

Delio, Michelle, 'Al Qaeda Website Refuses to Die', *Wired News*, 7 April 2003.

Department of Homeland Security, 'The National Strategy to Secure Cyberspace', (Washington, D.C.: Government Printing Office, March 2003).

Dishman, Chris, 'The Leaderless Nexus: When Crime and Terror Converge', *Studies in Conflict and Terrorism*, 28/3 (2005): 237–52.

Edwards, Paul N., 'Infrastructure and Modernity: Force, Time, and Social Organization in the History of Sociotechnical Systems', in Thomas J. Misa, Philip Brey and Andrew Feenberg (eds), *Modernity and Technology* (Cambridge, Massachusetts: MIT Press, 2003).

ElBoghdady, Dina, 'For Some, No Purchase Is Too Small For Plastic', *Washington Post*, 23 February 2005.

Farah, Douglas, 'Colombian Drug Cartels Exploit Tech Advantage', *Washington Post*, 15 November 1999.

Farah, Douglas, *Blood From Stones: The Secret Financial Network of Terror* (New York: Broadway Books, 2004).

Federal Communications Commission, 'FCC Adopts Notice of Proposed Rulemaking and Declaratory Ruling Regarding Communications Assistance for Law Enforcement Act' (Washington, DC: 4 August 2004).

Ferguson, Yale H. and Richard W. Mansbach, *Remapping Global Politics: History's Revenge and Future Shock* (Cambridge: Cambridge University Press, 2004).

Forno, Richard, 'MS to Micro-Manage Your Computer', *The Register*, 24 June 2002.

Galileo's World, 'Galileo Progress: New Alliances, ITTs', *GPS World*, 1 November 2003.

Giddens, Anthony, *The Consequences of Modernity* (Stanford: Stanford University Press, 1990).

Goldsmith, Jack and Tim Wu, *Who Controls the Internet? Illusions of a Borderless World* (Oxford: Oxford University Press, 2006).

Granovetter, Mark S., 'The Strength of Weak Ties', *American Journal of Sociology*, 78/6 (1973): 1360–1380.

Greene, Thomas C., 'ID Theft is Inescapable', *The Register*, 23 March 2005.

Haines, Lester, 'Kidnap-Wary Mexicans Get Chipped', *The Register*, 14 July 2004.

Henry, Ryan and C. Edward Peartree (eds), *The Information Revolution and International Security* (Washington, D.C.: Center for Strategic and International Studies, 1998).

Herrera, Geoffrey L., 'The Politics of Bandwidth: International Political Implications of a Digital Information Infrastructure', *Review of International Studies*, 28/1 (2002): 93–122.

Higgins, Andrew, Karby Leggett and Alan Cullison, 'How al Qaeda Put Internet in Service of Global Jihad', *Wall Street Journal*, 11 November 2002.

Huang, Gregory T., 'The Web's New Currency', *Technology Review*, December-January, 2004.

Hughes, Thomas P., 'The Evolution of Large Technological Systems', in Wiebe E. Bijker, Thomas P. Hughes and Trevor J. Pinch (eds), *Social Construction of Technological Systems: New Directions in the Sociology and History of Technology* (Cambridge, Massachusetts: MIT Press, 1987).

International Campaign Against Mass Surveillance, 'The Emergence of a Global Infrastructure for Mass Registration and Surveillance', April 2005.

Isenberg, David, 'Rise of the Stupid Network', <http://www.hyperorg.com/misc/stupidnet.html>, accessed 26 April 2006.

Kalathil, Shanthi and Taylor C. Boas, *Open Networks, Closed Regimes: The Impact of the Internet on Authoritarian Rule* (Washington, DC: Carnegie Endowment for International Peace, 2003).

Keck, Margaret E. and Kathryn Sikkink, *Activists Beyond Borders: Advocacy Networks in International Politics* (Ithaca, New York: Cornell University Press, 1998).

Kline, Ronald and Trevor Pinch, 'The Social Construction of Technology', in Donald A. MacKenzie and Judy Wajcman (eds), *The Social Shaping of Technology* (Milton Keynes: Open University Press, 1999).

Kobrin, Stephen J., 'Electronic Cash and the End of National Markets', *Foreign Policy*, 107 (1997): 65–77.

Kobrin, Stephen J., 'Economic Governance in an Electronically Networked Global Economy', in Rodney Bruce Hall and Thomas J. Biersteker (eds), *The Emergence of Private Authority in Global Governance* (New York: Cambridge University Press, 2002).

Labaton, Stephen, 'Easing of Internet Regulations Challenges Surveillance Efforts', *New York Times*, 22 January 2004.

Lachow, Irving, 'The GPS Dilemma: Balancing Military Risks and Economic Benefits', *International Security*, 20/1 (1995): 126–48.

LaMonica, Martin, 'IBM Car Tech to Nab Speeders', *CNET News.com*, 14 April 2005.

Landau, Susan, 'The Transformation of Global Surveillance', in Robert Latham (ed.), *Bombs and Bandwidth: The Emerging Relationship Between Information Technology and Security* (New York: The New Press, 2003).

Last, David, 'GPS and Galileo: Where Are We Headed?', paper given at the European Navigation Conference GNSS2004 (Rotterdam, 7–19 May 2004).

Latham, Robert (ed.), *Bombs and Bandwidth: The Emerging Relationship Between IT and Security* (New York: New Press, 2003).

Lessig, Lawrence, *Free Culture: The Nature and Future of Creativity* (New York: Penguin Books, 2004).

Lettice, John, 'EU Biometric RFID Scheme Unworkable, Says EU Tech Report', *Wired News*, 23 December 2004.

Levy, Steven, *Hackers: Heroes of the Computer Revolution* (Garden City, New York: Anchor Press, 1984).

Levy, Steven, 'E-Money (That's What I Want)', *Wired*, December 1994.
Litfin, Karen, 'Public Eyes: Satellite Imagery, The Globalization of Transparency, and New Networks of Surveillance', in James N. Rosenau and J. P. Singh (eds), *Information Technologies and Global Politics: The Changing Scope of Power and Governance* (Albany, NY: State University of New York Press, 2002).
Livingston, Steve and Lucas Robinson, 'Mapping Fears: The Use of Commercial High-Resolution Satellite Imagery in International Affairs', *Astropolitics*, 1/2 (2003): 3–25.
Lukasik, Stephen J., Seymour E. Goodman and David W. Longhurst, 'Protecting Critical Infrastructures Against Cyber-Attack', *Adelphi Papers*, 359 (30 September 2003).
Lynch, Marc, *Voices of the New Arab Public: Iraq, Al-Jazeera, and Middle East Politics Today* (New York: Columbia University Press, 2006).
Mara, Janis, 'Euro Scheme Makes Money Talk', *Wired News*, 9 July 2003.
Markoff, John and Lowell Bergman, 'Internet Attack Called Broad and Long Lasting by Investigators', *New York Times*, 10 May 2005.
McCullagh, Declan, 'FBI Pushes for Broadband Wiretap Powers', *CNET News.com*, 12 March 2004.
Meijer, Jeroen, 'Lights Going Out on the Internet? Not Just Yet', <http://www.circleid.com/posts/lights_going_out_on_the_internet_not_just_yet/>, accessed 21 May 2004.
Mishal, Shaul and Maoz Rosenthal, 'Al Qaeda as a Dune Organization: Toward a Typology of Islamic Terrorist Organizations', *Studies in Conflict and Terrorism*, 28/4 (2005): 275–93.
Orlowski, Andrew, 'MS Trusted Computing Back to Drawing Board', *The Register*, 6 May 2004.
Pierson, Paul, *Politics in Time: History, Institutions, and Social Analysis* (Princeton: Princeton University Press, 2004).
Powell, Walter W., 'Neither Market nor Hierarchy: Network Forms of Organization', *Research in Organizational Behavior*, 12 (1990): 295–336.
Ratliff, Evan, 'The Zombie Hunters', *The New Yorker*, 10 October 2005.
Ricciuti, Mike and Martin LaMonica, 'Longhorn Goes to Pieces', *CNET News.com*, 13 May 2004.
Richtel, Matt, 'In Texas, 28,000 Students Test an Electronic Eye', *New York Times*, 17 November 2004.
Ronfeldt, David and John Arquilla, 'Networks, Netwars, and the Fight for the Future', *First Monday*, 6/10 (2001).
Schneier, Bruce, 'Blaster and the August 14th Blackout', *Crypto-Gram Newsletter*, 15 December 2003.
Skowronek, Stephen, *Building a New American State: The Expansion of National Administrative Capacities, 1877–1920* (New York: Cambridge University Press, 1981).
Van Natta, Don, Jr., 'Terrorists Blaze a New Money Trail', *New York Times*, 28 September 2003.

Villeneuve, Nart, 'Project C: Tracking Internet Censorship in China', <http://www.chass.utoronto.ca/~citizenl/assets/articles/ProjectC-r1.pdf>, accessed 24 May 2004.

Walker, John, 'The Digital Imprimatur', <http://www.fourmilab.ch/documents/digital-imprimatur>, accessed 7 May 2004.

Wayner, Peter, 'Cybercash on Vacation', *Technology Review*, March 2005.

Weimann, Gabriel, 'www.terror.net: How Modern Terrorism Uses the Internet', (Washington, D.C.: United States Institute of Peace, March 2004).

Weimann, Gabriel, *Terror on the Internet: The New Arena, the New Challenges*, (Washington, D.C.: United States Institute of Peace, 2006).

Yould, Rachel, 'Beyond the American Fortress: Understanding Homeland Security in the Information Age', in Robert Latham (ed.), *Bombs and Bandwidth: The Emerging Relationship Between IT and Security* (New York: New Press, 2003).

Zetter, Kim, 'Feds Rethinking RFID Passport', *Wired News*, 26 April 2005.

Zimmer, Michael T., 'The Tensions of Securing Cyberspace: The Internet, State Power and the National Strategy to Secure Cyberspace', *First Monday*, 9/3 (2004).

Zittrain, Jonathan, 'Without a Net', *Legal Affairs* (January/February, 2006), < http://www.legalaffairs.org/printerfriendly.msp?id=960>, accessed 18 April 2007.

Zittrain, Jonathan and Benjamin Edelman, 'Empirical Analysis of Internet Filtering in China', <http://cyber.law.harvard.edu/filtering/china>, accessed 24 May 2004.

Chapter 5

Terrorist Use of the Internet and the Challenges of Governing Cyberspace

Maura Conway

Introduction

Information is the lifeblood of the international system. World politics today transcends simple international relations, and much of the change has taken place as a result of the spread of information infrastructures. The rapid expansion and diffusion of new International Communications Technologies (ICTs), particularly evident in the growth of the internet, contribute to the set of phenomena collectively labelled 'globalisation' and cut across traditional temporal and spatial boundaries. Yet the central and causal role of communications in the transformation of our world still tends to be neglected or minimised by most International Relations (IR) scholars. As recently as 2003, the editors of *Millennium*, in the introduction to a special issue devoted to 'IR in the Digital Age', observed that 'Whereas other social sciences have begun to address aspects of this issue, IR as a discipline is once again playing catch-up.'[1]

The ongoing advances in ICTs are significantly impacting the ways in which states and societies relate to one another. The information revolution underlines several challenges to global governance, chief amongst which are the following:

- The creation of electronic platforms where new, or hitherto less powerful, actors have emerged and influenced policy agendas while bypassing established channels of participation;
- The potential crisis of democratic accountability, legitimacy, and identity arising out of the empowerment of these;
- The changing conception of how states define their interests, their power bases, and their security;
- Mounting challenges to states' ability to govern and control the dissemination of information.[2]

Both global governance and the sub-set of issues that may be termed 'internet governance' are vast and complex issue areas. The difficulties of trying to 'legislate' at the global level – efforts that must encompass the economic, cultural, developmental, legal, and political concerns of diverse states and other stakeholders – are further

---

1 Eva Gross and Alvaro Mendéz, 'Editorial Note', *Millennium,* 32/3 (2003): iii.
2 Gross and Méndez, 'Editorial Note'.

complicated by the technological conundrums encountered in cyberspace. The unleashing of the so-called 'Global War on Terrorism' (GWOT) complicates things yet further.

Today, both sub-state and non-state actors are said to be harnessing – or preparing to harness – the power of the internet to harass and attack their foes. Clearly, international terrorism had already been a significant security issue prior to 11 September 2001 and the emergence of the internet in the decade before. Together, however, the events of 11 September 2001 and advancements in ICTs have added new dimensions to the problem. In newspapers and magazines, in film and on television, and in research and analysis, 'cyber-terrorism' has become a buzzword. Since the events of 11 September 2001, the question on everybody's lips appears to be 'is cyber-terrorism next?'.[3] It is generally agreed that the potential for a 'digital 9/11' in the near future is not great. This does not mean that IR scholars may continue to ignore the transformative powers of the internet. On the contrary, the internet came of age on 11 September 2001, as that was the day when the 'Digital Age' and the 'Age of Terror' converged.[4]

This chapter explores the difficulties of internet governance in the light of terrorists' increasing use of the medium. In particular, it details the clampdown on the burgeoning internet presence of extremist groups, undertaken by both state-based and sub-state actors, in the wake of the attacks of September 2001 in the US and of July 2005 in London. The ensuing governance challenges are many and varied, but include

- Debates over the role of various actors in the governance process, including national governments, hacktivists, and Internet Service Providers (ISPs);
- The appropriate legislative response to the terrorist internet presence;
- The debate over free speech vs. limits on speech;

The description and analysis of these challenges are at the centre of this chapter. First, however, it is worth considering what exactly is meant by the term 'internet governance'.

What is Meant by 'Internet Governance'?

The internet had unique governance structures during its development and early growth. It began life as a government project: in the late 1960s, the US government sponsored the establishment of the Defence Advanced Research Projects Agency (DARPA), which was charged with developing a resilient communication facility designed to survive a nuclear attack. By the 1980s, a wider community was using the facilities of this network, which had come to be referred to as the internet. In 1986, the Internet Engineering Task Force (IETF) was established to manage the further

---

3 Dorothy Denning, 'Is Cyber Terror Next?' in Craig Calhoun, Paul Price, and Ashley Timmer (eds), *Understanding September 11* (New York, 2001).

4 James Der Derian, 'The Question of Information Technology in International Relations', *Millennium*, 32/3 (2003): 441–456.

development of the internet through a cooperative, consensus-based decision-making process involving a wide variety of individuals. At this point, internet governance was relatively simple: 'There was no central government, no central planning, and no grand design.'[5] However, in 1994, the US National Science Foundation decided to involve the private sector by subcontracting the management of the Domain Name System (DNS) to Network Solutions Inc. (NSI). This angered many end users and resulted in a conflict, which was only resolved in 1998 with the establishment of a new organisation, the Internet Company for Assigned Names and Numbers (ICANN).[6]

Since the establishment of ICANN, the debate on internet governance has been characterised by the more direct involvement of national governments, mainly through the UN framework and institutions. The first World Summit on the Information Society (WSIS), held in Geneva in December 2003, officially placed the question of internet governance on diplomatic agendas. The Declaration of Principles and Action Plan adopted at WSIS 2003 proposed a number of actions in the field of internet governance, including the establishment of a Working Group on Internet Governance (WGIG).[7] This became necessary because each of the terms 'internet' and 'governance' was the subject of controversy as, indeed, was the concept of 'internet governance' itself.

It was the second part of the concept (i.e. 'governance') that was the subject of particular controversy, especially during the WSIS. Misunderstandings stemmed from terminological confusion arising out of the use of the term 'governance' as a synonym for 'government'. When the term 'internet governance' was introduced in the WSIS process, many countries linked it to the concept of government. One of the consequences was the belief that internet governance issues should be addressed primarily at the inter-governmental level with only the limited participation of other actors. What were the main reasons for this terminological confusion? Gelbstein and Kurbalija argue that it is not necessarily obvious to many that the term 'governance' does not mean 'government'. They point out, for example, that the term 'good governance' has been used by the World Bank to promote the reform of states by introducing more transparency, reducing corruption, and increasing the efficiency of administration and that, in this context, the term 'governance' was directly related to core government functions.[8]

In his analysis of internet governance, Klein draws on Robert Dahl's seminal text *Democracy and Its Critics* (1989), in which Dahl identifies what he views as the minimal conditions necessary for the establishment of an effective system of governance:

---

5 Eduardo Gelbstein and Jovan Kurbalija, *Internet Governance: Issues, Actors and Divides* (Geneva, 2005), p. 8.

6 Hans Klein, 'ICANN and Internet Governance: Leveraging Technical Coordination to Realize Global Public Policy', *The Information Society*, 18/3 (2002): 201.

7 See World Summit on the Information Society, *WSIS Plan of Action*, WSIS-03/GENEVA/DOC/5-E (Geneva, 2003), section 13b, <http://www.itu.int/wsis/docs/geneva/official/poa.html>, accessed 19 February 2007.

8 Gelbstein and Kurbalija, *Internet Governance*, p. 11.

The first is an *authority*. Governance requires a governor or a sovereign. An entity, be it an individual or a group, must make policy decisions that apply to the members of the polity. A second governance mechanism is *law*. Laws implement policy decisions. They might take the form of a tax, a license, or simply a binding rule. Third, there must be some mechanism for imposing *sanctions*. This allows for punishment of those who violate laws. Finally, governance requires the definition of *jurisdiction*. Jurisdiction defines the space over which the authority makes decisions and within which the laws apply and are enforced by the threat of sanctions. These four mechanisms make governance possible: the governing *authority* can make a policy decision that applies within its *jurisdiction*, embodying that decision in *law* and imposing *sanctions* on whomever disobeys [italics in original].[9]

Dahl's conception of governance is quite hierarchical, however, and closer to 'government' than perhaps many of those connected with the development of the internet – other than national governments – might find acceptable. Indeed, the WGIG has since published the following working definition of internet governance: 'Internet governance is the development and application by Governments, the private sector and civil society, in their respective roles, of shared principles, norms, rules, decision-making procedures, and programmes that shape the evolution and use of the Internet.'[10] This does not mean that the four issues identified by Dahl – authority, law, sanctions, jurisdiction – are of no importance; they arise repeatedly in any discussion of the relationship between terrorist use of the internet and internet governance; what the WGIG definition does draw our attention to, however, is the legacy of the early years of the internet's development and the resultant importance of actors-other-than- states in the internet governance process.

Terrorism and the Internet: A Brief History

For a considerable time, the terrorism-internet relationship consisted largely of fears about the potential for so-called 'cyber-terrorism'. In 1998, Mark Pollitt defined cyber-terrorism as 'premeditated, politically motivated attack[s] against information, computer systems, computer programs, and data which result in violence against non-combatant targets by sub-national groups or clandestine agents.'[11] On the basis of this definition, no act of cyber-terrorism has ever yet occurred; this has not mitigated against cyber-terrorism – conceived of as everything from sending pornographic e-mails to minors, posting offensive content on the internet, and defacing web pages, to using a computer to cause US$400 worth of damage, stealing credit card information, posting credit card numbers on the internet, and clandestinely redirecting internet traffic from one site to another[12] – receiving widespread coverage in newspapers, magazines, film, and television.

---

9 Klein, 'ICANN and Internet Governance', 194–5.

10 Working Group on Internet Governance (WGIG), *Report of the Working Group on Internet Governance* (Château de Bossey, 2005), p. 4.

11 Mark M. Pollitt, 'Cyberterrorism: Fact or Fancy?' *Computer Fraud and Security* (February 1998): 8–10, here 9.

12 See Maura Conway, 'What is Cyberterrorism? The Story So Far', *Journal of Information Warfare*, 2/2 (2003): 34–5.

Table 5.1 Cyber-terrorism in US newspapers before and after 11 September 2001

Newspaper	Pre-11 September 2001*	Post-11 September 2001**	Total
	(N)	(N)	(N)
The Washington Post	19	41	60
The New York Times	15	30	45
Philadelphia Inquirer	10	5	15
Miami Herald	4	7	11
International Herald Tribune	5	3	8

* From first recorded mention in June 1996 to 10 September 2001 (i.e., 63 months)
** 11 September 2001 to August 2004 (i.e., 36 months)
N = Number of articles mentioning the search words
Source: Compiled from Lexis-Nexis archives using the search words 'cyberterrorism' and 'cyber terrorism'.

Table 5.2 Cyber-terrorism in UK newspapers before and after 11 September 2001

Newspaper	Pre-11 September 2001*	Post-11 September 2001**	Total
	(N)	(N)	(N)
Financial Times	16	20	36
Guardian	11	20	31
Times	10	8	18
Independent	7	10	17
Mirror	3	10	13

* From first recorded mention in June 1996 to 10 September 2001(i.e., 63 months)
** 11 September 2001 to August 2004 (i.e., 36 months)
N = Number of articles mentioning the search words
Source: Compiled from Lexis-Nexis archives using the search words 'cyberterrorism' and 'cyber terrorism'

Cyber-threats became the object of increased attention from the US federal government in the 1990s. A particular concern was that enemies of the US, unable to defeat US forces on the conventional battlefield, would pursue alternative approaches to inflicting damage on the sole remaining superpower.[13] The events of 11 September 2001 were therefore doubly shocking for many US government officials: not only were the attacks appalling in themselves, but the conventional nature of the attacks was also completely unexpected. Far from reducing the fear of cyber attack however, for many the 11 September 2001 attacks only served to increase the credibility of the cyber-threat. In the weeks and months following 11 September 2001, in particular,

---

13 Neal A. Pollard, 'Indications and Warning of Infrastructure Attack', in Lars Nicander and Magnus Ranstorp (eds), *Terrorism in the Information Age: New Frontiers?* (Stockholm, 2004), p. 43.

the likelihood of a follow-up cyber-terror attack was widely referred to in the US press and was also taken up internationally (see Tables 5.1 and 5.2).

The one-sided nature of this analysis only became apparent to many when, in a little over four weeks in April and May 2004, the now-deceased Abu Musab al-Zarqawi, one-time leader of 'al-Qaida in Iraq', 'rocketed to worldwide fame, or infamy, by a deliberate combination of extreme violence and internet publicity'.[14] In early April 2004, Zarqawi posted online a 30-minute audio recording which explained who he was, why he was fighting, and details of the attacks for which he and his group were responsible. Zarqawi was interested in using the internet as a weapon, but not of the sort predicted by those hyping the threat of cyber-terrorism. Prior to the instigation of his internet-based PR campaign, each of Zarqawi's attacks had to kill large numbers of people in order to get noticed in the chaos and mounting daily death toll in Iraq. By going online, however, Zarqawi was able to both control the interpretation of his violent actions and achieve greater impact with smaller operations. By the end of April 2004, his group was regularly issuing communiqués via the internet. The first of these claimed responsibility for a suicide speedboat attack on Iraq's offshore oil export terminal in the Gulf which, although the operation failed, still shook oil markets because of Zarqawi's efforts at publicising the attack through the internet.

In May 2004, Zarqawi took things a step further and used the internet's force-multiplying power to the maximum effect when he was videotaped cutting off the head of a US hostage and had the footage posted online. The purpose of this video was to create images that would grab the attention of allies and enemies alike. In this respect, it was an undoubted success; Zarqawi risked very little in this undertaking, but accomplished 'as much if not more to undermine US plans as a bomb that killed 100 people in Najaf. And [at the same time] made himself a hero to jihadis across the world.'[15] The free availability of this and other grisly 'snuff movies' on the internet led to a realisation that the most important aspect of the terrorism-internet relationship was not the much vaunted 'cyber-terrorism', but those more mundane and everyday terrorist uses of the internet, from information provision to recruitment, which have a history stretching back for many years before Zarqawi's appearance on the internet.

In 1998, it was reported that approximately half of the (then) 30 groups designated as 'Foreign Terrorist Organisations' under the US Antiterrorism and Effective Death Penalty Act of 1996 operated websites. Today, virtually every active militant group – there are approximately 70 operating worldwide – has an online presence, and many groups are the subjects of more than one site. A majority of the 42 groups that appear on the US State Department's 2006 list of Designated Foreign Terrorist Organizations have an established online presence. A number of these groups have already shown a clear understanding of the power of the global information network to publicise their position. The Lebanese Hizbollah has clearly demonstrated this ability, as have the Tamil Tigers, al-Qaida, and numerous other

---

14 Paul Eedle, 'Al Qaeda's Super-Weapon: The Internet', paper presented at the conference Al-Qaeda 2.0: Transnational Terrorism After 9/11 (Washington, D.C., 1–2 December 2004).
15 Ibid.

political violence movements that maintain a web presence.[16] Unsurprisingly, in the post-11 September 2001 world, the latter are subject to much increased scrutiny. The remainder of this chapter is concerned with describing and analysing the attempts at internet governance instigated by those with concerns about increasing extremist use of the internet for the purposes of, amongst other things, information dissemination and thence recruitment. Much of the following is therefore concerned with what is called 'content control': efforts on the part of stakeholders to regulate what sort of material is available on the internet, including the removal of 'objectionable' materials currently accessible and the erection of barriers to the uploading of such materials in the future.

Content Control Issues

Who is Responsible for Content Policy?

When it comes to terrorism, governments are generally held to be the main players in the area of content control, as it is they who prescribe what should be controlled and how. Some groups of individual users, such as hacktivists, are also keen to play their part, however, and indeed have had some success in disrupting the online presence of a number of terrorist organisations. In practical terms, of course, both legislated content control and private initiatives require the participation of private enterprises, particularly Internet Service Providers (ISPs) and search engine companies, and pressure has increasingly been brought to bear on such firms, both by nation-states and private groups and individuals, to regulate terrorism-related content. In addition, the availability of appropriate control technologies is also a matter for discussion.

Three Approaches to Content Policy

Content policy is generally approached from one of three standpoints: 1.) Human rights (freedom of expression and right to communicate), 2.) Government (legislated content control), 3.) Technology (tools for content control).

Freedom of expression and the right to seek, receive, and impart information is a fundamental human right, according to Article 19 of the UN's Universal Declaration of Human Rights (1948). On the other hand, the Declaration also recognises that freedom of expression is counter-balanced by the right of states to limit freedom of expression for the sake of morality, public order, and general welfare (Article 29).

---

16 For an exploration of Hizbollah's internet presence, see Maura Conway, 'Cybercortical Warfare: Hizbollah's Internet Strategy', in Sarah Oates, Diana Owen, and Rachel Gibson (eds), *The Internet and Politics: Citizens, Voters and Activists* (London, 2005), pp. 100–17; an analysis of the LTTE's websites is contained in Shyam Tekwani's 'The Tamil Diaspora, Tamil Militancy, and the Internet', in K.C. Ho, Randolph Kluver, and Kenneth C.C. Yang (eds), *Asia.Com: Asia Encounters the Internet* (London, 2003). A comparative analysis of a number of English-language terrorist websites is to be found in Maura Conway, 'Terrorist Web Sites: Their Contents, Functioning, and Effectiveness', in Philip Seib (ed.), *Media and Conflict in the Twenty-First Century* (New York, 2005), pp. 185–215.

Thus, both the discussion and the implementation of Article 19 must be put in the context of establishing a proper balance between these two concerns. This ambiguous international regime opens many possibilities for different interpretations of norms relating to speech, and ultimately for different implementations.

Content control is very much bound up with free-speech issues and concerns regarding restrictions on freedom of expression. Controls on internet-based speech are especially contentious in the US context, where the First Amendment guarantees broad freedom of expression, even the right to publish hate speech and similar material.[17] Achieving a proper balance between content control and freedom of expression has therefore proven to be a considerable challenge, and much of the recent internet governance debate, including court cases and legislation, has been concerned with finding this balance. Whereas the US Congress has inclined towards stricter content control, particularly in the wake of the events of 11 September 2001, the US Supreme Court has sought to uphold First Amendment protections. This commitment to freedom of expression is what largely shapes the US position in the international debate on internet governance. So while the US has signed on to the Cybercrime Convention, it is constitutionally barred from signing the Additional Protocol to this convention that deals with the criminalisation of acts of a racist and xenophobic nature committed through computer systems.[18] In other words, while the Additional Protocol is now available to EU governments and other signatories, adding to other hate crimes statutes under which they may prosecute terrorist groups and their supporters who publish hate material online, the same legal options are not available to the US authorities.[19]

It is for this reason that many terrorist groups' sites are hosted in the US. For example, a Connecticut-based ISP was at one time providing co-location and virtual hosting services for a Hamas site in data centres located in Connecticut and Chicago.[20] While sites such as those maintained by Hamas have been subject to more intense scrutiny following the events of September 2001, similar websites had already been the subject of debate in the US even before the events of 11 September 2001. In 1997, controversy erupted when it was revealed that the State University of New York (SUNY) at Binghamton was hosting the website of the Revolutionary Armed Forces of Colombia (FARC), and that a *Tupac Amaru* (MRTA) solidarity site was operating out of the University of California at San Diego (UCSD). SUNY officials promptly shut down the FARC site. In San Diego, officials decided in favour of free speech, and the *Tupac Amaru* site remained in operation on UCSD's servers for some

---

17 For a general introduction to the legal protection of speech in the US, UK, and elsewhere, see Eric Barendt's *Freedom of Speech* (Oxford, 1987).

18 The full text of the Additional Protocol to the Convention on Cybercrime is accessible online at <http://conventions.coe.int/Treaty/EN/Treaties/Html/189.htm>, accessed 19 February 2007.

19 Yaman Akdeniz, *Stocktaking on Efforts to Combat Racism on the Internet* (Geneva, 2006), pp. 10–1.

20 Jay Lyman, 'Terrorist Web Site Hosted by US Firm', *NewsFactor Network*, 3 April 2002, <http://www.newsfactor.com/perl/story/17079.html>, accessed 19 February 2007.

years.[21] It is not illegal to host such a site, even if a group is designated a 'Foreign Terrorist Organisation' by the US Department of State, as long as a site is not seeking financial contributions nor providing financial support to the group. Other content is generally considered to be protected speech under the First Amendment of the US Constitution.

Constitutional guarantees notwithstanding, states are not technologically impotent when faced with political violence groups seeking to use the internet for information dissemination purposes. Rather, states have access to myriad technologies with which they can limit and constrain how dissidents are able to use the internet. The successful use of the internet for recruitment and other types of political action is based on the assumption that both users and audiences have access to the messages communicated via the internet. States can therefore constrain the effectiveness of these cyber-based strategies by limiting user and audience access to internet technologies, either by actively censoring internet content or by controlling the internet infrastructure, or by some combination of the two.[22] The common element for governmental filtering is generally an index of websites that citizens are blocked from accessing. If a website appears on this list, access will not be granted. Technically speaking, the filtering typically utilises router-based IP blocking, proxy servers, and DNS redirection. Filtering of content is carried out in many countries: in addition to those countries, such as China, Saudi Arabia, and Singapore, which are usually associated with such practices, other countries increasingly practice censorship also.[23] For example, Australia has a filtering system for specific national pages, while the German state of North-Rhine-Westphalia requires ISPs to filter access to mainly, but not solely, neo-Nazi sites.[24]

Three Types of Content

Discussions about content also usually focus on three types. The first type consists of content where a global consensus regarding its control exists. Control of the

---

21 Robert Collier, 'Terrorists Get Web Sites Courtesy of US Universities', *San Francisco Chronicle*, 9 May 1997. The site hosted by UCSD was at <http://burn.ucsd.edu/~ats/mrta.htm>, but is no longer operational; however the official homepage of the MRTA (in Europe) may still be accessed at <http://www.voz-rebelde.de>, accessed 19 February 2007.

22 W. Sean McLaughlin, 'The Use of the Internet for Political Action by Non-State Dissident Actors in the Middle East', *First Monday*, 8/11 (2003): 9.

23 For an account of China's Internet content policy, see Charles Li's 'Internet Content Control in China', *International Journal of Communications Law and Policy*, 8 (Winter 2003/04); W. Sean McLoughlin discusses Saudi Arabia's approach in 'The Use of the Internet for Political Action', while Singapore's policy is discussed in Gary Rodan's 'The Internet and Political Control in Singapore', *Political Science Quarterly*, 113/1 (1998): 63–89.

24 On the Australian position, see Carolyn Penfold, 'Nazis, Porn, and Politics: Asserting Control Over Internet Content', *JILT: The Journal of Information Law and Technology*, 2 (2001), while links to documents related to the German decision may be accessed via Robert W. Smith, 'Administrative Court in Düsseldorf Affirms Blocking Order in North Rhine-Westphalia', *Heise Online*, 15 June 2005, <http://www.heise.de/english/newsticker/news/60662>, accessed 19 February 2007.

dissemination of child pornography online is the area in which the greatest amount of consensus currently exists.[25] While incitement or organisation of terrorist acts are prohibited by international law (*ius cogens*) – that is, a general consensus about the need to remove this content from the Net has been established – disputes still arise. This is because there is no globally accepted definition of terrorism, which makes it difficult, not to say impossible, to come to any agreement as to what exactly might constitute terrorism-support in any given instance.

In terms of controls, the second type of content that is generally discussed is that which might be sensitive for particular countries, regions, or ethnic groups due to their particular religious and/or cultural values. There can be little doubt that globalized, high-volume, and more intensive communication challenges cultural and religious values held in differing regional, national, and local spaces. In fact, most internet court cases are concerned with this type of content. Germany has very developed jurisprudence in this area, with many court cases against those responsible for websites hosting Nazi materials. In the Yahoo! Case, a French court requested that Yahoo.com (USA) prohibit French citizens from accessing parts of a website selling Nazi memorabilia. Most content control in Asia and the Middle East is officially justified as the protection of specific cultural values.[26] This usually includes blocking access to pornographic and gambling sites, but also those of a radical political nature.

This brings the discussion to the third type of content, which consists of politically and ideologically sensitive materials. In essence, this involves internet censorship. There is a dilemma here between the 'real' and 'cyber' worlds. Existing rules about speech, promulgated for application in the real world, *can* be implemented on the internet. This is probably best illustrated within the European context where, for example, the EU Council Framework Decision on Combating Racism and Xenophobia explicitly indicates 'what is illegal off-line is illegal on-line.'[27] However, one of the arguments put forward by those who believe that the internet requires specific legislation tailored to its specific characteristics is that quantity (i.e. intensity of communication, number of messages, etc.) makes a qualitative difference. In this view, the problem of hate and terrorism-related speech is not that no regulation against it has been enacted, but that the share and spread of the internet render cyber-based hate and terrorism different kinds of legal problems than their 'real world' equivalents. In particular, more individuals are exposed to this type of speech and it

---

25 See Marie Eneman, 'The New Face of Child Pornography', in Mathias Klang and Andrew Murray (eds), *Human Rights in the Digital Age* (London, 2005), pp. 27–40; also Akdeniz, *Stocktaking on Efforts to Combat Racism on the Internet*, pp. 8–9.

26 For a discussion of the situation in Asia see, for example, Ida M. Azmi, 'Content Regulation in Malaysia: Unleashing Missiles on Dangerous Web Sites', *JILT: Journal of Information Law and Technology*, 3 (2004), while the Middle East situation is explored in Gary E. Burkhart and Susan Older, *The Information Revolution in the Middle East and North Africa* (Santa Monica, 2003) and in Marcus Franda, *Launching Into Cyberspace: Internet Development and Politics in Five World Regions* (Boulder, 2002), Chapter 3.

27 Commission of the European Union, Proposal for a Council Framework Decision on Combating Racism and Xenophobia (Brussels, 2001), pp. 6 and 8.

is difficult to enforce existing rules. Therefore, the difference that the internet brings is mainly related to problems of enforcement, not the rules themselves.[28]

The Contemporary Legislative Landscape

The legal vacuum in the field of content policy that characterised early internet use provided national governments with high levels of discretion in content control. National regulation in the field of content policy may provide better protection for human rights and resolve the sometimes-ambiguous roles of ISPs, enforcement agencies, and other players, but such laws may also prove highly divisive. In recent years, many countries have for the first time introduced internet content policy legislation. Some of this legislation was introduced as a result of the boom in internet use and the perceived need to protect the interests of user-citizens; however, a large amount of content policy was also hastily promulgated in the wake of 11 September 2001 on the basis of perceived risks to national security. Civil libertarians and others point to the knee-jerk nature and dubious efficacy of some such policies.

The US Position

In the immediate aftermath of 11 September 2001, the FBI was involved in the official closure of hundreds – if not thousands – of US-based internet sites. For instance, several radical internet radio shows, including *IRA Radio*, *Al Lewis Live* and *Our Americas*, were pulled by an Indiana ISP in late September 2001 after the FBI contacted them and advised that their assets could be seized for promoting terrorism. The New York-based *IRA Radio* was accused of raising funds for the Real IRA. The site contained an archive of weekly radio programmes said to back the dissident Irish republicans.[29] The archive of political interviews from the programme *Al Lewis Live*, hosted by iconoclastic actor/activist Lewis,[30] drew some 15,000 hits a day. *Our Americas* was a Spanish-language programme about rebels in Latin America.[31] However, because these and many of the other sites that were closed didn't directly incite violence or raise money, they were not contravening US law and many were therefore up and running again relatively shortly after they had been shut down.

Of all the legislation promulgated in the wake of 11 September 2001, the most relevant in terms of internet governance is the Uniting and Strengthening America

---

28 Gelbstein and Kurbalija, *Internet Governance*, pp. 127–8; Akdeniz, *Stocktaking on Efforts to Combat Racism on the Internet*, pp. 3–4, p. 11.

29 Ian Cobain, 'FBI Closes Website Linked to Real IRA', *The Times* (London), 8 October 2001: 8.

30 Janet Kornblum, 'Radical Radio Shows Forced from the Net', *USA Today*, 25 October 2001: 3D, <http://www.usatoday.com/tech/news/2001/10/16/ebrief.htm>, accessed 19 February 2007. Lewis was formerly Grandpa on the 1960s hit TV show 'The Munsters'!

31 *Al Lewis Live* can still be heard on Pacifica Radio in the United States. The IRA Radio site was allowed back online in March 2002 at <http://www.iraradio.com>. However, it appears to have closed down again some time after February 2003. Site archives are available via the Internet Archive. The other sites mentioned remain offline.

by Providing Appropriate Tools Required to Intercept and Obstruct Terrorism Act of 2001 (USA PATRIOT Act), which makes it illegal to advise or assist terrorists, such as via an internet site. The case of Babar Ahmad is an interesting one in this regard. Ahmad, a British citizen, was the publisher of two prominent jihadi websites, azzam.com and qoqaz.com, which were hosted in the US and through which he is accused of raising money for Islamic militants in Chechnya and elsewhere. The UK government has agreed to a US extradition request and Ahmad is to be tried in the US on charges relating to his use of the internet for terrorism-related purposes, which fall under the heading of 'conspiracy to provide material support to terrorists'. This includes not just the solicitation of financial support referred to above, but also, according to an affidavit filed in US District Court in Connecticut in 2004, urging all Muslims to 'use every means at their disposal to undertake military and physical training for jihad' and providing 'explicit instructions' about how to raise funds and funnel these to violent fundamentalist organizations through conduits such as Benevolence International Fund, a front organization operating as a charity.

Similar charges as those pending against Ahmad have been brought against other US residents. However, due to the high levels of speech protection in the US referred to earlier, at least two defendants have so far been tried and freed without charge on the basis of similar complaints: these are Sami Omas al-Hussayen, a Ph.D. candidate in computer science at the University of Idaho who established and maintained a radical website, and Sami Amin al-Arian, a professor at the University of South Florida who was tried on charges relating to, amongst other things, his utilization of the internet to publish and catalogue acts of violence committed by Palestinian Islamic Jihad. Babar Ahmad's trial will serve as yet another test of the new US anti-terrorism law that makes it a crime to provide material support in the form of expert advice or assistance to terrorists, including IT support. Clearly, Ahmad's case will be one to watch in terms of its impact on terrorism-related internet-based speech in the US.[32]

The UK Position

The July 2005 London bombings provided the spur for the British government to act against terrorist websites operating out of the UK. In the immediate aftermath of the attacks, the then-home secretary, Charles Clarke, indicated in a parliamentary speech that he would be seeking to extend the state's powers 'to deal with those who foment terrorism, or seek to provoke others to commit terrorist acts'. In his speech, Clarke noted specifically that 'running websites or writing articles that are intended to foment or provoke terrorism' were activities that would fall within the ambit of these new powers.[33] His plans were endorsed by Britain's Association of Chief Police Officers, who in turn requested that new legislation be drawn up giving law

---

32 Maura Conway, 'Terrorism and the Internet: New Media, New Threat?', *Parliamentary Affairs*, 59/2 (2006): 295–6.

33 The full text of Clarke's remarks may be accessed online at <http://www.publications.parliament.uk/pa/cm200506/cmhansrd/cm050720/debtext/50720-04.htm>, accessed 19 February 2007.

enforcement agencies 'powers to attack identified websites'.[34] The UK Prevention of Terrorism Bill 2005 narrowly avoided defeat in Westminster in October 2005; opposition centered on two key measures: new police powers to detain suspects for up to 90 days without charges[35] and a proposed offense of 'encouragement or glorification of terrorism'. With regard to the 'glorification of terrorism', such a measure would clearly criminalize the establishment, maintenance, and hosting of many websites currently operational within the UK.

The major criticism, of course, is that the latter clause may serve to stifle legitimate political speech. Several other measures included in the bill that may also impact terrorist internet use in the UK, such as the outlawing of 'acts preparatory to terrorism' and the giving or receiving of 'terrorism training', went largely uncontested in parliamentary debates.[36] In the event, the Blair government was defeated on the detention issue. However, the remainder of the bill's provisions went into force on receiving royal assent on 30 March when the bill became the Terrorism Act 2006.[37] What impact the new legislation will have on terrorism-related materials produced by or disseminated to UK citizens via the internet is unknown at the time of writing.

International Initiatives

At the international level, the main content control initiatives have been undertaken by European countries with strong legislation in the area of hate speech, with European regional institutions trying to impose those same rules in cyberspace. The key international legal instrument addressing the issue of content is the Council of Europe's Additional Protocol on the Cybercrime Convention. The protocol specifies various types of hate speech that should be prohibited on the internet, including racist and xenophobic materials, justification of genocide, and crimes against humanity.[38] The Organization for Security and Co-operation in Europe (OSCE) is active in this field also. In June 2003, the OSCE Meeting on Freedom of Media and the Internet adopted the Amsterdam Recommendations on Freedom of the Media and the Internet. The recommendations promote freedom of expression and attempt

---

34 The APCO proposals are outlined in a press release available online at <http://www.acpo.police.uk/asp/news/PRDisplay.asp?PR_GUID={423FD3C2-2791-403A-B5D0-8FC6B5476B0B}>, accessed 19 February 2007.

35 One of the main reasons suggested for the former was that suspects needed to be detained without charge for longer than 14 days because of the difficulty and complexity of decrypting computer hard drives, a suggestion which has been challenged by both the UK Intelligence Services Commissioner and the UK Interception of Communications Commissioner.

36 Conway, 'Terrorism and the Internet'; see also Ian Cram, 'Regulating the Media: Some Neglected Freedom of Expression Issues in the United Kingdom's Counter-Terrorism Strategy', *Terrorism and Political Violence*, 18/2 (2006): 343–8.

37 The full text of the Act may be viewed at the website of the UK's Office of Public Sector Information <http://www.opsi.gov.uk/acts/acts2006/20060011.htm>, accessed 19 February 2007. See, in particular, Part 1, Section 3, 'Application of ss. 1 and 2 to internet activity, etc'.

38 See Akdeniz, *Stocktaking on Efforts to Combat Racism on the Internet*, pp. 18–24.

to reduce censorship on the internet. In June 2004, the OSCE organised a Conference on the Relationship between Racist, Xenophobic, and Anti-Semitic Propaganda on the Internet and Hate Crimes. The focus of this event was on the potential misuses of the internet and freedom of expression. These OSCE events provided a wide range of academic and policy views addressing these two aspects of content control, though no new rules were instituted as a result of these discussions.

The EU has also undertaken several initiatives in the context of content control, adopting the European Commission Recommendation against Racism via the Internet. On a more practical level, the EU also introduced the EU Safer Internet Action Plan, which resulted in the establishment of a European network of hotlines, known as Inhope, for reporting illegal content. At the present time, the major type of illegal content focused upon is child pornography and paedophilia.[39] However, there is nothing stopping national governments or EU bodies from instituting a similar reporting system for terrorism-related content. Shortly after 11 September 2001, for example, the British domestic Security Service (MI5) took the unprecedented step of posting an appeal for information about potential terrorists on dissident Arab websites. The message, in Arabic, was placed on sites that the authorities knew were accessed by extremists, including Islah.org, a Saudi Arabian opposition site, and Qoqaz.com, a Chechen site that advocated *jihad*. MI5 were hopeful of eliciting information from persons on the margins of extremist groups or communities who were sufficiently shocked by the events of 11 September 2001 to want to contact the agency. The agency had intended to post the message on a further 15 sites known to be accessed by radicals, but many of these were shut down by the FBI in the aftermath of the attacks.

The Role of Private Actors

Legislating for terrorism-related content on the internet is clearly the domain of governments. However, because of the nature of the internet, private companies and groups are never far from the frontlines. In this section, the focus is on actors-other-than-states and their contributions to the effort to eradicate terrorism-related materials from the internet. Two groups, in particular, are focused on here: internet search companies and hacktivists.

Geo-location Software

One of the properties of the internet is said to be that it overcomes national borders and erodes the principle of sovereignty. In his famous 'Declaration of the Independence of Cyberspace' (1996), John Perry Barlow sent the following message to national governments: 'You are not welcome among us. You have no sovereignty where we gather. You have no moral right to rule us nor do you possess any methods of enforcement we have true reason to fear. Cyberspace does not lie within your

---

39 Ibid., pp. 24–6.

Terrorist Use of the Internet and the Challenges of Governing Cyberspace 109

borders.'⁴⁰ Since Barlow's declaration, there have been many changes, both in terms of the development of the internet and in the wider world. In analyses of internet governance, one of the key arguments frequently advanced was that the decentralised nature of the internet made attempts at censorship redundant. Today, this is in many respects untrue: the internet includes many techniques and technologies that can provide effective control. Having said this, from a technology standpoint, control mechanisms can also be bypassed. In states with government-directed content control, technically-savvy users have found ways around such controls.

Today, it is still difficult to identify exactly who is behind any given computer screen, but it is fairly straightforward to identify through which Internet Service Provider (ISP) the internet was accessed. The latest national laws worldwide require ISPs to identify their users and, if requested, to provide necessary information about them to authorities. Numerous governments have also announced plans to more closely monitor those who access the internet in public places, particularly internet cafes. Increased surveillance of the latter is now taking place in Italy, India, Thailand, and a host of other countries; the explanation generally offered is 'national security'. Interestingly, the more the internet is anchored in geography, the less unique its governance will be. For example, with the possibility to geographically locate internet users and transactions, the complex question of jurisdiction on the internet can be solved more easily through existing laws.

One technical solution is geo-location software, which filters access to particular internet content according to the national origin of users. The Yahoo! Case was important in this respect, since the group of experts involved indicated that in 90 per cent of cases, Yahoo! would be able to determine whether sections of one of its websites hosting Nazi memorabilia were being accessed from France. This technological assessment helped the court to come to a final decision. Geo-location software companies claim that they can currently identify the home country without mistake and the accessing city in about 85 per cent of cases, especially if it is a large city. Such software can therefore help internet content providers filter access according to nationality and thus avoid court cases in foreign jurisdictions.⁴¹

Content Control Through Search Engines

There are significant differences between the availability and the accessibility of online materials: the fact that particular web-based content is available on the internet does not mean that it can be easily accessed by large numbers of users. The bridge between the end user and web content is usually a search engine. Therefore, if a particular website cannot be found on Google, or another major search engine, its visibility is seriously diminished. It has been widely reported that one of the first instances of censorship through search engines was carried out by the Chinese authorities in conjunction with Google, Inc. If users entered prohibited words into Google, they would lose their IP connectivity for a few minutes. Also, on German

---

40 The full text of the Declaration is available online at <http://homes.eff.org/~barlow/Declaration-Final.html>, accessed 19 February 2007.
41 Gelbstein and Kurbalija, *Internet Governance*, p. 125.

and French versions of Google, it is not possible to search for and find websites with Nazi materials. This indicates a certain level of self-censorship on the part of Google in order to avoid possible court cases. In terms of terrorist websites, many internet companies voluntarily purged sites perceived as terrorist in the wake of 11 September 2001. For example, Yahoo! pulled dozens of sites in the Jihad Web Ring, a coalition of 55 *jihad*-related sites, while Lycos Europe established a 20-person team to monitor its websites for illegal activity and to remove terrorism-related content.[42]

The transition from the hit economy to the link economy, in the late 1990s, meant that an organization's internet reputation no longer depended on its site design, but was rather a product of the organisation's showing in 'reputable' websites.[43] As Rogers points out, the 'chaos' of the internet may be viewed as a product of the lack of source authority in an information free-for-all. However, while search engines such as Google have to some extent resulted in 'a new form of basic Web epistemology' by providing an indication of the status of information according to measurable reputability dynamics as determined by the web,[44] this works less well in terms of searches for terrorist sites as opposed to sites containing more mainstream views. Let's take the example of the New People's Army (NPA), a group operating in the Philippines, which appears on the US State Department's list of Designated Foreign Terrorist Organizations. With some 25,000 pages with something to say about the NPA, all being listed by engines, returning sites with frequent NPA keywords, one might expect that search engines with link authority logics (such as Google) would return www.philippinerevolution.org at the top of the returns. This is not the case, however; instead of the NPA themselves being viewed by internet users as the most reliable source of information about their group, the US government is instead the most frequently consulted source of information about the organisation, and the same is true of a number of the other groups that appear on the US list (see Table 5.3).

This brief discussion of search engines and their impact on internet governance illustrates two things. First, major search engines are wont to err on the side of caution when it comes to their operation in 'foreign' jurisdictions and tend to comply with applicable legislation in those states in order to avoid legal challenges. While such policies of compliance can be viewed as political in character and have thus come under fire, particularly from free-speech advocates, the second point is less contentious, as it relates more to search engine architecture than informed political or economic decisions made by internet companies: the basis on which the most popular search engine, Google, operates serves to obscure the websites of many terrorist groups. Clearly, this is unlikely to be a deterrent to persons intent on searching out these sites, but it does prevent the casual surfer from stumbling upon them by accident, thus reducing the audience for such sites.

---

42 Stephanie Gruner and Gautam Naik, 'Extremist Sites Under Heightened Scrutiny', *The Wall Street Journal Online*, 8 October 2001; Julia Scheeres, 'Blacklisted Groups Visible on Web', *Wired News*, 19 October 2001.

43 Robert Rogers, 'Operating Issue Networks on the Web', *Science as Culture*, 11/2 (2002): 191–214, here 205.

44 Ibid.: 200.

Table 5.3 Google search for terrorist group information (10 April 2005)

Search term(s)	No. of hits returned	Top returned site
'Aum Shinrikyo'	79,300	Apologetics Index http://www.apologeticsindex.org/a06.html
'Basque Homeland and Liberty'	370	Profile, International Policy Institute for Counter-Terrorism (Israel) http://www.ict.org.il/inter_ter/orgdet.cfm?orgid=8
'Revolutionary Armed Forces of Colombia'	94,300	Profile, International Policy Institute for Counter-Terrorism (Israel) http://www.ict.org.il/inter_ter/orgdet.cfm?orgid=37
'FARC'	919,000	FARC Official Site
'Hamas'	2,340,000	Hamas Official Site
'Hizbollah'	188,000	Hizbollah Official Site
'Kahane Chai'	16,500	Profile, International Policy Institute for Counter-Terrorism (Israel) http://www.ict.org.il/inter_ter/orgdet.cfm?orgid=19
'LTTE'	436,000	LTTE Official Site
'New People's Army'	25,000	'Philippines' NPA Redesignated as Terrorist Group' (US Embassy, Japan) http://japan.usembassy.gov/e/p/tp-20040811-11.html
'PKK'	1,410,000	Profile, US Department of State http://library.nps.navy.mil/home/tgp/kurds.htm
'Kongra-Gel'	47,300	Kongra-Gel Official Site
'Sendero Luminoso'	94,600	Library Guide to SL, University of North Carolina http://ils.unc.edu/~marsc/sendero.htm
'Shining Path'	120,000	Council on Foreign Relation's (US) Terrorism Q&A http://cfrterrorism.org/groups/shiningpath.html

Hackers and Hacktivists

The events of 11 September 2001 acted as the spur for many private groups and individuals to take to the internet in search of 'terrorist' websites to disrupt. Computer hackers were particularly well placed to engage in this sort of activity. In the immediate aftermath of the attacks, for example, a group calling itself 'The Dispatchers' proclaimed that they would destroy web servers and internet access in Afghanistan and also target nations that support terrorism. The group of 60 people, led by a 21-year-old security worker from Ohio, proceeded to deface hundreds of websites and launch Distributed Denial of Service (DoS) attacks[45] against targets

---

45 Distributed Denial of Service (DDoS) attacks are actions by distributed computers that prevent any part of another computer system from functioning in accordance with its intended purpose. DDoS attacks generally employ armies of 'zombie' machines taken over and controlled by a single master to overwhelm the resources of a target with floods of packets.

ranging from the Iranian Ministry of the Interior to the Presidential Palace of Afghanistan. Another group, known as Young Intelligent Hackers Against Terror (YIHAT), claimed in mid-October 2001 to be negotiating with one European and one Asian government to 'legalize' the group's hacking activities in those states. The group's founder, Kim Schmitz, claimed the group had breached the systems of two Arabic banks who had allegedly done business with Osama Bin Laden, although a bank spokesperson denied any penetration had occurred. The group, whose stated mission was to impede the flow of money to terrorists, issued a statement on its website requesting that corporations make their networks available to group members for the purpose of providing the 'electronic equivalent to terrorist training camps'. Later, their public website was taken offline, apparently in response to attacks from other hackers.[46]

Not all hacking groups were supportive of the so-called 'hacking war'. On 14 September 2001, the Chaos Computer Club, an organization of German hackers, called for an end to the protests and for all hackers to cease vigilante actions. A well-known group of computer enthusiasts, known as Cyber Angels, who promote responsible behaviour, also spoke out against the hacking war. They sponsored television advertisements in the US urging hackers to help gather information and intelligence on those who were participating in this hacktivism.[47] In any event, the predicted escalation in hack attacks[48] did not materialize. In the weeks following the attacks, web page defacements were well publicized, but the overall number and sophistication of these remained rather low. One possible reason for the non-escalation of attacks could be that many hackers – particularly those located in the US – were wary of being negatively associated with the events of 11 September 2001 and curbed their activities as a result.

It has never been all plain sailing for terrorist users of the internet, even prior to 11 September 2001. Their homepages have been subject to intermittent DoS and other hack attacks, and there have also been strikes against their ISPs that have resulted in more permanent difficulties. In 1997, for example, an e-mail bombing was conducted against the Institute for Global Communications (IGC),[49] a San Francisco-based ISP, hosting the web pages of the *Euskal Herria* or *Basque Country Journal,* a publication edited by supporters of the Basque group Homeland and Liberty (ETA). The attacks against IGC commenced following the assassination of a popular town councillor in northern Spain by ETA. The protesters wanted the site pulled from the internet. To accomplish this, they bombarded the IGC with thousands of fake e-mails routed through hundreds of different mail relays, spammed IGC staff and customer accounts, clogged their web page with bogus credit card orders, and threatened to

---

46 Denning, 'Is Cyber Terror Next?' The site was located at <http://www.kill.net>.

47 C. Hauss and A. Samuel, 'What's the Internet Got to Do With It? Online Responses to 9/11', paper presented at the American Political Science Association Annual (APSA) Annual Convention (Boston, 29 August–1 September 2002); National Infrastructure Protection Center, *Cyber Protests Related to the War on Terrorism: The Current Threat* (Washington, D.C., 2001).

48 Institute for Security Technology Studies (ISTS), *Cyber Attacks During the War on Terrorism: A Predictive Analysis* (Dartmouth College, 2001).

49 Online at <http://www.igc.org/igc/gateway/index.html>, accessed 19 February 2007.

employ the same tactics against other organizations using IGC services. IGC pulled the *Euskal Herria* site on 18 July 1997, but not before archiving a copy of the site enabling others to put up mirrors. Shortly thereafter, mirror sites appeared on half a dozen servers on three continents. Despite this, the protesters' e-mail campaign raised fears of a new era of censorship imposed by direct action from anonymous hacktivists. Furthermore, approximately one month after the IGC had pulled the controversial site off its servers, Scotland Yard's Anti-Terrorist Squad shut down Internet Freedom's UK website for hosting the journal. Scotland Yard claimed to be acting against terrorism.[50] The so-called 'cyber-war' that raged between Israelis and Palestinians and their supporters in 2000 was a mere nuisance in comparison with such targeted and sustained campaigns, although more recently, a more sustained targeting of pro-Palestinian and also jihadist websites has emerged.

Since 11 September 2001 a number of web-based organizations have been established to monitor terrorist websites. One of the most well-known of such sites is Internet Haganah,[51] self-described as 'an internet counterinsurgency'. Also prominent is the Washington, D.C.-based Search for International Terrorist Entities (SITE) Institute[52] that, like Internet Haganah, focuses on Muslim terror groups. Clients of SITE's fee-based intelligence service are said to include the FBI, the Office of Homeland Security, and various media organizations. But what are the goals of these private organizations? SITE is a for-profit concern, while Internet Haganah survives on donations and advertising revenue. SITE's co-founder and director, Rita Katz, has commented: 'It is actually to our benefit to have some of these terror sites up and running by US companies. If the servers are in the US, this is to our advantage when it comes to monitoring activities.'[53] Aaron Weisburd, who runs Internet Haganah out of his home in Southern Illinois, says his goal is to keep the extremists moving from address to address: 'The object isn't to silence them – the object is to keep them moving, keep them talking, force them to make mistakes, so we can gather as much information about them as we can, each step of the way.'[54] On the Haganah website, the mark of victory is a little blue graphic of an AK-47 assault rifle, each of which represents another terrorist website put out of commission (at least temporarily). Weisburd's *modus operandi* is to first research a site, he then

---

50 Dorothy Denning, 'Activism, Hacktivism, and Cyberterrorism: The Internet as a Tool for Influencing Foreign Policy', in John Arquilla and David Ronfeldt (eds), *Networks and Netwars: The Future of Terror, Crime, and Militancy* (Santa Monica, 2001), pp. 239–88, here pp. 270–1. For more information on the e-mail bombing and IGC's response to it see the institute's website <http://www.igc.apc.org>. See also the press release issued by Internet Freedom UK in response to the shutting of their operations by Scotland Yard at <http://www.fitug.de/debate/9709/msg00018.html>, accessed 19 February 2007. The group's website is located at <http://www.netfreedom.org/>.

51 In Hebrew, 'Haganah' means defence. Internet Haganah is online at <http://www.haganah.org.il/haganah/index.html>.

52 The SITE website is at <http://www.siteinstitute.org/>.

53 As quoted in John Lasker, 'Watchdogs Sniff Out Terror Sites', *Wired News*, 25 February 2005.

54 Ibid.; see also Gary Bunt, *Islam in the Digital Age: E-Jihad, Online Fatwas and Cyber Islamic Environments* (London, 2003), pp. 24 and 93.

makes a 'whois' inquiry. If there is evidence of extremism, he contacts the hosting company and urges the host to remove the site from its servers. If successful, Internet Haganah may purchase the domain name so the address can never be used again. Since its inception in 2003, Internet Haganah has taken credit for or claims to have assisted in the shutdown of more than 600 sites it alleges were linked to terrorism.

Information Gathering and Content Control

Thus far, the focus in this chapter has been on the control of content posted online by terrorists and their sympathisers and on the challenges faced by those wishing to regulate such speech. In terms of the terrorism-internet relationship, however, controlling content may include a lot more than simply trying to disrupt or close down extremist websites. One interesting approach is to explore the use of the internet by extremists for information-gathering purposes, and the responses of governments and other actors. Information-gathering is thought to be one of the main uses of the internet for extremists.

These information-gathering activities rely not on the operation of the extremists' own websites, but on the information contributed by others to 'the vast digital library' that is the internet.[55] There are two major issues to be addressed here. The first may be termed 'data mining' and refers to terrorists using the internet to collect and assemble information about specific targeting opportunities.[56] The second issue is 'information-sharing,' which refers to more general online information collection by terrorists.

Data Mining

In January 2003, US Defense Secretary Donald Rumsfeld warned in a directive sent to military units that too much unclassified, but potentially harmful material was appearing on Department of Defense (DoD) websites. Rumsfeld reminded military personnel that an al-Qaida training manual recovered in Afghanistan states: 'Using public sources openly and without resorting to illegal means, it is possible to gather at least eighty per cent of information about the enemy.' He went on to say that 'at more than 700 gigabytes, the DoD web-based data makes a vast, readily available source of information on DoD plans, programs and activities. One must conclude our enemies access DoD websites on a regular basis.'[57]

---

55 Gabriel Weimann, *WWW.terror.net: How Modern Terrorism Uses the Internet* (Washington, D.C., 2004), p. 6.

56 Others exploring terrorist use of the Net have employed the term 'data mining' in a less expansive fashion to refer to the systematized analysis of large bodies of data using specialist computer software. For an introduction to the latter, see Mary De Rosa, *Data Mining and Data Analysis for Counterterrorism* (Washington, D.C., 2004), <http://www.csis.org/tech/2004_counterterrorism.pdf>, accessed 22 March 2007.

57 Declan McCullagh, 'Military Worried About Web Leaks', *CNET News*, 16 January 2003.

In addition to information provided by and about the armed forces, the free availability of information on the internet about the location and operation of nuclear reactors and related facilities was of particular concern to public officials post 11 September 2001. Roy Zimmerman, director of the Nuclear Regulatory Commission's (NRC) Office of Nuclear Security and Incident Response, said the 11 September 2001 attacks had highlighted the need to safeguard sensitive information. In the days immediately after the attacks, the NRC took their website off–line altogether. When it was restored weeks later, it had been purged of more than 1,000 sensitive documents. Initially, the agency decided to withhold documents if 'the release would provide clear and significant benefit to a terrorist in planning an attack.' Later, the NRC tightened the restriction, opting to exclude information 'that could be useful or could reasonably be useful to a terrorist'. According to Zimmerman, 'it is currently unlikely that the information on our website would provide significant advantage to assist a terrorist.'[58]

The measures taken by the NRC were not exceptional. According to a report produced by OMB Watch,[59] since 11 September 2001, thousands of documents and tremendous amounts of data have been removed from US government sites. The difficulty, however, is that much of the same information remains available on private-sector websites.[60] Patrick Tibbetts points to the Animated Software Company's website, which has off-topic documents containing the locations, status, security procedures, and other technical information concerning dozens of US nuclear reactors,[61] while the Virtual Nuclear Tourist site contains similar information. The latter site is particularly detailed on specific security measures that may be implemented at various nuclear plants worldwide.[62] Many people view such information as a potential gold mine for terrorists.[63] Their fears appear well founded given the capture of al-Qaida computer expert Muhammad Naeem Noor Khan in Pakistan in July 2004, which yielded a computer filled with photographs and floor diagrams of buildings in the US that terrorists may have been planning to attack.[64] The Australian press has also reported that a man charged with terrorism offences

---

58 Mike M. Ahlers, 'Blueprints for Terrorists?' *CNN.com*, 19 November 2004.

59 Office of Management and Budget (OMB) Watch is a watchdog group based in Washington, D.C. Their home page is at <http://www.ombwatch.org>.

60 McCullagh; Gary D. Bass, and Sean Moulton, 'The Bush Administration's Secrecy Policy: A Call to Action to Protect Democratic Values', working paper (Washington, D.C., 2002).

61 See <http://www.animatedsoftware.com/environm/no_nukes/nukelist1.htm>, accessed 19 February 2007.

62 Patrick S. Tibbetts, 'Terrorist Use of the Internet and Related Information Technologies', unpublished paper (Fort Leavenworth, 2002), p. 15. The Nuclear Tourist website is at <http://www.nucleartourist.com/>.

63 See Chapter 6 of Dan Verton's *Black Ice* (New York, 2003), which is entitled 'Web of Terror: What al-Qaeda Knows About the US'; it provides a wide-ranging, though somewhat breathless, survey of the potential dangers posed by Web-based information.

64 David Jehl and Douglas Johnston., 'Reports That Led to Terror Alert Were Years Old, Officials Say', *New York Times*, 3 August 2004; Dan Verton and Lucas Mearian, 'Online Data a Gold Mine for Terrorists', *ComputerWorld*, 6 August 2004.

there had used Australian government websites to get maps, data, and satellite images of potential targets.[65]

Terrorists can also use the internet to learn about anti-terrorism measures. Gabriel Weimann suggests that a simple strategy like conducting word searches of online newspapers and journals could allow a terrorist to study the means designed to counter attacks, or the vulnerabilities of these measures. Weimann provides the example of newspaper articles detailing attempts to slip contraband items through airport security. He mentions a report, which noted that at Cincinnati airport, contraband slipped through over fifty per cent of the time. 'A simple Internet search by terrorists would uncover this shortcoming, and offer the terrorists an embarkation point for their next operation.'[66] A number of authors have also lambasted reports on various online news sites which noted that US law enforcement agencies were tracing calls made overseas to Al Qaida cells using phone cards, cell phones, phone booths, or internet-based phone services. These authors were concerned that exposing the targeting techniques of law enforcement agencies would allow the terrorists to alter their operating procedures accordingly.[67]

Sharing Information

Policymakers, law enforcement agencies, and others are also concerned about the proliferation of 'how to' web pages devoted to explaining, for example, the technical intricacies of making homemade bombs. Many such devices may be constructed using lethal combinations of otherwise innocuous materials; today, there are hundreds of freely available online manuals containing such information. As early as April 1997, the US Department of Justice had concluded that the availability of this information played a significant role in facilitating terrorist and other criminal acts:

> It is readily apparent from our cursory examination that anyone interested in manufacturing a bomb, dangerous weapon or weapon of mass destruction can easily obtain detailed instructions for fabricating and using such a device. Available sources include not only publications from the so called underground press but also manuals written for legitimate purposes, such as military, agricultural, industrial and engineering purposes. Such information is *also readily available to anyone with access to a home computer equipped with a modem* [italics mine].[68]

---

65 Australian Broadcasting Corporation (ABC), 'NSW Considers Limits on Government Website', *ABC Online*, 28 April 2004.

66 Gabriel Weimann, 'Terror on the Internet: The New Arena, the New Challenges', paper presented at the annual meeting of the International Studies Association (ISA) (Montreal, Canada, 17 March 2004), p. 15.

67 Christopher Andrew, 'Counsel of War', *The Times* (T2 Supplement), 4 October 2001: 2–3; Timothy L. Thomas, 'Al Qaeda and the Internet: The Danger of '"Cyberplanning"', *Parameters*, Spring (2003): 114; Weimann, 'Terror on the Internet', p. 15.

68 US Department of Justice, Report On The Availability of Bombmaking Information, the Extent to Which Its Dissemination Is Controlled by Federal Law, and the Extent to Which Such Dissemination May Be Subject to Regulation Consistent With the First Amendment to the United States Constitution (Washington, D.C., 1997), pp. 15–6.

Jessica Stern provides details of one such manual, *Bacteriological Warfare: A Major Threat to North America* (1995), which is described on the internet as a book for helping readers survive a biological weapons attack and is subtitled 'What Your Family Can Do Before and After.' However, it also describes the reproduction and growth of biological agents and includes a chapter entitled 'Bacteria Likely To Be Used By the Terrorist.' The text is available for download, in various edited and condensed formats, from a number of sites,[69] while hard copies of the book are available for purchase over the internet from major online book sellers for as little as US$13. Its author is one Larry Wayne Harris, a microbiologist and former neo-Nazi who at one time purchased three vials of the bacterium that causes bubonic plague.[70]

More recently, an al-Qaida laptop found in Afghanistan had been used to visit the website of the French Anonymous Society (FAS) on several occasions. The FAS site publishes a two-volume *Sabotage Handbook* that contains sections on planning an assassination and anti-surveillance methods, amongst other resources.[71] Another manual, *The Mujahadeen Poisons Handbook* (1996), authored by Abdel-Aziz, is available via the Hamas-Palestinian Information Center's Arabic-language website. The 'handbook' details in 23 pages how to prepare various homemade poisons, poisonous gases, and other deadly materials for use in terrorist attacks. A much larger manual, nicknamed *The Encyclopedia of Jihad* and prepared by al-Qaida, runs to thousands of pages; distributed via the internet, it offers detailed instructions on how to establish an underground organization and execute terror attacks.[72] Further, BBC News reported that at least one jihadist website had posted careful instructions on how to use mobile phones as detonators for explosives prior to the Madrid train bombings in 2004, the perpetrators of which subsequently employed this method of detonation.[73]

This kind of information is sought out not just by sophisticated terrorist organizations, but also by disaffected individuals prepared to use terrorist tactics to advance their idiosyncratic agendas. In 1999, for instance, right-wing extremist David Copeland planted nail bombs in three different areas of London: multiracial Brixton, the largely Bangladeshi community of Brick Lane, and the gay quarter in Soho. Over the course of three weeks, he killed three people and injured 139. At his trial, he revealed that he had learned his deadly techniques from the internet by downloading copies of *The Terrorist's Handbook* and *How to Make Bombs: Book Two*. Both titles are still easily accessible.[74] According to the US Bureau of Alcohol,

---

69 See, for example, <http://www.uhuh.com/reports/harris/book.htm>, accessed 19 February 2007.

70 Jessica Stern, *The Ultimate Terrorists* (Cambridge, 1999), p. 51.

71 Thomas, 'Al Qaeda and the Internet: 115; Weimann, *WWW.terror.net*, p. 9. The two-volume handbook is available for download from a number of Internet sites including <http://sabotage.org/handbook/>, accessed 19 February 2007.

72 Weimann, *WWW.terror.net*, p. 9; see also Rodney A. Smolla, 'From Hit Man to Encyclopaedia of Jihad: How to Distinguish Freedom of Speech from Terrorist Training', *Loyola Entertainment Law Review*, 22/2 (2002).

73 Gordon Corera, 'A Web Wise Terror Network', *BBC News* (World Edition), 6 October 2004, <http://news.bbc.co.uk/2/hi/in_depth/3716908.stm>, accessed 19 February 2007.

74 Weimann, *WWW.terror.net*, p. 10.

Tobacco, and Firearms, federal agents investigating at least 30 bombings and four attempted bombings between 1985 and June 1996 recovered bomb-making literature that the suspects had obtained from the internet. None of these were terrorism-related, but many involved minors.[75]

Gabriel Weimann provides the example of a further deadly bomb attack, which occurred in Finland in 2002, and was also carried out by a minor. The brilliant chemistry student, who called himself RC, spent months discussing bomb-making techniques with other enthusiasts on a Finnish website devoted to bombs and explosives. RC posted numerous queries on topics like manufacturing nerve gas at home. And he often traded information with the site's moderator, who used the screen name Einstein and whose postings carried a picture of his own face superimposed on Osama bin Laden's body, complete with turban and beard. Then RC exploded a bomb that killed seven people, including himself, in a crowded Finnish shopping mall. The site's sponsor, a computer magazine called *Mikrobitti*, immediately shut down the website used by RC, known as the Home Chemistry Forum. However, a backup copy, with postings by teenagers who used aliases like Ice Man and Lord of Fire, was immediately reposted, on a read-only basis.[76]

The Open Source Threat?

The threat posed by the easy availability of bomb-making and other 'dangerous information' is a source of heated debate. Patrick Tibbetts warns against underestimating the feasibility of such threats. He points out that captured al-Qaida materials include not only information compiled on 'home-grown explosives', but also indicate that this group is actively seeking out the data and technical expertise necessary to pursue chemical, biological, radiological, and nuclear (CBRN) weapons programs. According to Ken Katzman, a terrorism analyst for the Congressional Research Service, much of the material in these captured documents was probably downloaded from the internet.[77] As a result, many have called for laws restricting the publication of bomb-making instructions on the internet, while others have pointed out that this material is already easily accessible in bookstores and libraries.[78] In fact, much of this information has been available in print media since at least the late 1960s with the publication of William Powell's *The Anarchist Cookbook* and other, similar titles.

Jessica Stern has observed: 'In 1982, the year of the first widely reported incident of tampering with pharmaceuticals, the Tylenol case, only a few poisoning manuals were available, and they were relatively hard to find.'[79] This is doubtless true; they were hard to find, but they *were* available. As Stern herself concedes, currently, how-to manuals on producing chemical and biological agents are not just available on the

---

75 Anti-Defamation League (ADL), 'Terrorist Activities on the Internet', *Terrorism Update* (Winter 1998).
76 Weimann, 'Terror on the Internet': 15.
77 Tibbetts, 'Terrorist Use of the Internet and Related Information Technologies', p. 17.
78 ADL, 'Terrorist Activities on the Internet'.
79 Stern, p. 50.

internet, but are advertised in paramilitary journals sold in magazine shops all over the US.[80] According to a US government report, over 50 publications describing the fabrication of explosives and destructive devices are listed in the Library of Congress and are available to any member of the public, as well as being easily available commercially.[81]

Despite assertions to the contrary,[82] the infamous *Anarchist Cookbook* (1971) is not available online, although it is easily purchased from online retailers. According to Ken Shirriff, author of 'The Anarchist Cookbook FAQ,' there are various files available on the internet that rip off the name 'Anarchist Cookbook' and have somewhat similar content, but are not the real *Anarchist Cookbook*. There are other files that do contain parts of the content from the original *Anarchist Cookbook*, often mixed with other material, but the entire unedited publication is not available online. The original author, William Powell, had this to say in 2001: 'I conducted the research for the manuscript on my own, primarily at the New York City Public Library. Most of the contents were gleaned from Military and Special Forces Manuals.'[83] The anonymous authors of websites claiming to post the *Cookbook* and similar texts often include a disclaimer that the processes described should not be carried out. This is because many of the 'recipes' have a poor reputation for reliability and safety. One author points out that at least one of the recipes for poison gas contained in *The Mujahadeen Poison Handbook* was nothing more than the standard procedure for making a stink bomb.[84]

In terms of obtaining information about the construction of CBRN weapons from the internet, it is generally agreed that much of this type of information is also flawed, while some is, in fact, pure imagination. Although some relatively accurate information on the construction of such weapons *is* available online, raw data on such a process is not particularly valuable. Putting together a terrorist operation requires elaborate planning, as demonstrated by the 11 September 2001 hijackers. Organizations with the structure and control over their members required for such planning might also be expected to have the resources for developing and distributing their own proprietary tactical materials. As, indeed, al-Qaida has done.[85] However, even when a terrorist outfit draws inspiration and data from materials published on the internet, these materials often duplicate other materials already available in other public fora. In addition, while on the surface, information about scientific processes

---

80 Ibid., p. 51.

81 US Department of Justice, *Report On The Availability of Bombmaking Information*, p. 5. The same report mentions that one Kansas bomber got his bomb instructions from the August 1993 *Reader's Digest*, pp. 6–7.

82 See, for example, Weimann's *WWW.terror.net*, p. 9.

83 Ken Shirriff, *Anarchist Cookbook FAQ* <http://www.righto.com/anarchy/>, accessed 19 February 2007.

84 George Smith, 'The Recipe for Ricin, Part II: The Legend Flourishes', *National Security Notes*, 4 March 2004. See also George Smith, 'The Recipe for Ricin: Examining the Legend', *National Security Notes*, 20 February 2004.

85 Portions of an Al Qaeda Training Manual are available via the Federation of American Scientists site at <http://www.fas.org/irp/world/para/manualpart1.html>, accessed 22 March 2007.

may be more technical than information regarding terrorist tactics, the same analysis ultimately applies. Actually utilizing a formula for poison gas or a nuclear device, for example, requires not only the cultivation of a body of knowledge and professional judgment, but also the financial resources to build and maintain a physical plant for the manufacture and distribution of the weapon. Developing the expertise and the infrastructure to exploit the information gathered thus demands a significant investment of time and money. Individuals with sufficient skills and resources to exploit the information are unlikely to need the published formula to carry out their plans. Similarly, persons lacking such expertise cannot benefit from the information even when it is published on the internet or elsewhere. The upshot of this is that attempts to stop the flow of 'harmful' information have no useful purpose and would, in any case, doubtless inspire what Peter Margulies has termed 'an endless virtual fun-house of mirror sites.'[86]

Perhaps the most likely online 'recipes' to be of use to terrorists are those related to hacking tools and activities. Such information is also likely to be considerably more accurate than bomb-making information, for example; this is because the internet is both the domain and tool of hackers. In testimony before the US House Armed Services Committee in 2003, Purdue University professor and information assurance expert Eugene Spafford said that bulletin boards and discussion lists could teach hacking techniques to anyone: 'We have perhaps a virtual worldwide training camp,' he testified.[87] Terrorists have been known to exploit this resource. In 1998, Khalid Ibrahim, who identified himself as an Indian national, sought classified and unclassified US government software and information, as well as data from India's Bhabha Atomic Research Center, from hackers communicating via Internet Relay Chat (IRC). In conversations taken from IRC logs, Ibrahim claimed to be a member of Harkat-ul-Ansar,[88] a militant Kashmiri separatist group. Confirming Ibrahim's true identity was difficult; the most compelling evidence that he was acting on behalf of Harkat-ul-Ansar was a US$1,000 money order he sent to a teenage hacker in the US in an attempt to buy stolen military software. Although he used several anonymous Hotmail accounts to send his e-mails, Ibrahim always accessed the web from an internet service provider in New Delhi. He approached members of various cracking teams looking for sensitive information. In one transcript of an internet chat conversation between Ibrahim and crackers, Ibrahim threatens to have the youths killed if they reported him to the FBI. In the event, it appears that almost all of Ibrahim's efforts to buy information were rebuffed.[89]

Finally, it is important to keep in mind that removal of technical information from public websites is no guarantee of safeguarding it. In essence, this effort is akin to 'closing the barn door after the horse has bolted'. Intelligence and technical data obtained by terrorist operatives prior to 11 September 2001 can be archived,

---

86 Peter Margulies, 'The Clear and Present Internet: Terrorism, Cyberspace, and the First Amendment', *UCLA Journal of Law and Technology*, 8/2 (2004): 74–6.

87 Eugene Spafford, Testimony before the US House Armed Services Committee, Subcommittee on Terrorism, Unconventional Threats and Capabilities, 24 July 2003, p. 31.

88 Harkat-ul-Ansar is on the State Department's list of FTOs.

89 Niall McKay, 'Do Terrorists Troll the Net?' *Wired*, 4 November 1998.

stored, and distributed surreptitiously irrespective of government or private attempts to squelch its presence on the internet in 2006. Indeed, these materials can be loaded onto offshore or other international web servers that cannot be affected by US legislation, rendering futile any attempt to halt their spread outside the reach of US law enforcement.[90] This point is made in a recent RAND report whose authors believe that the threat posed by open-source data is small. The 2004 report advises that federal officials should consider reopening public access to about three dozen websites withdrawn from the internet after the 11 September 2001 attacks because the sites pose little or no risk to US national security. Baker et al. report that the overwhelming majority of federal websites that reveal information about airports, power plants, military bases, and other potential terrorist targets need not be censored because similar or better information is easily available elsewhere. RAND's National Defense Research Institute identified 629 internet-accessible federal databases that contain critical data about specific locations. The study, conducted between mid-2002 and mid-2003, found no federal sites that contained information a terrorist would need to launch an attack. It identified four databases where restricting access probably would enhance national security; none remain available to the public. These included two websites devoted to pipelines, one to nuclear reactors, and one to dams. The researchers recommended that officials evaluate 66 databases with some useful information, but they did not anticipate restrictions would be needed, because similar or better data could be easily obtained elsewhere.[91]

Conclusion: Where Do We Go From Here?

What is the future of the internet? It is generally agreed that it is difficult to predict outcomes for the internet because of the complicated relationships between secrecy and openness, security and insecurity, freedom and oppression, the public and the private, the individual and the community, etc. It is commonly agreed also that the potential for a 'digital 9/11' in the near future is not great. This does not mean that IR scholars may continue to ignore the transformative powers of the internet. On the contrary, as of 11 September 2001, the internet has come of age. Both terrorism and the internet are significant global phenomena, reflecting and shaping various aspects of world politics (sometimes separately but oftentimes in unison). Due to its global reach and rich multilingual context, the internet has the potential to influence in manifold ways many different types of political and social relations. Unlike the traditional mass media, the internet's open architecture has restricted efforts by governments to regulate internet activities, which, in turn, has provided Netizens with immense freedom and space to shape the internet in their own likeness: a patchwork of peoples, ideas, hierarchies, ideologies, images, etc.

---

90 Tibbetts, 'Terrorist Use of the Internet and Related Information Technologies', p. 17.
91 John C. Baker et al., *Mapping the Risks: Assessing the Homeland Security Implications of Publicly Available Geospatial Information* (Santa Monica, 2004); John C. Baker et al., 'America's Publicly Available Geospatial Information: Does It Pose a Homeland Security Risk?' *Rand Research Brief*, RB-9045-NGA (2004).

In large part, internet users learn by doing. Once users figure out what the Net is good for – donating to charity, disseminating information, communicating securely, etc. – on their own terms, they quickly begin to develop new uses, and the volume and sophistication of traffic on the internet is increased. This, in turn, contributes to an unprecedented independence on the part of the users as information gatherers and producers. Included within this cohort are terrorists who are not limiting themselves to the traditional means of communication; they increasingly employ the new media to pursue their goals. The terrorists of today, like those of yesteryear, are keen to exploit the traditional mass media while also recognizing the value of more direct communication channels. As has been pointed out, 'if what matters is openness in the marketplace of ideas [...] then the Web delivers an equal opportunity soapbox' (Norris 2001, 172).

As far back as 1982, Alex Schmid and Janny De Graaf conceded that

> If terrorists want to send a message, they should be offered the opportunity to do so without them having to bomb and kill. Words are cheaper than lives. The public will not be instilled with terror if they see a terrorist speak; they are afraid if they see his victims and not himself [...] If the terrorists believe that they have a case, they will be eager to present it to the public. Democratic societies should not be afraid of this.[92]

Not everybody is in agreement with this position, however. Over time, both state- and non-state actors have endeavoured to curb the availability of terrorism-related materials online with varying degrees of success. Authoritarian governments have met with some success in this regard by deploying technologies that constrain their citizens' ability to access certain sites. There are fewer options for restriction available to democratic governments, however, and although more restrictive legislation has recently been promulgated in a number of jurisdictions, it is not yet clear that it will be any more successful than previous attempts at controlling, for example, cyber-hate. In terms of terrorist websites, however, those private initiatives instituted by a range of sub-state actors in conjunction with ISPs have been much more successful. The activities of individual hacktivists, such as Aaron Weisburd of Internet Haganah, raise a number of important issues relating to limits on speech and who has the ability to institute these limits, however. These same limits and their efficacy are also central to the discussion on removing of information from the public internet, whether about bomb-making or computer hacking, that could be deemed of use to terrorists. The ability of private political and economic actors to bypass the democratic process and to have materials they find politically objectionable erased from the internet is a matter for concern, as is the removal by government agencies of information that was previously publicly accessible online. Such endeavours may, in fact, cause us to think again about the matter of legislation, not just in terms of putting controls in place – perhaps, for example, outlawing the posting and dissemination of beheading videos – but also writing into law more robust protections for radical political speech.

---

92 Alex P. Schmid and Janny De Graaf, *Violence as Communication: Insurgent Terrorism and the Western News Media* (London, 1982), p. 170.

References

Ahlers, Mike M., 'Blueprints for Terrorists?' *CNN.com*, 19 November 2004, <http://www.cnn.com/2004/US/10/19/terror.nrc/>, accessed 19 February 2007.

Akdeniz, Yaman, *Stocktaking on Efforts to Combat Racism on the Internet*, E/CN.4/2006/WG.21/BP.1 (Geneva: UN Commission on Human Rights, 2006), <http://www.cyber-rights.org/reports/ya_un_paper_int_06.pdf>, accessed 19 February 2007.

Andrew, Christopher, 'Counsel of War', *The Times* (T2 Supplement), 4 October 2001.

Anti-Defamation League (ADL), 'Terrorist Activities on the Internet.' *Terrorism Update* (Winter 1998), <http://www.adl.org/Terror/focus/16_focus_a.asp>, accessed 19 February 2007.

Australian Broadcasting Corporation (ABC), 'NSW Considers Limits on Government Website', *ABC Online*, 28 April 2004.

Azmi, Ida M., 'Content Regulation in Malaysia: Unleashing Missiles on Dangerous Web Sites', *JILT: Journal of Information Law and Technology*, 3 (2004), <http://www2.warwick.ac.uk/fac/soc/law/elj/jilt/2004_3/azmi/>, accessed 19 February 2007.

Baker, John C. et al., *Mapping the Risks: Assessing the Homeland Security Implications of Publicly Available Geospatial Information* (Santa Monica: Rand, 2004), <http://www.rand.org/publications/MG/MG142/>, accessed 19 February 2007.

Baker, John C. et al., 'America's Publicly Available Geospatial Information: Does It Pose a Homeland Security Risk?' *Rand Research Brief*, RB-9045-NGA (2004), <http://www.rand.org/publications/RB/RB9045/>, accessed 19 February 2007.

Barendt, Eric, *Freedom of Speech* (Oxford: Clarendon Press, 1987).

Bass, Gary D. and Sean Moulton, 'The Bush Administration's Secrecy Policy: A Call to Action to Protect Democratic Values', working paper (Washington, D.C.: OMB Watch, 2002), <http://www.ombwatch.org/rtk/secrecy.pdf>, accessed 19 February 2007.

Bunt, Gary, *Islam in the Digital Age: E-Jihad, Online Fatwas and Cyber Islamic Environments* (London: Pluto Press, 2003).

Burkhart, Gary E. and Susan Older, *The Information Revolution in the Middle East and North Africa* (Santa Monica: Rand, 2003), <http://www.rand.org/publications/MR/MR1653/MR1653.pdf>, accessed 19 February 2007.

Cobain, Ian, 'FBI Closes Website Linked to Real IRA', *The Times* (London), 8 October 2001: 8.

Collier, Robert, 'Terrorists Get Web Sites Courtesy of US Universities', *San Francisco Chronicle*, 9 May 1997.

Commission of the European Union, *Proposal for a Council Framework Decision on Combating Racism and Xenophobia* (Brussels: European Commission, 2001), <http://europa.eu.int/eur-lex/en/com/pdf/2001/com2001_0664en01.pdf>, accessed 19 February 2007.

Conway, Maura, 'Terrorism and the Internet: New Media, New Threat?', *Parliamentary Affairs*, 59/2 (2006): 1–16.

Conway, Maura, 'Terrorist Web Sites: Their Contents, Functioning, and Effectiveness', in Philip Seib (ed.), *Media and Conflict in the Twenty-First Century* (New York: Palgrave, 2005), pp. 185–215.

Conway, Maura, 'Cybercortical Warfare: Hizbollah's Internet Strategy', in Sarah Oates, Diana Owen and Rachel Gibson (eds), *The Internet and Politics: Citizens, Voters and Activists* (London: Routledge, 2005), pp. 100–17.

Conway, Maura, 'What is Cyberterrorism? The Story So Far', *Journal of Information Warfare*, 2/2 (2003): 33–42.

Corera, Gordon, 'A Web Wise Terror Network', *BBC News* (World Edition), 6 October 2004, <http://news.bbc.co.uk/2/hi/in_depth/3716908.stm>, accessed 19 February 2007.

Cram, Ian, 'Regulating the Media: Some Neglected Freedom of Expression Issues in the United Kingdom's Counter-Terrorism Strategy', *Terrorism and Political Violence*, 18/2 (2006): 335–55.

Dahl, Robert A., *Democracy and Its Critics* (New Haven, CT: Yale University Press, 1989).

Denning, Dorothy, 'Is Cyber Terror Next?' in Craig Calhoun, Paul Price, and Ashley Timmer (eds), *Understanding September 11* (New York: New Press, 2001), <http://www.ssrc.org/sept11/essays/denning.htm>, accessed 19 February 2007.

Denning, Dorothy, 'Activism, Hacktivism, and Cyberterrorism: The Internet as a Tool for Influencing Foreign Policy', in John Arquilla and David Ronfeldt (eds), *Networks and Netwars: The Future of Terror, Crime, and Militancy* (Santa Monica: Rand, 2001), pp. 239–88, <http://www.rand.org/publications/MR/MR1382/MR1382.ch8.pdf>, accessed 19 February 2007.

Der Derian, James, 'The Question of Information Technology in International Relations', *Millennium*, 32/3 (2003): 441–56.

De Rosa, Mary, *Data Mining and Data Analysis for Counterterrorism* (Washington DC: Center for Strategic and International Studies), <http://www.csis.org/tech/2004_counterterrorism.pdf>, accessed 22 March 2007.

Eedle, Paul, 'Al Qaeda's Super-Weapon: The Internet', paper presented at the conference Al-Qaeda 2.0: Transnational Terrorism After 9/11, New America Foundation (Washington, D.C., 1–2 December 2004), <http://www.outtherenews.com/modules.php?op=modload&name=News&file=article&sid=89&topic=7>, accessed 19 February 2007.

Eneman, Marie, 'The New Face of Child Pornography', in Mathias Klang and Andrew Murray (eds), *Human Rights in the Digital Age* (London: Glasshouse Press, 2005).

Franda, Marcus, *Launching Into Cyberspace: Internet Development and Politics in Five World Regions* (Boulder and London: Lynne Rienner, 2002).

Gelbstein, Eduardo and Jovan Kurbalija, *Internet Governance: Issues, Actors and Divides* (Geneva: DiploFoundation, 2005), <http://www.diplomacy.edu/isl/ig/>, accessed 19 February 2007.

Gross, Eva and Alvaro Mendéz, 'Editorial Note', *Millennium*, 32/3 (2003).

Gruner, Stephanie and Gautam Naik, 'Extremist Sites Under Heightened Scrutiny', *The Wall Street Journal Online*, 8 October 2001, <http://zdnet.com.com/2100-1106-530855.html?legacy=zdnn>, accessed 19 February 2007.

Hauss, C. and Samuel, A., 'What's the Internet Got to Do With It? Online Responses to 9/11', paper presented at the American Political Science Association Annual (APSA) Annual Convention (Boston, 29 August – 1 September 2002).

Jehl, David and Douglas Johnston, 'Reports That Led to Terror Alert Were Years Old, Officials Say', *New York Times*, 3 August 2004.

Klein, Hans, 'ICANN and Internet Governance: Leveraging Technical Coordination to Realize Global Public Policy', *The Information Society*, 18/3 (2002): 193–207.

Kornblum, Janet, 'Radical Radio Shows Forced from the Net', *USA Today*, 25 October 2001.

Lasker, John, 'Watchdogs Sniff Out Terror Sites.' *Wired News*, 25 February 2005, <http://www.wired.com/news/privacy/0,1848,66708,00.html>, accessed 19 February 2007.

Li, Charles, 'Internet Content Control in China', *International Journal of Communications Law and Policy*, 8 (Winter 2003/04), <http://www.ijclp.org/8_2004/pdf/charlesli-paper-ijclp-neu.pdf>, accessed 19 February 2007.

Lyman, Jay, 'Terrorist Web Site Hosted by US Firm', *NewsFactor Network*, 3 April 2002, <http://www.newsfactor.com/perl/story/17079.html>, accessed 19 February 2007.

Margulies, Peter, 'The Clear and Present Internet: Terrorism, Cyberspace, and the First Amendment', *UCLA Journal of Law and Technology*, 8/2 (2004), <http://www.lawtechjournal.com/articles/2004/04_041207_margulies.pdf>, accessed 19 February 2007.

McCullagh, Declan, 'Military Worried About Web Leaks', *CNET News*, 16 January 2003, <http://news.com.com/2100-1023-981057.html>, accessed 19 February 2007.

McKay, Niall, 'Do Terrorists Troll the Net?' *Wired*, 4 November 1998, <http://www.wired.com/news/politics/0,1283,15812,00.html>, accessed 19 February 2007.

McLaughlin, W. Sean, 'The Use of the Internet for Political Action by Non-State Dissident Actors in the Middle East', *First Monday*, 8/11 (2003), <http://www.firstmonday.org/issues/issue8_11/mclaughlin/index.html>, accessed 19 February 2007.

National Infrastructure Protection Center, *Cyber Protests Related to the War on Terrorism: The Current Threat* (Washington, D.C.: National Infrastructure Protection Center, 2001), <http://www.iwar.org.uk/cip/resources/nipc/cyberprotestupdate.htm>, accessed 19 February 2007.

Penfold, Carolyn, 'Nazis, Porn, and Politics: Asserting Control Over Internet Content', *JILT: The Journal of Information Law and Technology*, 2 (2001), <http://elj.warwick.ac.uk/jilt/01-2/penfold.html>, accessed 19 February 2007.

Pollard, Neal A., 'Indications and Warning of Infrastructure Attack', in Lars Nicander and Magnus Ranstorp (eds), *Terrorism in the Information Age: New Frontiers?* (Stockholm: National Defence College, 2004).

Pollitt, Mark M., 'Cyberterrorism: Fact or Fancy?' *Computer Fraud and Security*, (February 1998): 8–10.

Powell, William, *The Anarchist Cookbook* (Arkansas: Ozark PR LLC, 2003 [1971]).

Rodan, Garry, 'The Internet and Political Control in Singapore', *Political Science Quarterly*, 113/1 (1998): 63–89.

Rogers, Robert, 'Operating Issue Networks on the Web', *Science as Culture*, 11/2 (2002): 191–214.

Scheeres, Julia, 'Blacklisted Groups Visible on Web', *Wired News*, 19 October 2001.

Schmid, Alex P. and Janny De Graaf, *Violence as Communication: Insurgent Terrorism and the Western News Media* (London: Sage, 1982).

Smith, George, 'The Recipe for Ricin: Examining the Legend', *National Security Notes*, 20 February 2004, <http://www.globalsecurity.org/org/nsn/nsn-040220.htm>, accessed 19 February 2007.

Smith, George, 'The Recipe for Ricin, Part II: The Legend Flourishes', *National Security Notes*, 4 March 2004, <http://www.globalsecurity.org/org/nsn/nsn-040304.htm>, accessed 19 February 2007.

Smith, Robert W., 'Administrative Court in Düsseldorf affirms blocking order in North Rhine-Westphalia', *Heise Online*, 15 June 2005, <http://www.heise.de/english/newsticker/news/60662>, accessed 19 February 2007.

Smolla, Rodney A., 'From Hit Man to Encyclopedia of Jihad: How to Distinguish Freedom of Speech from Terrorist Training', *Loyola Entertainment Law Review*, 22/2 (2002), <http://elr.lls.edu/issues/v22-issue2/smolla.pdf>, accessed 19 February 2007.

Spafford, Eugene, *Testimony before the US House Armed Services Committee, Subcommittee on Terrorism, Unconventional Threats and Capabilities*, 24 July 2003, <http://commdocs.house.gov/committees/security/has205260.000/has205260_0f.htm>, accessed 19 February 2007.

Stern, Jessica, *The Ultimate Terrorists* (Cambridge: Harvard University Press, 1999).

Tekwani, Shyam, 'The Tamil Diaspora, Tamil Militancy, and the Internet', in K.C. Ho, Randolph Kluver, and Kenneth C.C. Yang (eds), *Asia.Com: Asia Encounters the Internet* (London: Routledge, 2003).

Thomas, Timothy L., 'Al Qaeda and the Internet: The Danger of "Cyberplanning"', *Parameters*, (Spring 2003), <http://carlisle-www.army.mil/usawc/Parameters/03spring/thomas.htm>, accessed 19 February 2007.

Tibbetts, Patrick S., 'Terrorist Use of the Internet and Related Information Technologies', unpublished paper (Fort Leavenworth: United States Army Command and General Staff College, 2002), <http://stinet.dtic.mil/cgi-bin/fulcrum_main.pl?database=ft_u2&searchid=0&keyfieldvalue=ADA403802&filename=%2Ffulcrum%2Fdata%2FTR_fulltext%2Fdoc%2FADA403802.pdf>, accessed 19 February 2007.

US Department of Justice, *Report On The Availability of Bombmaking Information, the Extent to Which Its Dissemination Is Controlled by Federal Law, and the Extent to Which Such Dissemination May Be Subject to Regulation Consistent With the First Amendment to the United States Constitution* (Washington, D.C.: US Department of Justice, 1997), <http://cryptome.org/abi.htm>, accessed 19 February 2007.

Verton, Dan and Lucas Mearian, 'Online Data a Gold Mine for Terrorists', *ComputerWorld*, 6 August 2004, <http://www.computerworld.com/securitytopics/security/story/0,10801,95098,00.html>, accessed 19 February 2007.

Verton, Dan, *Black Ice: The Invisible Threat of Cyberterrorism* (New York: McGraw Hill, 2003).

Weimann, Gabriel, *WWW.terror.net: How Modern Terrorism Uses the Internet* (Washington, D.C.: United States Institute of Peace, 2004), <http://www.usip.org/pubs/specialreports/sr116.pdf>, accessed 19 February 2007.

Weimann, Gabriel, 'Terror on the Internet: The New Arena, the New Challenges', paper presented at the annual meeting of the International Studies Association (ISA), (Montreal, Canada, 17 March 2004), <http://archive.allacademic.com/publication/pro1_index.php>, accessed 19 February 2007.

Working Group on Internet Governance (WGIG), *Report of the Working Group on Internet Governance* (Château de Bossey: WSIS, 2005), <http://www.wgig.org/docs/WGIGREPORT.pdf>, accessed 19 February 2007.

World Summit on the Information Society (WSIS), *WSIS Plan of Action*, WSIS-03/GENEVA/DOC/5-E (Geneva: WSIS, 2003), <http://www.itu.int/dms_pub/itu-s/md/03/wsis/doc/S03-WSIS-DOC-0005!!PDF-E.pdf>, accessed 19 February 2007.

Chapter 6

Improving Information Security in Companies: How to Meet the Need for Threat Information

Manuel Suter

Introduction

In discussing the impact of new information and communication technology (ICT) on the security of states, it is sometimes neglected that the inherent insecurity of information technologies primarily affects companies and private users. ICT plays a central role in many enterprises and enables them to work as networks, simplifying internal as well as external communication. The development of this new technology has, however, also heralded the arrival of a new set of problems. In the 1980s, everyone was talking about the emergence of computer viruses; nowadays, these are a worldwide phenomenon and only one of many threats to the information security of companies. Despite the installation and implementation of various technical and organizational protection measures, the risk of information security breaches has increased constantly over the past years.

Apparently, companies are not investing enough in information security, or even worse, the investments in question are ineffective. The realization that investment in information security was often insufficient or ineffective led to the emergence of a new field of research called the economics of security.[1] Studies in this discipline go beyond the traditional technical approaches in explaining the ongoing problems of information insecurity. They try to identify economic and social reasons underlying the problem. In this chapter, I pursue that approach taking recourse to the instruments of political science. It is the contention of this chapter that a political science analysis of cyber-security should not be confined to scrutiny of the effects of new developments on the security of states, but should also examine how states can improve the security of the economy as a whole.

While current research has identified various economic causes of information insecurity (e.g., perverse incentives, network externalities, the existence of monopolies, etc.), I will focus on the lack of threat information. It is presumed that companies fail to implement efficient security strategies mainly because they do not have enough reliable information about the quality and quantity of threats.

---

1 For an overview on that field of research, see <http://www.cl.cam.ac.uk/~rja14/econsec.html>, accessed 19 April 2007.

Anderson states: 'These risks cannot be managed better until they can be measured better.'[2] Nobody knows the costs of future attacks; thus, companies cannot weigh the benefits against the costs in order to determinate their optimal level of investment. In consequence, they 'often simply react to a breach or compromise and spend what it takes to solve the existing problem'[3]. Hence, companies rarely implement a sustainable and efficient strategy for the protection of their information, and it is therefore rather unsurprising that new vulnerabilities are continuously emerging. Obviously, companies require quantitative information in order to be able to manage risk conventionally. Since the benefits of security investments are defined as avoided damages, companies have to know the probability and the costs of such damages.

The most obvious way of getting this information is to conduct information security surveys among companies. Many such surveys have been or are being conducted worldwide by various institutions; but as I will show in the first part of the chapter, most of them fail to provide reliable information about the frequency and the costs of information security breaches. It is difficult to record accurate data because some attacks are hard to discover, and some firms may hesitate to provide information about information breaches they have suffered. It is therefore very difficult to calculate the costs of these incidents. Nevertheless, some of the results of the existing surveys provide interesting insights. I will discuss the findings of some of the most important international surveys and show how information security surveys could even be a more useful instrument of risk analysis if they differentiated between the various types of companies.

Despite the data of surveys (and because of their unreliability), there is still a lot of uncertainty about the adequate strategy to protect information. In addition, the quality and quantity of threats are evolving very fast, and there is a confusingly broad range of alternatives for potential countermeasures. It is therefore difficult to establish which protection measure is adapted, and which strategy is the most efficient. The only way to learn more about which measures are successful and which are unsuitable is for different companies to exchange their experiences. This is also the underlying idea of information-sharing. This concept was developed by governments to better protect the critical infrastructures, and thus refers mainly to the exchange of information among large companies and between large companies and the state.

There is a considerably volume of literature on the subject of information-sharing. In the second part of this chapter, I will review the key arguments of the concept and discuss its chances and challenges. Subsequently, I will examine the practical implementation of the theoretical concept and discuss two examples of information-sharing among large firms.

As I will show, the existing examples of information-sharing must be ascribed mainly to governmental initiative. States have a distinct interest in improving the information security of companies, as the security of the whole society depends on a functioning information infrastructure. Particularly important is the security

---

2 Ross Anderson and Tyler Moore, 'The Economics of Information Security', *Science*, 314 (2006), p. 610.

3 Brent Rowe, *Economic Analysis of Cyber Security* (New York, 2006), p. 1.

of the so-called critical infrastructures (e.g., energy/power, information and telecommunication technologies, health services, banking and finance, etc.).[4] Due to the deregulation of markets, these critical infrastructures are today often in the hands of private companies. Unsurprisingly, states try to foster information-sharing among the owners and operators of critical infrastructures in order to render them more secure. Thus, in the third part of the chapter, I will examine the options available to governments in strengthening information-sharing.

Unlike information-sharing among large firms, the exchange of knowledge among small and medium-sized firms (SMEs) has been studied far less. Although the key arguments for information-sharing also apply to SMEs, there is one important difference: There are simply many more SMEs than there are large firms. The implementation of the concept of information-sharing – which is highly dependent on trust – is therefore different in the case of SMEs, considering that they cannot easily be assembled in small and clearly arranged information-sharing associations. Therefore, I will conclude by discussing potential designs for information-sharing associations for SMEs and by examining one of the rare examples of such a body.

Surveys as Instrument of Risk Assessment

The precondition for adequate and effective risk management is to know the threats. As the threats to the information security of enterprises are numerous and rapidly evolving, this is a rather demanding task. On the other hand, it can be ascertained that the main features of the threats are resilient. In essence, all threats relate to confidentiality, availability, and data integrity. Furthermore, some patterns of attacks reappear remarkably often. For example, viruses have been known for years, but are still at the base of many newer attacks. Even those forms of attacks that have only emerged recently are fairly well-known.[5] They are broadly discussed not only in professional journals, but also in daily newspapers. In sum, it can be assumed that most companies are more or less familiar with the relevant threats to their information security.

But although the threats are known, companies may find it very difficult to assess the risk to their information security, because they lack knowledge about the frequency and the potential damages of the respective threat. Thus, what is needed is a set of metrics for the probability and the harmfulness of the individual threats to information security.

---

4   The definition of critical infrastructure varies from country to country. For an overview on national and international protection policies, see Isabelle Abele-Wigert and Myriam Dunn, *International CIIP Handbook 2006 Vol.I: An Inventory of 20 National and 6 International Critical Information Infrastructure Protection Policies* (Zurich, 2006).

5   For an overview on current threats, see, e.g., Hossein Bidgoli et al. (eds), *Handbook of Information Security, Volume 1–3* (New Jersey, 2006).

Metrics for Threats to Information Security

This demand for quantitative threat and vulnerability information is widely recognized. It was already asserted by the report of the President's Commission on Critical Infrastructure Protection (PCCIP) in 1997.[6] Almost ten years later, however, companies still lack accurate quantitative data. This deficiency is mainly due to difficulties in collecting data. Unlike conventional theft, information security breaches are rarely reported to the police, so there is no central agency that counts the frequency of incidents.

Quantitative information about the frequency of security breaches and the extent of subsequent losses is therefore usually derived by surveys. There are currently plenty of such surveys available; however, most of them are conducted by commercial IT-security companies and serve marketing purposes, rather than being conceived as scientific endeavours to establish facts. Yet, some surveys, in particular those conducted by governmental agencies or by well-known magazines, have gained credibility over the years.[7] According to Brent Rowe, among these recognized surveys, differentiation between two main sources of data is needed: there are surveys on the costs associated with past attacks, as well as surveys collecting attack and vulnerability statistics.[8]

It is particularly difficult to estimate the costs of the damages caused by information security breaches. The losses incurred in various incidents are highly dependent upon different factors. For example, the value of stolen information depends upon the identity of the thief. If information is stolen by a competitor, the costs are much higher than in the case of intrusion by a harmless 'script kiddy'. In addition, the losses resulting from a breakdown of a specific service can be reduced if there is an alternative plan of operation. Consequently, these surveys are sometimes exposed to charges of unreliability and exaggeration.[9] Even if such accusations may be too hard, it can clearly be ascertained that the reliability of cost estimations is highly questionable.

The attack and vulnerability statistics – which are the basis for cost estimations – are less contested. The main criticism is that data on past incidents is useless for predicting future trends, given the rapid change of threats to information security. But as Kevin J. Soo Hoo states, such arguments are baseless when the expectations of such surveys remain realistic:

---

6 President's Commission on Critical Infrasturcture Protection (PCCIP), *Critical Foundation: Protecting America's Infrastructures* (Washington DC, 1997), p. 27.

7 For an overview on existing statistics in the US, see Rowe 'Economic Analysis of Cyber Security', pp. 16–24.

8 Ibid.

9 As example for these critics, see Ira Winkler, 'Time to End the CSI/FBI survey?', *Computerworld Security*, 9 November 2006. The tendency of exaggeration in the security engineering community is also mentioned by Ross Anderson, *Unsettling Parallels Between Security and the Environment* (Berkeley, Workshop on Economics and Information Security 2002).

They are predicated on an expectation that past data must have near perfect predictive powers. [...] Using past data to predict the future has been likened to driving forward while only looking in the rearview mirror. Gentle curves in the road can be predicted and followed, but sharp turns are unforeseeable. Thus, the use of past data should be tempered by the understanding that it provides only a partial answer.[10]

A more serious objection again concerns the reliability of collected data. The problem with threats like spyware, Trojan horses, or the abuse of wireless networks is the fact that they are designed to abuse a system without attracting any attention. Thus, they are usually not noticed until well after the event, or sometimes not at all. In this case, they obviously do not appear in any statistics. Furthermore, evidently only the reported breaches are measurable. But companies may be reluctant to report incidents – first, because they fear possible damage to their reputation or even legal liability, and secondly, because they want to avoid undermining the confidence of customers in their services. Therefore, statistics of incidents may tend to understate the problem, and the reliability of the data should again be considered questionable.

Existing Statistics and the Lack of Differentiation

Because of the above-mentioned sources of error, data on information security breaches is uncertain in many respects. However, interpreted carefully, surveys on information security breaches in companies can deliver important information on the threats facing companies, as well as insight into the use of security measures. In comparing the most established of the existing surveys,[11] trends in information security threats can be detected. For instance, all of the surveys under consideration show that the most widespread threat still comes from the various forms of malware (viruses, spyware, worms, and Trojan horses). Another shared finding is the importance of conventional theft. The statistics point out that theft of laptops or other hardware is one of the most serious threats to information security. Finally, the comparison between the existing statistics highlights that more sophisticated attacks (like Denial-of–Service Attacks or system penetration), which also have a more serious impact, are encountered far less often.

Accordingly, there are common findings about the risk management of companies. The surveys all indicate the nearly uniform use of firewalls and antivirus software in companies. Meanwhile, more complex technologies such as intrusion detection and biometric systems are rarely used.

Such insights are interesting and particularly helpful for researchers in the field of information security. With access to the data of surveys, it is possible to

---

10 Kevin J. Soo Hoo, *How Much is Enough? A Risk-Management Approach to Computer Security* (Stanford, 2002), p. 33.

11 The following surveys are considered: Computer Security Institute (CSI) and Federal Bureau of Investigation (FBI), *2006 CSI/FBI Computer Crime and Security Survey*; National Hi-Tech Crime Unit (NHTCU), *Hi-Tech Crime: The Impact on UK Business 2005*; CIO Magazine and PricewaterhouseCoopers, *The Global State of Information Security 2006*; Department of Trade and Industry (DTI) and Pricewaterhouse Coopers, *Information Security Breaches survey 2006*.

create rankings on the frequency of the different threats and on the diffusion of countermeasures. Thereby companies may gain an overview of threats and clues for protection measures. Accurate quantitative data – which is needed for the purpose of efficient risk management – is still not available, however.

In order to gain more accurate and reliable data, the quality of surveys would have to be ameliorated. Unfortunately, most of the surveys don't differentiate between different types of companies. Significant differences such as the number of employees, the business sector, or the company's reputation can be expected to affect the probability of a company encountering attacks, as well as its level of risk management. The size of firms, in particular, is likely to have a strong impact. Large businesses have larger networks and use IT technologies more intensively than small and medium-sized companies. Apart from that, larger firms are more attractive for attacks, because from a hacker's point of view, carrying out sophisticated attacks only really worth the effort if the company in question generates sufficient revenues or has sufficient assets to make it worth targeting or appropriating. Obviously, more money can be taken from bigger companies than from smaller ones. The impact of the size is confirmed by the CIO/CSO study 'The Global State of Information Security in 2006'. As the results of this survey show, the bigger companies suffer more security breaches and bigger losses than small and medium-sized enterprises. But that doesn't mean that the small and medium-sized companies are better at securing their networks than their bigger counterparts. Large companies devote more financial and human resources to safeguard their information security. Hence, the authors of the study conclude:

> ... the gap between mid- and large-market might have been even wider if the larger companies had not followed more strategic security practices. The lesson here is that midsized companies might reduce the number of security breaches they experience (and the damage caused by them) if they did the same.[12]

Precisely the same observations could be made in a survey on information security in Swiss companies. The survey showed that the more sophisticated attacks in technical terms like system penetration, DoS-attacks or website defacement mainly affect large firms with over 250 employees, even thought they invest considerably more resources into risk management. It also scrutinized the impact of business activity. The assumption was that companies operating in e-commerce are more likely to encounter an incident. Again, the supposition was clearly confirmed by the results. Firms that purchase goods online or sell goods via their website are at much higher risk of targeted attacks. Firms conducting commercial activities via the internet are more attractive for hackers, because they can try to scam the customers' money during payment (a recent and well-known example of internet scams are phishing attacks).[13]

---

12 CIO Magazine and PricewaterhouseCoopers, 'The Global State of Information Security', p. 9.

13 Manuel Suter, *Information Security in Swiss Companies: A Survey on Threats, Risk Management and Forms of Joint Action* (Zurich, 2006), p. 18.

As mentioned, other factors can also be expected to influence the risk of an incident. Such factors may include the level of technical innovation, the market position, or the degree of popularity of a company. Depending on the profile of a company, it faces very different threats. Therefore, future surveys should take into account the differences between the various firms. Without such specifications, estimations of the frequency of individual incidents and the average losses caused by these threats are of limited use for risk assessment of individual companies. In addition, differentiation would also help to increase the reliability of data.

But although future surveys could gain reliability, they can hardly ever be a sufficiently useful instrument for risk assessment in companies as long as it is not possible to calculate the costs more accurately. Thus, in order to find the adequate level of risk management, companies rely on other sources of information. The most promising option is direct information-sharing among firms. By sharing information about security vulnerabilities and solutions, companies could minimize the costs of information security expenditures as well as the costs of security breaches. In the next section, I will therefore discuss the concept of information-sharing and show examples of information-sharing alliances among large firms.

The Concept of Information-sharing

The idea of information-sharing was already contained in the 1997 report of the President's Commission on Critical Infrastructure Protection (PCCIP). It was suggested to 'provide an information sharing and analysis capability to support [corporate] efforts to mitigate risk and effectively respond to adverse events, including cyber, physical, and natural events.'[14] This report, and the subsequent Presidential Decision Directive (PDD) 63, leveraged the idea of information-sharing. The idea quickly received a lot of attention. Accordingly, there is a considerable volume of literature on the subject of information-sharing. Referring to studies on trade associations, researchers try to assess the benefits and potential of sharing knowledge and have identified impediments to that form of joint action. Below, I will review the most important arguments of these studies.

The Benefits of Information-sharing

The advocates of information-sharing argue that pooling knowledge about best practices and exchanging experiences of incidents will significantly reduce the problem of information insecurity. As Gordon, Loeb, and Lucyshyn point out, information-sharing potentially minimizes the costs of security breaches as well as the costs of information security expenditures. They write:

> In the absence of information sharing, each firm independently sets its information security expenditures at a level where the marginal benefits equal the marginal costs. It is shown that when information is shared, each firm reduces the amount spent on information

---

14 Government Accountability Office (GAO), *Critical Infrastructure Protection: Improving Information Sharing with Infrastructure Sectors* (Washington D.C., 2004), p. 8.

security activities. Nevertheless, information sharing can lead to an increased level of information security. [...] The level of information security that would be optimal for a firm in the absence of information sharing can be attained by the firm at a lesser cost when computer security information is shared.[15]

Members of information-sharing alliances profit from the experiences of all other members and are therefore better informed. This enables them to react rapidly and adequately to security breaches and renders their risk management more effective.

Gal-Or and Ghose prove in their analysis of the economics of information-sharing that benefits may not only be derived from minimizing security expenditures, but also from an increase in the demand for the final products. They argue that consumers prefer to buy a product in companies with high levels of security. Therefore, when a firm increases its investments in information security (by implementing new technologies or by enhancing the effectiveness of its measures through information-sharing), we can expect an increase of the demand for the final product as soon as the clients are aware of the better security of the products.[16]

A further economic incentive for sharing information is the effect of deterrence. Schechter and Smith demonstrate how thieves planning to penetrate a system in order to steal information might evaluate their potential gains: If a company shares information with the law enforcement agencies or with other firms, it thereby enhances the probability that the thief will be captured when he attacks others. Thus, thieves are likely not to include this company in their set of possible targets. As we see, sharing of information may not have an immediate benefit for the victim of an attack, but raises its reputation as an unattractive and dangerous target and therefore lowers the likelihood of future attacks.[17]

Impediments to Information-sharing

Beside the advantages of information-sharing described above, however, there are also strong economic impediments to information-sharing. Due to these impediments, firms may appraise the costs of information-sharing as being higher that the benefits. The highest costs would be incurred if information on vulnerabilities and security breaches were disseminated publicly. This could result in new attempts by hackers to exploit the vulnerabilities, and above all, in a loss of reputation. Companies value their reputation highly, as customers will be reluctant to transact businesses with firms that are perceived to be as being insecure. Cavusoglu, Mishra, and Raghunathan demonstrate that the announcement of a security breach is negatively correlated to

---

15 Lawrence A. Gordon, Martin P. Loeb, and William Lucyshyn, 'Sharing Information on Computer Systems Security: An Economic Analysis' *Journal of Accounting and Public Policy*, 22 (2003), p. 461.

16 Esther Gal-Or and Anindya Ghose, *The Economic Incentives for Sharing Security Information* (Pittsburgh, 2004), p. 10.

17 Stuart E. Schechter and Michael D. Smith, *How Much Security is Enough to Stop a Thief? The Economics of Outsider Theft via Computer Systems and Networks* (Cambridge, 2003).

the market value of the targeted firm.[18] Additionally, sharing delicate information is risky, because public dissemination of secret information could also violate laws in the context of the protection of privacy.[19]

In summary, while the benefits of sharing information are hard to quantify – as it is difficult to assess the value of more effective protection in the future – the potential costs are evident and become manifest immediately. Thus, the reluctance of companies to share information with other firms is understandable.

Another barrier to information-sharing is the problem of free-riding. Companies are more concerned about their own profit than about social welfare. Members of information-sharing associations may therefore avoid the costs of developing security measures in anticipation of obtaining information about effective protection from other members. As a result of free-riding, all firms will tend to underinvest in information security and are reluctant to share information for free.[20] The problem of free-riding can be resolved by introducing incentive mechanisms (e.g., financial rewards for information) or by making the disclosure of information a condition for membership in the information-sharing association.

While free-riding might be prevented, the problem of business competition among companies poses another serious challenge. In the literature on information-sharing, the rivalrous character of knowledge about effective protection of information is often neglected. Possession of better knowledge in information security may provide an important competitive advantage: Assuming that a company has found a cheap and effective way to keep its e-commerce service up and running and well-protected, it can reduce the charges for the service. All else being equal, this company will thus be able to provide its service at a lower price than its competitor, and therefore will have no interest in sharing its knowledge of efficient protection with anyone. Aviram and Tor point out the negative consequences of the rivalrous nature of information for the likelihood of information-sharing:

> The axiom that sharing information among competitors [...] is non-rivalrous is a gross oversimplification. An analytical framework that fails to take into account the private cost to a firm of allowing its competitor to benefit from an information exchange [...] will overestimate the likelihood of information sharing.[21]

---

18 Huseyin Cavusoglu, Mishra Birendra, and Srinivasan Raghunathan, 'The Effect of Internet Security Breach Announcements on Market Value: Capital Market Reactions for Breached Firms and Internet Security Developers', *International Journal of Electronic Commerce*, 9/1 (2004), p. 94. See also Katherine Campbell et al., 'The Economic Cost of Publicly Announced Information Security Breaches: Empirical Evidence from the Stock Market', *Journal of Computer Security*, 11/3 (2003), 431–48.

19 Lewis M. Branscomb and Erwann O. Michel-Kerjan, 'Public-Private Collaboration on a National and International Scale', in Philip E. Auerswald et al. (eds), *Seeds of Disaster, Roots of Response* (Cambridge, 2006), pp. 395–404.

20 Gordon, Loeb, and Lucyshyn, 'Sharing Information on Computer Systems Security: An Economic Analysis', pp. 461–85.

21 Amitai Aviram and Avishalom Tor, *Overcoming Impediments to Information Sharing* (Cambridge, 2003), p. 12.

Because some firms profit directly from the ignorance of other companies, they are not interested in sharing information. This behaviour, called 'strategic reduction of cooperation',[22] is a particularly useful option for large firms competing against smaller companies.

For all intents and purposes, strategic reduction of cooperation is the complement strategy to free-riding. In the case of free-riding, small firms usually benefit from information provided by large firms, whereas in the case of reduction of cooperation, large firms benefit from the problems of small firms.[23] Both strategies result in a decreasing likelihood of information-sharing.

The discussion of the impediments to information-sharing has revealed two crucial points: first, companies fear the potential costs of information-sharing and are therefore reluctant to join information-sharing associations. Consequently, information-sharing depends on external incentives, which may be offered by the government. Second, information-sharing is unlikely to occur between firms with unequal capacities and resources due to the strategic behaviour of companies. This means that information-sharing associations can only encompass a restricted number of companies, and small and medium-sized enterprises cannot simply join existing information-sharing associations of large firms. I will come back to these points later in this chapter. First, I will present examples of existing information-sharing associations in order to examine the implementation of theory into practice.

Examples of Information-sharing: CERTs and ISACs

The first implementation of the concept of information-sharing dates back to 1988. The US government created a Computer Emergency Response Team (CERT)[24] at Carnegie Mellon University. Since then, the US model of CERTs has been replicated all over the world.[25] The function of CERTs can be compared to that of a fire department. They are ready to help in case of incidents, but are also actively engaged in prevention by providing information, warnings, and advice to their constituency.[26] The size of CERTs and of their constituency varies to great extent;

---

22 Aviram and Tor call this behaviour degradation: 'This form of strategic behaviour – taking actions that inflict a greater harm on one's rival than inflicted on oneself [...] us known in the antitrust literature as "raising rivals" cists. When this action takes the form of refusing cooperation or compatibility (in our case, declining to share information), we call it degradation.' (footnotes omitted). Amitai and Tor, 'Overcoming Impediments to Information Sharing', p. 18.

23 Gal-Or and Ghose , 'The Economic Incentives for Sharing Security Information', p. 26.

24 Another often used name is Computer Security Incident Response Team (CSIRT), but there are further similar names and acronyms. For further information see Killcrece Georgia et al., *State of the Practise of Computer Security Incident Response Teams (CSIRTs)* (Pittsburgh, 2003).

25 For a list of existing CERTs all over the world, see <http://www.first.org/members/teams/>.

26 Moira J. West Brown et al., *Handbook for Computer Securtiy Incident Response Teams (CSIRTs)* (Pittsburgh, 2003), p. 2.

some large firms have their own CERT, while other CERTs are responsible for several organizations.[27]

But despite structural differences, all CERTs are designed as centers of expertise conducted by information security specialists. That also means that CERTs are not formed for the purpose of fostering horizontal information-sharing among companies. Companies profit from the expert knowledge of CERTs, but do not share their experiences via CERTs with other companies. CERTs are an early implementation of the concept of information-sharing, but they cannot be quoted as an example of horizontal information-sharing in the narrow sense.

Better examples for horizontal information-sharing among companies are the Information Sharing Analysis Centers (ISACs). The foundation of ISACs was decided in the aforementioned Presidential Decision Directive 63. In this directive, President Bill Clinton followed the recommendations of the report of the President's Commission on Critical Infrastructure Protection, which suggested the promotion of such ISACs.[28] The exact wording of the directive is:

> The National Coordinator [...] shall consult with owners and operators of the critical infrastructures to strongly encourage the creation of a private sector information sharing and analysis center. The actual design and functions of the center [...] will be determined by private sector, in consultation with and with assistance from the Federal Government. Within 180 days of this directive, the National Coordinator [...] shall identify possible methods of providing federal assistance to facilitate the startup of an ISAC.[29]

Today, most of the US firms in question are members of an ISAC.[30] The function of an ISAC is to collect and share information about security, incidents, and best practices among ISAC members (companies of the same business sector) and other ISACs. ISACs are presumed to be a promising way of fostering the efficiency of risk management by exchanging experiences and knowledge. They were promoted by the government to improve the risk management in terms of information security of the owners and operators of critical infrastructure.

Unlike CERTs, which are mainly based on the expertise of information security experts, the success of ISACs depends on the willingness of their members to share information. Hence, the arguments presented above for the benefits and challenges of information-sharing from the private company's point of view refer mostly to the examples of ISACs. They are of great interest for researchers in the field of information-sharing, particularly because the state supports their formation, but doesn't intervene once they have been established. The companies are free to arrange their ISACs as they wish, and the ISACs of the various sectors display very different

---

27 Thomas Holderegger, 'The Aspect of Early Warning in Critical Information Infrastructure Protection (CIIP)', in Myriam Dunn and Victor Mauer (eds), *International CIIP Handbook 2006 Vol. II* (Zurich, 2006), pp. 111–35.

28 President's Commission on Critical Infrastructure Protection (1997), *Critical Foundation: Protecting America's Infrastructures*, pp. 27–33.

29 White House, *Protecting America's Critical Infrastructure: White Paper on PDD 63* (Washington D.C., 1998).

30 Abele-Wigert and Dunn, *International CIIP Handbook 2006 Vol. I*, pp. 328–30.

structures.[31] Researchers have examined the success of different ISACs in order to elaborate the most appropriate designs for future information-sharing associations.

These examples also make clear that information-sharing is not easy to establish. Both CERTS and ISACs have been formed only due to governmental efforts; and governmental support remains an important factor: Due to the impediments to information-sharing discussed above, some researchers remain sceptical with regard to the success of ISACs. Gal-Or and Ghose write: 'ISACs do not seem to have well-designed incentives to prevent firms from free-riding. [...] Thus, there is a possibility that even after entering an alliance, firms might renege on sharing security breach information with other member firms.'[32] Therefore, it is presumed that governments have to keep providing incentives for information-sharing. In the following section, I will take a look at the different possibilities of governmental support.

State Assistance for Information-sharing

Both the theoretical arguments and the practical examples show that incentives are needed in order to make it disadvantageous for companies to renege on information-sharing agreements. Since the market is failing to create strong enough incentives, researchers in the field of information-sharing suggest that additional incentives have to be provided by the government.[33]

The state is traditionally responsible for safeguarding various elements of the national infrastructure that are of central importance to the wellbeing of the population. Given that in our modern society, that wellbeing relies heavily on the functioning of critical infrastructure, the information security of these infrastructures has become an important task for the state. Fostering information-sharing is regarded as the centrepiece of this policy. But there is a broad scope of conceivable measures that states could undertake in this regard. They range from simple approval and promotion of information-sharing to the regulation or even prescription of cooperation. In this section, I will therefore discuss the implications of the different potential actions.

Regulation and Legislation

The most obvious way to overcome the problems of market failure is direct regulation. The government could intervene directly, using its legislative power and forcing the companies to share information. For instance, governments could make information-sharing mandatory for owners and operators of critical infrastructures. However, there is a widespread agreement that direct governmental regulation will not be

---

31 Daniel B. Prieto, 'Information Sharing with the Private Sector: History, Challenges, Innovation, and Prospects', in Auerswald et al. (eds), *Seeds of Disaster, Roots of Response* (Cambridge, 2006), pp. 415–22.

32 Gal-Or and Ghose, 'The Economic Incentives for Sharing Security Information', p. 26.

33 Gordon, Loeb, and Lucyshyn, 'Sharing Information on Computer Systems Security: An Economic Analysis', pp. 478ff.

effective.[34] Despite governmental enforcement, free-riding and refusal to cooperate would still be possible, since governments will never be able to control the validity of all of the information supplied by companies. Instead of sharing no information at all, companies under governmental constraint will share incomplete or even false information. This could hardly be considered an enhancement of security.

However, direct regulation may have a positive effect. The mere perspective of governmental intervention may be sufficient to foster information-sharing within the private sector. The report 'Critical Information Infrastructure Protection and the Law' points out this indirect effect of potential regulation:

> The mere threat of such regulation could motivate vendors and corporations to self-regulate, providing their own standards and audit policies. The heightened interest in ISACs in 2002 is an indicator that the private sector is moving toward self-regulation. The government could periodically review such self-regulation efforts and provide reports showing deficiencies that would need to be corrected by a given deadline if regulation is to be avoided.[35]

Thus, direct regulation is an instrument of last resort for governments to enforce information-sharing. It would probably not be effective, but the mere prospect of such regulation can serve to foster closer cooperation in the private sector.

Apart from direct regulation, states could also encourage the exchange of information by legislative measures. States have enacted laws to prevent the building of trusts, in favour of free competition. Such legislation may hamper information-sharing and have to be reviewed. For instance, US antitrust agencies facilitated the compliance of ISACs with antitrust laws by issuing 'business review letters' in which they state that they have no intention to challenge the ISAC. In the same way, legislation on disclosure of information can also be important. Information-sharing is more likely if the information-sharing association is exempt from disclosure under state and local laws.[36]

We can conclude that direct regulation is hardly the appropriate way to facilitate information-sharing. However, the legislative power of states should be used to create 'safe harbours' for information-sharing by granting exemptions form antitrust and disclosure laws, so that companies are free to share any data.[37]

---

34 Walter S. Baer, 'Rewarding IT Security in the Marketplace', *Contemporary Security Policy*, 24/1 (2003), pp. 204ff.

35 Steward D. Personick and Cynthia Patterson (eds), *Critical Information Infrastructure Protection and the Law: An Overview of Key Issues* (Washington DC, 2003), p. 60.

36 Amitai Aviram, *Network Responses to Network Threats: The Evolution into Private Cyber-Security Associations* (Florida, 2004), p. 16.

37 Kenneth N. Cukier, Viktor Mayer-Schoenberger, and Lewis M. Branscomb, *Ensuring, (and Insuring?) Critical Information Infrastructure Protection* (KSG Working Paper, 2005), p. 17.

Incentives for Information-sharing and Public-Private Partnerships

Besides regulation and legislation, government can also foster information-sharing by providing lucrative incentives for companies. The most obvious form of providing incentives are direct subsidies or tax breaks for members of information-sharing associations. But such economic policy instruments are quite hard to handle and usually generate high costs for the government. In addition, governments will hardly be able to control the efficiency of information-sharing.[38]

Instead, governments usually prefer to offer non-pecuniary subsidies. A particular successful incentive is the exclusive provision of security-related governmental information for members of information-sharing associations. Membership in such an association entails preferential access to government information, which is in general very valuable for companies. The close collaboration of the US government with the CERTs and the ISACs of all sectors is a good example for this form of subsidy.[39] This kind of collaboration among government and private companies is usually done in the framework of a Public-Private Partnership (PPP). Information-sharing between government and private sector in such PPPs is favourable for both parties. On account of direct communication, private actors can respond to the requirements of the government in a more flexible way and thereby avoid direct regulation. In turn, governments prefer the cooperation model to pecuniary subsidies, as it allows them to maintain a certain degree of control.[40] In the domain of Critical Information Infrastructure Protection, PPPs are established in many countries. They are seen as the best and most sustainable way of protecting the CII.[41]

However, governments cannot cooperate with all forms of information-sharing associations to the same extent, and in particular, cannot share sensitive information with all kinds of companies. As governments are primarily interested in the security of critical infrastructures, they focus on information-sharing and PPPs with companies operating such an infrastructure (e.g., ISACs). But apart from information-sharing with these associations, governments could also provide incentives to foster the exchange of security-related information between small and medium-sized firms. Although governments do not usually establish PPPs with SMEs, they can offer them incentives to exchange information as well. I will therefore continue by discussing information-sharing associations among SMEs.

Information-sharing Associations for SMEs

As mentioned above, the requirement for information-sharing was first identified in the 1997 report of the Presidential Commission on Critical Infrastructure Protection

---

38 Jan J. Andersson and Andreas Malm, 'Public Private Partnership and the Challenge of Critical Infrastructure Protection', in Myriam Dunn and Victor Mauer (eds), *International CIIP Handbook 2006, Vol. II* (Zurich, 2006), p. 150.

39 Aviram, 'Network Responses to Network Threats', p. 15.

40 Andersson and Malm, 'Public-Private Partnerships and the Challenge of Critical Infrastructure Protection', p. 151.

41 Abele-Wigert and Dunn, *International CIIP Handbook 2006, Vol. I*, p. 393.

(PCCIP). From the beginning, the concept of information-sharing was designed for cooperation between large companies and the government. Accordingly, the existing literature discusses the question of information-sharing with regard to operators or owners of critical infrastructures, and most of the arguments refer to large companies. But as we have seen in the first section of this chapter, information security and the exchange of security-related information are becoming more and more important for the whole economy.

The question arises whether the concept of information-sharing associations such as ISACs – including a strong involvement of the government and originally designed for better protection of critical infrastructures – is also applicable to SMEs. To In order to answer this question, the pros and cons of information-sharing have to be reviewed with regard to the SMEs. Subsequently, I will identify potential models for information-sharing among SMEs and discuss the example of the so-called Warning Advice and Reporting Points (WARPs) in the UK.

The Benefits and Costs of Information-sharing Associations for SMEs

As mentioned in the first section of this chapter, threats to information security can affect different companies to very different extents. Large firms face much higher risks than SMEs, but they invest also more financial and human resources in the problem. The large firms are interested in sharing expert knowledge. They are interested not so much in general information-security issues, but in know-how about the implementation of highly complex and technically demanding security measures.

Small and medium-sized firms, on the other hand, face smaller risks, but are often not prepared at all. As many SMEs also depend on a functioning IT infrastructure, they would stand to gain much more from information-sharing than large firms. Due to their limited resources, SMEs are particularly interested in finding effective ways of risk management and would profit from pooling experiences. Nevertheless, information-sharing is rarely established among these firms.

One reason for the absence of information-sharing associations for SMEs might be that the costs of information-sharing are too high for SMEs. For example, it is presumed that the costs of announcing security breaches are higher for small companies than for large firms, because 'investors penalize smaller firms more than larger firms when a security breach occurs.'[42] Furthermore, the constitution of an information-sharing association also entails costs. Because the SMEs are usually not confronted with high expenditures for their information security, they tend to be reluctant to incur the costs of information-sharing. In addition, market failure (free-riding and strategic reduction of cooperation) raises problems for information-sharing among SMEs as much as for large firms.

---

42 Cavusoglu, Birendra, and Raghunathan, 'The Effect of Internet Security Breach Announcements on Market Value', p. 95.

The Potential Design of Information-sharing Associations for SMEs

But the most important reason for the lack of information-sharing among SMEs is the absence of governmental support. Governments have supported CERTs and ISACs, but have done little to foster the exchange of information among SMEs. It stands to reason that states hesitate to support SMEs in this regard, because – unlike in the case of Public-Private Partnerships with large firms operating critical infrastructures – governments cannot enter into close collaboration with SMEs, as this would result in innumerable PPPs and too high costs. It is also impossible to provide SMEs with exclusive security-related information, because such information is normally too delicate to be spread so widely.

Hence, the state can barely provide incentives for information-sharing among SMEs. The role of the state is restricted to promotion and coordination of information-sharing. At the most, governments could bear the initial costs of building up the information-sharing association. In fact, when it comes to setting up information-sharing associations for SMEs, state support would appear to be necessary, given that firms only tend to participate in such associations when they have proven their usefulness.

Because the government can only provide initial aid, it cannot act as a controlling authority that guarantees the engagement of every member. The members of information-sharing associations for SMEs have to enforce the norms of information-sharing (i.e., every member should participate actively in the process of information-sharing and no company should conceal relevant information) among themselves. Such enforcement is only feasible if sanctions are envisaged for non-compliance. Therefore, information-sharing associations for SMEs are best designed among members who share other common interests. Amitai Aviram points out the importance of preexisting structures for private legal systems (PLS), of which information-sharing associations are an example:

> ... when a PLSs attempts to enforce a high enforcement-cost norm, the PLS is unlikely to form unless it relies on a preexisting basis. On the other hand, such norms were far more likely to be successfully enforced by PLSs that had a significant existing functionality applying to the same people whose behavior the new norm intends to affect. [...] Since it seems that network security norms tend to incur high enforcement costs, a POS enforcing them is unlikely to form spontaneously. It may form over a preexisting functionality[43]

According to this argument, information-sharing associations should be formed among companies that have preexisting relations. These relations may be manifold in nature and may include trade associations or regional business associations. Because information-sharing is unlikely among companies with disparate resources, only preexisting relations among similar businesses can be of use in establishing information-sharing associations. Because of the various factors that determine the level of threats and their potential impacts on companies (i.e. the size of firms, the business sector they operate in, etc.), the ideal design for information-sharing

---

43 Aviram and Tor, 'Overcoming Impediments to Information Sharing', p. 42.

associations among SMEs would involve companies that are similar in many respects and share preexisting relations.

The Example of WARPs

In the UK, the National Infrastructure Security Co-ordination Centre (NISCC) developed the model of Warning, Advice and Reporting Points (WARPs) to foster information-sharing among SMEs and other users who are not covered by the established CERT teams. According to the NISSC, 'a WARP is a community based service where members can receive and share up-to-date advice on information security threats, incidents and solutions'.[44] WARPs provide a trusted environment for the discussion of security-related questions. It is also possible to report incidents and ask for technical aid – in this respect, WARPs can be seen as the smaller counterparts of CERTs.[45] But unlike ISACs or CERTs, WARPs are not directly influenced by governmental action; a WARP is designed as a community of companies, and not as a Public-Private Partnership.

Nevertheless, the government provides incentives for companies to form and join WARPs. The NISCC has developed a freely usable toolbox that supports the formation of a WARP. It also runs a website where the existing or planned WARPs are listed and promoted. The WARP program supports all registered WARPs '[s]o long as they are looking after the needs of their users, following the WARP Code of Practice, and delivering the three basic WARP services of Warning, Advice, and Reporting'.[46] In sum, the NISCC provides comprehensive support for the formation and operation of WARPs, without entering into direct partnerships with the companies.

Currently, there are 19 registered operational or developing WARPs in the UK. Most of them are composed of local authorities or public service providers (apparently, the promotion of WARPs by the NISCC was primarily effective in the public sector), but there are also WARPs for SMEs, such as MYSWARP, which is operated by the Mid Yorkshire Chamber of Commerce & Industry.[47]

The promoters and operators of WARPs are aware of the importance of the composition of the constituency. Typically, WARPs are operated on behalf of a preexisting community. Members of these communities share common interests or are designed with a regional focus. In such communities, it is much easier to build up the trust necessary to share delicate, security-related information, and it is much easier to detect and sanction free-riding. In addition, WARPs are obviously designed with regard to the needs of the members and therefore often comprise organizations with similar characteristics.[48]

---

44 The WARP Website: <http://www.warp.gov.uk/Index/indexintroduction.htm>.

45 Mehis Hakkaja, 'The Evolution of WARPs', *ENISA Quarterly*, No. 4 (2006).

46 The WARP Website <http://www.warp.gov.uk/Index/indexfutureofwarps.htm>, accessed 19 April 2007.

47 For the list of registered WARPS, see <http://www.warp.gov.uk/Index/WARPRegister/indexcurrentwarps.htm>. The WARP of the Mid Yorkshire Chamber of Commerce & Industry can be found here: <http://www.mywarp.org/>.

48 Bob Askwith, 'WARP Case Study: Experience Setting up a WARP', *NISCC Quarterly*, 1 (2006).

As we can see, the design of WARPs corresponds mainly to the theoretical considerations of information-sharing among SMEs. They are promoted and supported by the government, but are not designed as Public-Private Partnerships, and they are formed among organizations with similar needs and preexisting relations. Therefore, it will be very interesting to observe the progress of WARPs in the future.

Conclusion

Considering the frequency of information security breaches, it would appear that many companies are not investing adequately in their information security. Instead of implementing systematic risk management by weighing benefits (i.e., avoided damages) against investment costs, they often simply react to security breaches. This lack of anticipatory risk management is mainly due to the lack of information. Because companies do not know the probability and potential costs of incidents, they cannot assess the risk. In addition, they have often no information about the effectiveness of the various possible countermeasures. The objective of this chapter has been to show how this flaw can be eradicated.

First, I discussed the usefulness of information security surveys. I pointed out that it is very hard to gain reliable and accurate data, and that the existing surveys fail to differentiate between the various types of firms. Nevertheless, I argued that surveys can provide important insights and are helpful tools that enable companies to perform a better assessment of risks.

The second option for overcoming the lack of information is the exchange of experiences. I therefore scrutinized the concept of information-sharing and its implementation in practice. The theoretical arguments and the practical examples both showed that there are strong economic impediments to information-sharing. Hence, information-sharing associations rely on governmental support.

Since states have a fundamental interest in improving the security of the owners and operators of critical infrastructures, they are often engaged in information-sharing associations that are designed as Public-Private Partnerships. Within these partnerships, the governments provide information that is valuable for the companies, and thus offer crucial incentives for these companies to join information-sharing associations. Furthermore, in this way, governments retain a certain degree of control over the process of information-sharing and may prevent companies from pursuing defective strategies (e.g., free-riding) in order to minimize their costs.

PPPs are an adequate format for fostering information-sharing among owners and operators of critical infrastructures, but evidently, governments cannot enter into partnerships with smaller companies that are less important from a macroeconomic perspective. However, information-sharing would also be profitable for small and medium-sized enterprises. I therefore discussed a potential design for information-sharing associations between SMEs. I argued that governments could also foster these associations by promoting and coordinating them in the early stages. The support of governments in this case could be described as help for self-help.

In sum, we can conclude that it is possible to provide the companies with more information. When better surveys are available and information-sharing is established, companies will be able to pursue proactive rather than reactive strategies against security breaches, and will thus contribute to improving the security of the economy as a whole. But both of these elements, the conduct of surveys and the establishment of information-sharing, are difficult tasks that can hardly be achieved without governmental support. Thus, mutual assistance between governments and companies should be considered a crucial precondition for the improvement of information security.

References

Abele-Wigert, Isabelle and Myriam Dunn, *International CIIP Handbook 2006 Vol. I: An Inventory of 20 National and 6 International Critical Information Infrastructure Protection Policies* (Zurich: Center for Security Studies, 2006).

Anderson, Ross, *Unsettling Parallels Between Security and the Environment* (Berkeley: Workshop on Economics and Information Security, 2002).

Anderson, Ross and Tyler Moore, 'The Economics of Information Security', *Science*, 314 (2006): 610–13.

Andersson, Jan J. and Andreas Malm, 'Public-Private Partnerships and the Challenge of Critical Infrastructure Protection', in Dunn, Myriam and Victor Mauer (eds), *International CIIP Handbook 2006 Vol. II: Analyzing Issues, Challenges, and Prospects* (Zurich: Center for Security Studies, 2006).

Askwith, Bob, 'WARP Case Study: Experience Setting up a WARP', *NISCC Quarterly*, 1 (2006).

Auerswald, Philip. E. et al. (eds), *Seeds of Disaster, Roots of Response: How Private Action Can Reduce Public Vulnerability* (Cambridge: Cambridge University Press, 2006).

Aviram, Amitai, *Network Responses to Network Threats: The Evolution into Private Cyber-Security Associations*, Public Law and Legal Theory Working Paper No. 115 (Florida: Florida State University College of Law, 2004).

Aviram, Amitai and Avishalom Tor, *Overcoming Impediments to Information Sharing* (Cambridge: Harvard Law School, 2003).

Baer, Walter S., 'Rewarding IT Security in the Marketplace', *Contemporary Security Policy*, 24/1 (2003): 190–208.

Bidgoli, Hossein et al. (eds), *Handbook of Information Security, Volumes 1–3* (New Jersey: Hoboken, 2006).

Branscomb, Lewis. M. and Erwann O. Michel-Kerjan, 'Public-Private Collaboration on a National and International Scale', in Auerswald, Philip E. et al. (eds), *Seeds of Disaster, Roots of Response: How Private Action Can Reduce Public Vulnerability* (Cambridge: Cambridge University Press, 2006).

Campbell, Katherine et al., 'The Economic Cost of Publicly Announced Information Security Breaches: Empirical Evidence from the Stock Market', *Journal of Computer Security*, 11/3 (2003): 431–48.

Cavusoglu, Huseyin, Mishra Birendra, and Srinivasan Raghunathan, 'The Effect of Internet Security Breach Announcements on Market Value: Capital Market Reactions for Breached Firms and Internet Security Developers', *International Journal of Electronic Commerce*, 9/1 (2004): 69–104.

CIO Magazine and PricewaterhouseCoopers, 'The Global State of Information Security 2006', *CIO Magazine*, September 2006, <http://www.csoonline, .com/read/090106/fea_exec.html>, accessed 19 April 2007.

Computer Security Institute (CSI) and Federal Bureau of Investigation (FBI) (2006), *2006 CSI/FBI Computer Crime and Security Survey* (San Francisco: CSI, 2006).

Cukier, Kenneth N., Viktor Mayer-Schoenberger, and Lewis M. Branscomb, *Ensuring, (and Insuring?) Critical Information Infrastructure Protection*, John F. Kennedy School of Government Faculty Research Working Paper, Working Paper RWP05-055 (Cambridge: John F. Kennedy School of Government, 2005).

Department of Trade and Industry (DTI) and Pricewaterhouse Coopers, *Information Security Breaches Survey 2006* (London, UK Department of Trade and Industry, 2006).

Dunn, Myriam and Victor Mauer (eds), *International CIIP Handbook 2006 Vol. II: Analyzing Issues, Challenges, and Prospects* (Zurich: ETH Center for Security Studies, 2006).

Gal-Or, Esther and Anindya Ghose, *The Economic Incentives for Sharing Security Information* (Pittsburgh: University of Pittsburgh and Carnegie Mellon University, 2004).

Gordon, Lawrence A., Martin P. Loeb, and William Lucyshyn, 'Sharing Information on Computer Systems Security: An Economic Analysis', *Journal of Accounting and Public Policy*, 22 (2003): 461–85.

Government Accountability Office (GAO), Critical Infrastructure Protection: Improving Information Sharing with Infrastructure Sectors (Washington D.C.: US General Accounting Office, 2004).

Hakkaja, Mehis, 'The Evolution of WARPs', *ENISA Quarterly*, No. 4 (2006).

Holderegger, Thomas, 'The Aspect of Early Warning in Critical Information Infrastructure Protection (CIIP)', in Dunn, Myriam and Victor Mauer (eds), *International CIIP Handbook 2006 Vol. II* (Zurich: Center of Security Studies, 2006).

Killcrece, Georgia et al., *State of the Practise of Computer Security Incident Response Teams (CSIRTs)* (Pittsburgh: Carnegie Mellon Software Engineering Institute, 2003).

National Hi-Tech Crime Unit (NHTCU), *Hi-Tech Crime: The Impact on UK Business 2005* (London: NOP World Business and Technology, 2005).

Personick, Steward D. and Cynthia A. Patterson (eds), *Critical Information Infrastructure Protection and the Law: An Overview of Key Issues* (Washington DC: National Academic Press, 2003).

President's Commission on Critical Infrastructure Protection, *Critical Foundation: Protecting America's Infrastructures* (Washington, D.C.: US Government Printing Office, 1997).

Prieto, Daniel B., 'Information Sharing with the Private Sector: History, Challenges, Innovation, and Prospects', in Auerswald, Philip E. et al. (eds), *Seeds of Disaster,*

Roots of Response: How Private Action Can Reduce Public Vulnerability (Cambridge: Cambridge University Press, 2006).

Rowe, Brent, *Economic Analysis of Cyber Security* (New York: Air Force Research Laboratory, 2006).

Schechter, Stuart E., *Computer Security Strength & Risk: A Quantitative Approach* (Cambridge: Harvard University, 2004).

Schechter, Stuart E. and Michael D. Smith, *How Much Security is Enough to Stop a Thief? The Economics of Outsider Theft via Computer Systems and Networks* (Cambridge, Harvard University, 2003).

Soo Hoo, Kevin J., *How Much is Enough? A Risk-Management Approach to Computer Security* (Stanford: Consortium for Research on Information Security and Policy, 2000).

Suter, Manuel, *Information Security in Swiss Companies: A Survey on Threats, Risk Management and Forms of Joint Action* (Zurich: Center for Security Studies, 2006).

West Brown, Moira J. et al., *Handbook for Computer Security Incident Response Teams (CSIRTs)* (Pittsburgh: Carnegie Mellon Software Engineering Institute, 2003).

White House, *Protecting America's Critical Infrastructure: White Paper on PDD 63* (Washington DC: White House Press, 1998).

Winkler, Ira, 'Time to End the CSI/FBI Survey?', *Computerworld Security*, 9 November 2006.

Chapter 7

The Role of the State in Securing the Information Age – Challenges and Prospects

Myriam Dunn Cavelty and Victor Mauer

A commentator once said about securing the information age that it was 'a Gordian knot around which many stakeholders circle, pulling on the strands that seem most promising and causing the entire thing to tighten even more snugly rather than loosen to reveal its internal structure'.[1] Even though this quote dates back to 1999, it still rings true today. The conundrum of security in the information age and the state's role in it represents a major challenge to many actors from a variety of communities, and its inner secrets are far from being revealed.

The essays in this volume have contributed to mapping the diverse layers, actors, approaches, and policies of the cyber-security realm. However, while it is increasingly apparent that the dynamic integration of new information technologies into a multimedia system of communication has an influence on the international system, there is far less consensus about the theoretical and practical implications of the often-contradictory developments, and our understanding of the consequences of the information revolution for international relations and security still remains rather limited. The primary reason for this is that the outcome of the expected changes can by no means be easily comprehended. Instead, they are intriguingly complex, contradictory, and a lot less explicit than some scholars like to envisage. The complexity and volatility of the development severely impedes attempts to comprehend it. While it might just be too early to say with any confidence where the world is heading, and while the pervasive uncertainty may be resolved over time, we believe it far more likely that ambiguity has become the defining feature of our times, and is therefore more than just a passing inconvenience soon to be resolved. In this concluding chapter, we will address this issue and ask ourselves what this means for the posture of the state in the information age.

Specifically, we have addressed the topical complex of information, power, and security in this volume and have found that one of the key issues in the debate is the role of the nation-state in a changing environment. The developments of the past decade have in fact led many observers to assume that the forces driving global

---

1 Holly Porteous, 'Some Thoughts on Critical Information Infrastructure Protection', *Canadian IO Bulletin*, 2/4, October 1999, <http://www.ewa-canada.com/Papers/IOV2N4.htm>.

change are acutely undermining the state and its political freedom of action. State power, according to some observers, is being eroded by the effects of the information revolution. It is true enough that when it comes to securing the information age, governments are challenged to operate in unfamiliar ways, sharing influence with experts in the IT community, with businesses, and with non-profit organisations, because the ownership, operation, and supply of the critical systems are in the hands of a largely private industry.

However, it has in fact become evident in the last couple of years that rather than becoming obsolete, the traditional nation-state is adapting its role and functions to changing circumstances. Cyberspace is shaped by policies; it is not some natural feature or a 'thing' that grows wild and free naturally, as John Perry Barlow suggests in his 'Declaration of the Independence of Cyberspace'.[2] In the last couple of years, states have ceaselessly shaped the extra-territorial realm of the internet to the best of their ability. Indeed, there is every reason to assert that states are collectively enforcing their authority in cyberspace. Consequently, we have not witnessed the end of the nation-state, but a return to overlapping authorities, including various forms of governance structures.

The Role of the State in Securing the Information Age

However, the information age also presents the state with many difficulties and challenges. Throughout this volume, we have pointed to implications of the information age for security. First of all, protecting society against asymmetrical threats that arise partly from the information revolution has become *the* central security policy concern today. The importance and relevance of the issue for the security community is largely based on the fact that the information infrastructure – the combination of computers and communications systems that serve as the underlying infrastructure for organisations, industries, and the economy – has become a key asset in today's security environment.[3] All critical infrastructures are increasingly dependent on the information infrastructure for a variety of information management, communications, and control functions. This dependence has a strong national-security component, since information infrastructure enables both economic vitality and military and civilian government operations. In particular, the information infrastructures of the government and the military depend on commercial telecommunications providers for everything from logistics and transport to various other functions.[4] Current trends, such as the opening and liberalisation of the markets, globalisation processes that stimulate the cross-national interconnection of infrastructures, and widespread access to telecommunications networks, are heightening the security requirements of the infrastructures in countries across the entire world.

---

2   John Perry Barlow, *A Declaration of the Independence of Cyberspace* (1996).

3   Computer Science and Telecommunications Board, National Research Council, *Trust in Cyber-space* (Washington, D.C., 1999).

4   Stewart D. Personick and Cynthia A. Patterson (eds), *Critical Information Infrastructure Protection and the Law: An Overview of Key Issues* (Washington, D.C., 2003), p. 1.

At the same time, new forms of warfare have focused the minds of a variety of actors on the importance of information in the strategic world. The concentration on the information domain leads to a change in how wars are fought and to new conceptions of power in international relations. In modern conflicts, the military uses language, images, and information to assault the mind, damage the morale, and affect the volition of the enemy: information operations generally expand the battlefield to encompass the minds of the world's population. Herein, they blur the boundaries between civilian and military objectives and systems, and also between war and peace, since many aspects of information operations are conducted on a permanent basis.

How then can states, faced with transnational and transversal challenges, ensure security in the information age? In a changed strategic context of security policy, the demand that critical infrastructures be protected adequately raises an interesting question: Who should carry responsibility for protecting them? Clearly, the state is not the only international actor that provides public services such as security, welfare, education, and law. But the scale of the threat and the complexity of the task at hand call for a leading role of the state. At the same time, it is obvious that like other security issues, the vulnerability of modern societies – caused by dependency on a spectrum of highly interdependent information systems – has global origins and implications. To begin with, the information infrastructure transcends territorial boundaries, so that information assets that are vital to the national security and to the essential functioning of the economy of one state may reside outside of its sphere of influence on the territory of other nation-states. Additionally, 'cyberspace' – a huge, tangled, diverse, and universal blanket of electronic interchange – is present wherever there are telephone wires, cables, computers, or human-made electromagnetic waves, which severely curtails the ability of individual states to regulate or control it alone. Thus, there can be no question that the world-wide scope of the internet demands an international approach, even though each cyber-criminal is a physical entity in a physical location with an internet connection.

It has been argued that one fruitful approach to the problem of cyber-security is to focus mainly on economic and market aspects of the issue.[5] There are many strong arguments to be made for the idea that global economic development, steered in the right direction, may be the most suitable force to address the problem – rather than a strong focus on security measures of all sorts. By applying an economic viewpoint, the insecurity of the internet can be compared to environmental pollution, and cyber-security can be shown to have strong traits of a 'public good' that will be underprovided or not provided at all in a privatized market. In economics, a public good is a good that it is difficult or even impossible to produce for private profit.[6] Public goods provide a very important example of market failure, in the sense that

---

[5] Ross Anderson, 'Why Information Security is Hard: An Economic Perspective', in IEEE Computer Society (ed.), *Proceedings of the 17th Annual Computer Security Applications Conference* (New Orleans, 10–14 December 2001), <http://www.ftp.cl.cam.ac.uk/ftp/users/rja14/econ.pdf>.

[6] Joseph E. Stiglitz, and Carl E. Walsh, *Principles of Microeconomics* (New York, 2004, 4th Edition), pp. 236–8.

individual behaviour seeking to gain profit from the market does not produce efficient results. The production of public goods results in positive externalities, which are not remunerated. In other words, because private organisations cannot reap all the benefits of a public good that they have produced, there will be insufficient incentive for them to produce it voluntarily. At the same time, consumers can take advantage of public goods without contributing sufficiently to their creation. This is called the free-rider problem.[7]

Economic studies propose a number of possible solutions to the free-rider problem. All of these offer interesting options for the provision of cyber-security in a globalising world – and all of them show that the traditional nation-state has a strong role to play. Some public choice theorists advocate government intervention and provision of public goods by the state. In other words, governments would have to make up the difference between the optimal level of cyber-security and the level that the private sector provides voluntarily. Also, if voluntary provision of public goods does not work, then the obvious solution is to make their provision mandatory.[8] One general solution to the problem is for governments or states to impose taxation to fund the provision of public goods. A government may also subsidise the production of a public good in the private sector.

In fact, there is another role for government, linked to a third solution to the free-rider problem, that might, in combination with some state intervention where truly needed, produce promising results: The *Coasian solution*, named for economist Ronald Coase.[9] The Coasian solution proposes a mechanism by which the potential beneficiaries of a public good band together and pool their resources based on their willingness to pay to create the public good. A government can serve as the convener, bringing parties to the table for such solutions. It can enforce – either through persuasion or, where necessary, through regulation – the sort of behaviour that many believe is needed. Moreover, government can use purchasing criteria to create a market for products that conform to certain specifications, like security standards.

Furthermore, governments should eliminate 'cyber-crime havens'. Different countries have different legal systems and criminal laws; therefore, arrangements and cooperation mechanisms between enforcement agencies are the appropriate way to deal with cyber-crime that crosses borders. States should review their laws in order to ensure that abuses of modern technology that are deserving of criminal sanctions are criminalised and that problems with respect to jurisdiction, enforcement powers, investigation, training, crime prevention, and international cooperation with respect to such abuses, are effectively addressed. Liaison between the law enforcement and

---

7 Myriam Dunn and Victor Mauer, 'Towards a Global Culture of Cyber-Security', in Myriam Dunn and Victor Mauer (eds), *The International CIIP Handbook 2006, Vol. II: Analyzing Issues, Challenges, and Prospects* (Zurich, 2006), pp. 189–206.

8 Mark Grady and Francesco Parisi, 'The Law and Economics of Cyber-security: An Introduction', George Mason University School of Law and Economics Working Paper Series No. 04–54 (November 2004).

9 Ronald Coase, 'The Lighthouse in Economics', *Journal of Law and Economics*, 17/2 (1974): 357–76.

prosecution officials of different states should be improved, including the sharing of experiences in addressing these problems.

Other solutions should consider furnishing an international organisation with sufficient funds to subsidise abatement, and empowering it with sharp enough teeth to penalise non-compliance. At the World Summit on the Information Society 2005 held in Tunis, it was suggested that perhaps the UN could govern the internet, and devise treaties to address issues such as cyber-security. Some support the idea, while others feel that it would add more bureaucracy and cause further delay in dealing with cyber-security issues if the treaty-making effort were to start from scratch, as UN treaty-making is inordinately cumbersome and certainly unduly time-consuming. An alternative method for moving towards a global framework would be to take an existing treaty and broaden its signatory base: This procedure is advocated by many who refer to the model of the Council of Europe Convention on Cyber-Crime. For the existing convention with its broad coverage to be put to a more global use and thus to save precious negotiation time, it would be necessary to focus on its built-in merits and flexibilities.[10]

To achieve this, a *global* culture of cyber-security would be needed, since a common understanding of threats and needs can only be fostered if all relevant stakeholders find a common language to address these issues. Equipped with such a common understanding, the many stakeholders will no longer have to pull on the strands that seem most promising, but will be able to systematically untangle those strands that have hitherto kept the community from developing a global culture of cyber-security. The 2003 WSIS Declaration of Principles calls for such a culture in order to strengthen the trust framework, including information security and network security, authentication, privacy, and consumer protection, all of which are prerequisites for the development of a strong information society, a goal pursued in many countries around the world.[11] The WSIS Plan of Action proposes to reach that goal mainly by promoting cooperation among governments and by getting them, in close cooperation with the private sector, to prevent, detect, and respond to cyber-crime and the misuse of information and communication technologies by developing guidelines and considering legislation, by strengthening institutional support, and by encouraging education and raising awareness.[12]

---

10 World Federation of Scientists Permanent Monitoring Panel on Information Security, 'Information Security in the Context of the Digital Divide: Recommendations submitted to the World Summit on the Information Society at its Tunis phase (16–18 November 2005)' Document WSIS-05/TUNIS/CONTR/01-E, 2 September 2005, p. 23.

11 World Summit on the Information Society, 'Declaration of Principles Building the Information Society: A Global Challenge in the New Millennium'. Document WSIS-03/GENEVA/DOC/4-E, 12 December 2003, <http://www.itu.int/wsis/docs/geneva/official/dop.html>.

12 World Summit on the Information Society, 'Plan of Action', Document WSIS-03/GENEVA/DOC/5-E, 12 December 2003, <http://www.itu.int/wsis/docs/geneva/official/poa.html>.

Ambiguous Transformations – Taking Complexity, Ambiguity, and Uncertainty Seriously

At the same time, complexity, ambiguity, and change are determining characteristics of the new world of information networks – and they are anathema to 'the state', which is by nature slow, rather conservative, and reactionary, and often seeks to maintain a status quo and an equilibrium. In order to understand and skilfully adapt to the changes around them, states need to develop new conceptual repertoires and adequate strategic tool kits that will better equip them to meet the challenges posed by the new threat picture, the speed with which the world is evolving, and the extreme global complexity that is emerging. In this conclusion, we want to suggest that uncertainty, ambiguity, and change should not necessarily be seen as adverse conditions. In fact, taking them at face value and discarding the belief that the environment will revert to the old days opens up new avenues of analysis and action.

We can state with certainty that complex problems are on the rise in, and due to, the information age. One possible explanation for complexity in the technical world can be found in the combination of two laws of technical innovation, namely Moore's Law and Metcalfe's Law, which describe phenomena that are widely credited as the stimuli driving the stunning growth of internet connectivity: Moore's Law states that the number of transistors per square inch on integrated circuits will double approximately every 18 months, which means that computing power increases exponentially over time. Metcalfe's Law states that the value of a communication system grows as the square of the number of users of the system, which leads us to expect an increasing number of networks, nodes, and links. According to one simple but straightforward definition, complexity is the sum of interdependencies plus change.[13] This means that complexity in information infrastructure systems is increasing, as the exponential growth of technological development leads to change, and as the increasing number of networks, nodes, and links creates growing interdependencies. In addition, the complexity of these systems grows with the extension of the geographical reach and the expansion of the services provided, the introduction of new components with richer functionality using diverse technologies, and the layering of systems over systems.[14]

It is almost ironic that in today's all-digital world, uncertainty should reappear as a major concern. Humanity has often developed technologies to regain control and ensure stability. Digital computing, for example, prevailed because of its ability to eliminate uncertainty in data representation and transformation, even after a vast number of computing steps. Now, however, the same technology seems to accelerate

---

13 Peter Gomez, 'Vom Umgang mit Komplexität: Denkfallen und Entscheidungshilfen', in Hansjürg Mey and Daniel Lehmann Pollheimer, *Absturz im freien Fall – Anlauf zu neuen Höhenflügen: Gutes Entscheiden in Wirtschaft, Politik und Gesellschaft* (Zürich, 2001), p. 151.

14 Nicholas Kyriakopoulos and Marc Wilikens, *Dependability and Complexity: Exploring Ideas for Studying Open Systems* (Ispra, 2000); Marcelo Masera and Mark Wilikens, 'Interdependencies with the Information Infrastructure: Dependability and Complexity Issues', paper given at the *5th International Conference on Technology, Policy, and Innovation* (Ispra, 2001).

changes and therefore feeds the complexity spiral.[15] In fact, we can put together a considerable list of contradictory phenomena that lead to hybrid outcomes: The information revolution empowers individuals as well as elites; it breaks down hierarchies and creates new power structures; it has a fragmentising as well as an integrating effect; it amplifies the capacity to analyse, but reduces reaction times; it offers better information, but also raises more questions about authenticity and security.[16] The most important characteristics of security in the information age thus seem to be complexity, ambiguity, and ensuing uncertainty, especially uncertainty as to the scope of future transformation and as to the most appropriate response to these developments.

Rather than concluding with the realisation that we live in complex times, as some authors do, we want to venture to discuss below *how* security is being transformed by complexity, ambiguity, and the ensuing uncertainty – as well as instances of continuity. This is no easy undertaking and involves a great deal of speculation, as one complexity researcher has noted: 'one consequence of emerging complexity is that you cannot see the end from the beginning [...] emerging complexity creates not one future but many.'[17] Nonetheless, the discipline of complexity sciences teaches us that complex systems of any sort exhibit a number of specific, non-exclusive features and behaviours. From these, some lessons can be drawn without falling into the trap of domesticating 'real-world demons in ill-fitting complex cages'[18] or of abusing metaphors.

For one thing, there are cause-and-effect relationships between the so-called 'agents' that form the system, but both the number of agents and the number of relationships defy categorisation or analytic techniques. Cause and effect, or inputs and outputs, are not proportional; the whole does not correspond to the sum of its parts, and is not even qualitatively recognisable in its constituent components. Tiny causes can have enormous effects. Small uncertainties are amplified, so that even though system behaviour is predictable in the short term, it is unpredictable in the long term.[19] Thus, extreme sensitivity to initial boundary conditions or historical paths makes detailed prediction impossible.[20] Initial behaviour patterns and outcomes often influence later ones, producing powerful dynamics that explain change over times and that cannot be captured by labelling one set of elements 'causes' and other

---

15 Uri Merry, *Coping with Uncertainty: Insights from the New Sciences of Chaos, Self-organization, and Complexity* (Westport, 1995), pp 81–2; M. Satyanarayanan, 'Coping with Uncertainty,' *IEEE Pervasive Computing*, 2/3 (2003), p. 2.

16 David J. Rothkopf, 'Cyberpolitik: The Changing Nature of Power in the Information Age.' *Journal of International Affairs*, 51/2 (1998): 331–56.

17 R.T. Pascale, 'Surfing the Edge of Chaos', *Sloan Management Review*, 40/3 (1999): 83–94.

18 G. Bowker, 'How to be Universal: Some Cybernetic Strategies 1943–1970', *Social Studies of Science*, 23/1 (1993): 107–28.

19 Merry, 'Coping with Uncertainty', pp. 26–7.

20 Kevin Mihata, 'The Persistence of 'Emergence', in Raymond A. Eve, Sara Horsfall, and Mary E. Lee (eds), *Chaos, Complexity, and Sociology: Myths, Models, and Theories* (Thousand Oaks, 1997), pp. 33–4.

'effects'.[21] Because specific dynamic system outputs cannot be predicted (in the long run), it is not possible to plan, via prediction, the outcomes of an intervention in a social system.[22]

First and foremost, our observations question the one assumption that pervades the practice and the theory of decision-making and policy formulation: the supposition that underlying relationships between cause and effect can be understood. This assumption of order takes for granted that from the study of physical (and observable) conditions, we can derive or discover general rules or hypotheses that can be empirically verified and that create a body of reliable knowledge, which can then be developed and expanded. This has a couple of implications that we want to discuss below.

Implications for Theory-building

The first result of ambiguity that we want to dwell on applies to the discipline of IR scholars. What becomes clear from the above is that 'grand' theorising about security in the information age is neither possible nor feasible. If we take the twin forces of complexity and change seriously, there can be no 'grand' theoretical project that distils complexity, ambiguity, and uncertainty into neat theoretical packages and categories. While looking at grand theories may have heuristic value, we should acknowledge that everything is in flux and that paradox and uncertainty prevail in today's environment. This means that even though we might aim to reflect on theoretical premises, any theorising will be limited in scope, and generalisations might be conditional rather than universal.

The complexity paradigm also focuses attention on the concept of the inherently unpredictable situation – a situation that is unpredictable by nature, not just by virtue of the limitations of the observer. This resonates well with the post-modern view that no determination is possible. The complexity sciences confirm that the observer and the observed cannot be detached from each other, and that observation itself is an ontological event. Additionally, the complex is assigned a specific epistemological meaning: It shows the limits of knowledge due to complexity and unpredictability. The positivist-empiricist idea, which still dominates the discipline, that a trained observer can encapsulate the complexity of the world into grand theoretical projects through a variety of rigorous procedures, is antithetical to the current circumstances. It is clear that analyses of causes and consequences always depend largely on the context. In the light of what we have argued above, this becomes even more relevant: if generalisation becomes difficult, the specific gains prominence.

The problem is, though, that it is very easy to slip into generalisations about 'technology'. In another sign of increasing complexity, the linking of computers with

---

21 Robert Jervis, 'Complex Systems: The Role of Interactions', in David S. Alberts and Thomas J. Czerwinski (eds), *Complexity, Global Politics, and National Security* (Washington D.C., 1997).

22 Mark Michaels, 'Seven Fundamentals of Complexity for Social Science Research', in A. Albert (ed.), *Chaos and Society. Frontiers in Artificial Intelligence and Applications*, Vol. 29, (Amsterdam, 1995), p. 23.

other technologies also makes it increasingly difficult to distinguish clearly between different media. It is very important to note that not every ICT wields the same impact. To be as precise as possible, we should focus on the impact of specific information technologies on specific areas and institutions of government (or vice versa, on the implications of particular forms of governance or government for particular information technologies), at particular points in time, rather than generalizing.[23] Taken to the extreme, we should constantly ask ourselves what kind of governance, what kind of information revolution, and what kind of international system we are looking at. As such an approach is clearly unachievable given that theorising calls for at least some generalisation, we should at least make the point here that context and perspective become as important as rationality. The issues discussed here are often not about 'objective' reality, but about perceptions and understanding. This means that any analysis will be aided by thinking about the ways in which different people might perceive the same situation. The advantage of such an approach is the understanding not only that there are different perspectives on an event or situation, but also that this understanding can be used to one's advantage.[24]

Implications for Politics

The second result of ambiguity and change is that governments are increasingly faced with situations where the common tools and techniques for analysing the environment are no longer sufficient. The most common technique in use is 'risk analysis' in the context of security issues. Risk is usually understood as a function of the *likelihood* of a given *threat source* displaying a particular potential *vulnerability*, and the resulting *impact* of that adverse event.[25] The label 'risk analysis', then, refers to the processes used to evaluate those probabilities and consequences, and also to investigations of how to incorporate the resulting estimates into the decision-making process. The risk assessment process also serves as a decision-making tool, in that its outcomes are used to provide guidance on the areas of highest risk, and to devise policies and plans to ensure that systems are appropriately protected.

Even though there are various methods of conducting a risk assessment, they often entail a very similar catalogue of objects, threats, vulnerabilities, and probabilities, and define links between them. All these approaches assume order in the form of linear cause-and-effect relationships. Risk assessment breaks problems down into smaller parts. However, one of the hallmarks of complex systems is that they display emergent behaviour that is a property of the system as a whole and that cannot be studied by taking the system apart.[26] Furthermore, risk assessment

---

23 David M. Hart, *Information Technology, Governance, and All That: What Do We Mean?*, <http://siyaset.bilkent.edu.tr/Harvard/hart2.htm>.

24 Cynthia F. Kurtz and Dave Snowden, 'The New Dynamics of Strategy: Sense-making in a Complex and Complicated World', *IBM Systems Journal*, 42/3 (2003): 462–83.

25 Gary Stoneburner, Alice Goguen, and Alexis Feringa, *Risk Management Guide for Information Technology Systems. Recommendations of the National Institute of Standards and Technology*, NIST Special Publication 800–30 (Washington, 2002), p. 8.

26 James P. Crutchfield, 'Is Anything Ever New? Considering Emergence', in G. Cowan, D. Pines, and D. Melzner (eds), *Complexity: Metaphors, Models, and Reality*, SFI Series in

originated in the technical context of limited or 'closed' systems. When discussing information networks, however, we are no longer dealing with closed systems in a centrally networked environment, but with systems that are part of global network environment that knows no bounds, no central control, and offers only limited insight into the underlying system structure. These unbounded systems also lack well-defined geographic, political, cultural, and legal and jurisdictional boundaries.[27] The international environment has become qualitatively different in such a way that new analytical techniques and methodologies are required to evaluate it.

Learning to recognise and appreciate complexity, ambiguity, and uncertainty is liberating in a way, because we can start focusing on different methods that might work well in situations where the assumption of order does not hold. Our aim should not be to reduce uncertainty, as traditional scientific methods do, but to accept it for what it is. We learn from the complexity sciences that complex spaces bring forth certain patterns, the details of which are unpredictable. Certainly, once a pattern has stabilised, its path appears logical, but it is only one of many that could have stabilised, each of which also would have appeared logical in retrospect. Relying on historically stable patterns of meaning implies that we will be insufficiently prepared to recognise and act upon such unexpected patterns in the future. However, these patterns are usually recognisable in their basic forms, and with practice, one can even learn to stabilise or disrupt them, and to shape desirable patterns by creating so-called 'attraction points'.[28] This means that decision-makers and researchers must learn to accept ambiguity, complexity, and uncertainty without fear if they are ever to make sense of the dynamics of the information age.

References

Allen, Julia H. and Carol A. Sledge, 'Information Survivability: Required Shifts in Perspective', *CrossTalk: The Journal of Defense Software Engineering*, July (2002): 7–9.

Anderson, Ross, 'Why Information Security is Hard: An Economic Perspective', in IEEE Computer Society (ed.), *Proceedings of the 17th Annual Computer Security Applications Conference* (New Orleans, 10–14 December 2001), <http://www.ftp.cl.cam.ac.uk/ftp/users/rja14/econ.pdf>, accessed 16 February 2007.

Barlow, John Perry, *A Declaration of the Independence of Cyberspace* (1996), <http://homes.eff.org/~barlow/Declaration-Final.html>, accessed 16 February 2007.

---

the Sciences of Complexity XIX (Redwood City, 1994), pp. 479–97.

27 R.J. Ellison, D.A. Fisher, R.C. Linger, H.F. Lipson, T. Longstaff, and N.R. Mead, *Survivable Network Systems: An Emerging Discipline*, technical report CMU/SEI-97-TR-013 (1997), pp. 4–6; Julia H. Allen and Carol A. Sledge, 'Information Survivability: Required Shifts in Perspective', *CrossTalk: The Journal of Defense Software Engineering,* July (2002), pp. 7–9.

28 Kurtz and Snowden, 'The New Dynamics of Strategy: Sense-Making in a Complex and Complicated World'.

Bowker, G., 'How to be Universal: Some Cybernetic Strategies 1943–1970', *Social Studies of Science*, 23/1 (1993): 107–28.
Coase, Ronald, 'The Lighthouse in Economics', *Journal of Law and Economics*, 17/2 (1974): pp. 357–76.
Computer Science and Telecommunications Board, National Research Council, *Trust in Cyber-space* (Washington, D.C.: National Academy Press, 1999).
Crutchfield, James P., 'Is Anything Ever New? Considering Emergence', in G. Cowan, D. Pines, and D. Melzner (eds), *Complexity: Metaphors, Models, and Reality*, SFI Series in the Sciences of Complexity XIX (Redwood City: Addison-Wesley, 1994), pp. 479–97.
Dunn, Myriam and Victor Mauer, 'Towards a Global Culture of Cyber-Security', in Myriam Dunn and Victor Mauer (eds), *The International CIIP Handbook 2006, Vol. II: Analyzing Issues, Challenges, and Prospects* (Zurich: Center for Security Studies, 2006), pp. 189–206.
Ellison, R.J., D.A. Fisher, R.C. Linger, H.F. Lipson, T. Longstaff, and N.R. Mead, *Survivable Network Systems: An Emerging Discipline*, Technical Report CMU/SEI–97–TR–013 (Pittsburgh, PA: Software Engineering Institute, Carnegie Mellon, 1997).
Gomez, Peter, 'Vom Umgang mit Komplexität: Denkfallen und Entscheidungshilfen', in Hansjürg Mey and Daniel Lehmann Pollheimer, *Absturz im freien Fall – Anlauf zu neuen Höhenflügen: Gutes Entscheiden in Wirtschaft, Politik und Gesellschaft* (Zürich: Vdf Hochschulverlag AG, 2001).
Grady, Mark and Francesco Parisi, 'The Law and Economics of Cyber-security: An Introduction', George Mason University School of Law and Economics Working Paper Series No. 04–54 (November 2004).
Hart, David M., *Information Technology, Governance, and All That: What Do We Mean?*, <http://siyaset.bilkent.edu.tr/Harvard/hart2.htm>, accessed 16 February 2007.
Jervis, Robert, 'Complex Systems: The Role of Interactions', in David S. Alberts and Thomas J. Czerwinski (eds), *Complexity, Global Politics, and National Security* (Washington: National Defense University Press, 1997).
Kurtz, Cynthia F. and Dave Snowden, 'The New Dynamics of Strategy: Sense-Making in a Complex and Complicated World', *IBM Systems Journal*, 42/3 (2003): 462–83.
Kyriakopoulos, Nicholas and Marc Wilikens, *Dependability and Complexity: Exploring Ideas for Studying Open Systems* (Ispra: Joint Research Centre, 2000).
Masera, Marcelo and Mark Wilikens, 'Interdependencies with the Information Infrastructure: Dependability and Complexity Issues', paper given at the *5th International Conference on Technology, Policy, and Innovation* (Ispra, 2001).
Merry, Uri, *Coping with Uncertainty: Insights from the New Sciences of Chaos, Self-organization, and Complexity* (Westport: Praeger, 1995).
Michaels, Mark, 'Seven Fundamentals of Complexity for Social Science Research', in A. Albert (ed.), *Chaos and Society. Frontiers in Artificial Intelligence and Applications*, Vol. 29 (Amsterdam: IOS Press, 1995), pp. 15–34.

Mihata, Kevin, 'The Persistence of 'Emergence', in Raymond A. Eve, Sara Horsfall, and Mary E. Lee (eds), *Chaos, Complexity, and Sociology: Myths, Models, and Theories* (Thousand Oaks: Sage Publications, 1997), pp. 30–8.

Pascale, R.T., 'Surfing the Edge of Chaos', *Sloan Management Review*, 40/3 (1999): 83–94.

Personick, Stewart D. and Cynthia A. Patterson (eds), *Critical Information Infrastructure Protection and the Law: An Overview of Key Issues* (Washington, D.C.: National Academies Press, 2003).

Porteous, Holly. 'Some Thoughts on Critical Information Infrastructure Protection', *Canadian IO Bulletin*, 2/4, October 1999, <http://www.ewa-canada.com/Papers/IOV2N4.htm>, accessed 16 February 2007.

Rothkopf, David J., 'Cyberpolitik: The Changing Nature of Power in the Information Age.' *Journal of International Affairs*, 51/2 (1998): 331–56.

Satyanarayanan, M., 'Coping with Uncertainty', *IEEE Pervasive Computing*, 02/3 (2003), p. 2.

Stiglitz, Joseph E. and Carl E. Walsh, *Principles of Microeconomics* (New York, 2004, 4th Edition).

Stoneburner, Gary, Alice Goguen and Alexis Feringa, *Risk Management Guide for Information Technology Systems*, Recommendations of the National Institute of Standards and Technology (Washington D.C.: NIST Special Publication 800–30, 2002).

World Federation of Scientists Permanent Monitoring Panel on Information Security, 'Information Security in the Context of the Digital Divide: Recommendations submitted to the World Summit on the Information Society at its Tunis phase (16 to 18 November 2005)', Document WSIS-05/TUNIS/CONTR/01-E, 2 September 2005, <http://www.itu.int/wsis/docs2/tunis/contributions/co1.doc>, accessed 16 February 2007.

World Summit on the Information Society, 'Plan of Action', Document WSIS-03/GENEVA/DOC/5-E, 12 December 2003, <http://www.itu.int/wsis/docs/geneva/official/poa.html>, accessed 16 February 2007.

World Summit on the Information Society, 'Declaration of Principles Building the Information Society: A Global Challenge in the New Millennium', Document WSIS-03/GENEVA/DOC/4-E, 12 December 2003, <http://www.itu.int/wsis/docs/geneva/official/dop.html>, accessed 16 February 2007.

Index

9/11 (2001) xii, 96
  censorship xii, 77–8
  hackers 111–14
  internet legislation 105–8
  and RFID technologies 86–7
Abu Ghraib prison 58
al-Qaida 82, 100, 114, 116, 118
al-Zarqawi, Abu Musa 100
ambiguity 158, 159
Anderson, Benedict, on print 52
anonymity, and cyberspace 76–9
anti-terrorist websites 113
asymmetric
  tactics 26–7
  vulnerability 26, 27

Barlow, John Perry, cyberspace
  manifesto 1, 5, 67, 108–9, 152
bin Laden, Osama 112
Blaster computer worm 72
Brunner, Elgin M. 1–18

CERTs (Computer Emergency Response
  Teams) 138–9
Chaos Computer Club 112
child pornography 104
China, information control xii, xiii, 84, 109
CI (Critical Infrastructures) 27
CIIP (Critical Information Infrastructure
  Protection) xiii
see also PCCIP
CIP (Critical Infrastructure Protection), US
  26
'clash of civilizations' 55
Coasian solution 154
Cold War 26, 27, 35
collective memory 49, 56
companies, information security
  strategy 130
  surveys 130

threat information 129–47
  see also information sharing; SMEs
complexity
  information infrastructure 156–7
  and unpredictability 158
constructivism 51
  and information networks 51–4
  in international relations 48, 51, 54
  meta-power, contribution to 54
  security 35–6
  Wendt on 48–9
Conway, Maura 95–127
credit card transactions, internet 81
cultural goods, trade in 59
cultural studies contribution,
  meta-power 49–50
culture, and security 54–5, 57
Cyber Angels 112
cyber-attacks 36–7, 72–3
  on IGC 112–13
cyber-security
  as economic problem 38
  ensuring 153–5
  global culture of xiii
  private/public collaboration 15
  state role 154–5
  UN, possible role 155
  see also information security
cyber-terrorism
  definition 98
  in newspapers
    post-September 11 99
    pre-September 11 99
cyber-threats x
  alleged increase 33–6
  uncertainty factor 35
cyberspace
  and anonymity 76–9
  definition 2

independence, Barlow's manifesto 1, 5, 67, 108–9, 152
   nature of 67
   ocean metaphor 68
   official surveillance 83
   placeless-ness hypothesis 69–73, 74–5, 76, 87–8
   reterritorialisation 75
   and sovereignty 14
   and territorial space 58, 68
   terrorist use 72
   see also internet

Dahl, Robert
   Democracy and Its Critics 97–8
   on governance 97–8
DARPA (Defense Advanced Research Projects Agency) 24, 96
data mining, internet 114–16
desecuritisation 38
Designated Foreign Terrorist Organizations 110
deterritorialisation, security 75, 88–9
DNS (Domain Name System) 97, 102
DoD (Department of Defense) website 114
DoS (Denial of Service) attacks 72, 73, 111–12, 134
Dunn Cavelty, Myriam 1–18, 19–44, 151–61

e-cash, failure 80–1
e-commerce 79–82
ETSI (European Telecommunications Standards Institute) xiii
EU, Safer Internet Action Plan 108
Europe, responses to terrorism 57

FARC (Revolutionary Armed Forces of Colombia), internet site 102
Foucault, Michel, on knowledge 50
France, information control xii, 110
free-riding, information sharing 137, 154

Galileo satellite system 85, 86
geo-location software 108–9
Germany, information control xii, 110
GIE (Global Information Economy) 58–61
global governance, information revolution, challenges by 95

globalization, and ICT 71, 95
GLONASS satellite system 85
GNSS (Global Navigation Satellite System), examples 85–6
Google, search for terrorist groups 110–11
Google Earth 85
governance
   conditions for 97–8
   Dahl on 97–8
   see also global governance; internet governance
GPS (Global Positioning System) 85, 86
   applications 87
GWOT (Global War on Terrorism) 57, 96

hackers
   post-9/11 activities 111–14
   virtual community of 73
hacking
   meaning 72
   and security 73
Hamas internet site 102
hate material 102
Herrera, Geoffrey L. 67–93
Hizbollah 100
Hull, Cordell 46
Huntington, Samuel, 'clash of civilizations' 55
hyper-space, vs territorial space 53

Ibrahim, Khalid 120
ICANN (Internet Company for Assigned Names and Numbers) 97
ICT (Information and Communication Technologies)
   and globalization 71, 95
   impact, variable 159
   limitations 5
   pervasiveness 1–2, 27–8, 72
   and security 71
   vulnerability 11–12, 72
   see also internet
identity
   construction of 49
   and security 54–5
IGC (Institute for Global Communications), cyber attack on 112–13
information
   'how to', on internet 116–21

Index

as power resource 8–10
information age 21
  role of state 151–60
  security
    grand theories 158
    scope 22
  semantic problems 20
information control
  China xii, xiii, 84, 109
  France xii, 110
  Germany xii, 110
  Iran xi–xii
  UK 106–7
  US 105–6
information flows, threat of xi–xii
information infrastructure 21–8, 152
  complexity 156–7
  insecurity of 23–5
  vulnerability 77
  see also CIP
information networks
  and constructivism 51–4
  definition 45fn2
  Litfin on 51–2
  and meta-power 54
information revolution 2–4, 19
  consequences 4–8
  definition 4
  features 69
  global governance, challenges to 95
  international relations, implications for 151
  nation-state, threat to 8–9
  negative aspects 6–8
  origins 23
  positive aspects 5–6
  reality of 3–4
  security/governance implications 28–36
information security
  breaches
    damage 132
    statistics 133–5
  companies 129–47
  information sharing 135–46
  surveys 131–5
  threat
    information about 129–47
    measurement 132–3
    predictions 132–3
  see also cyber-security

information sharing
  benefits 135–6
  CERTs 138–9
  concept 135
  and critical infrastructures 131
  examples 138–40
  free-riding 137, 154
  incentives for 142
  information security 135–46
  ISACs 139–40
  legislation/regulation 140–1
  obstacles to 136–8
  PPPs 142
  reduction of cooperation 138
  SMEs 131, 142–6
  state help for 140
information warfare 7, 10–11
integrative theory x
interaction theory, need for 45
international relations
  'constructivist turn' 48, 51, 54
  information revolution, implications of 151
  paradigms 45
  and power, research on 46, 47
  sociological approach 49
  state-centric security model 59
internet
  anti-terrorist websites 113
  content control
    censorship 104
    child pornography 104
    cultural values, protection 104
    and free speech 102
    geo-location software 108–9
    hackers/hacktivists 111–14
    and hate material 102
    information gathering 114–21
    private actors 108–14
    search engines 109–11
    states 77–9, 84–5, 103
    terrorism, incitement to 104
  content policy 101–3, 105–8
  credit card transactions 81
  and criminal activity xi
  data mining 114–16
  'how to' information 116–21
  impact 2–3
  information, protection x–xi

insecurity of 24, 25
legislation
  international 107–8
  UK 106–7
  US 105–6
nature of 25
origins 24, 96–7
prerecorded music, sale of 80
revolutionary groups, use by 102–3
and terrorism 98–101, 110
Westphalian topology 84
see also cyberspace
internet governance 77, 96–8, 108–14
  definition 98
  and terrorism 14
Internet Haganah 113–14
Iran, information control xi–xii
ISACs (Information Sharing Analysis Centers) 139–40
IT (Information Technologies) 3
iTunes Music Store (iTMS) 80

knowledge, Foucault on 50
Krasner, Stephen, meta-power theory 47, 48
Krishna-Hensel, Sai Felicia ix–xiv

Litfin, Karen, on information networks 51–2
London bombings (2005) 106
Lycos Europe 110

McLuhan, Marshall, on media 52
Mauer, Victor 151–62
media, McLuhan on 52
meta-power 45, 46–9
  constructivism, contribution 54
  cultural studies contribution 49–50
  essence of 61–2
  examples 47, 58
  and information networks 54
  Krasner's theory 47, 48
  meaning 46–7
  see also power
Metcalfe's Law 156
Mohammed (Prophet), cartoons controversy 58
Moore's Law 156
MRTA (Túpac Amaru Revolutionary Movement) internet site 102
music, prerecorded, on internet 80

nation-state
  adaptation 152
  challenges to ix, x, 156
  identities, formation 55–6
  information revolution, threat by 8–9
  interests 55
  see also state
networks
  packed-switched 70, 76
  security, vs national security 56
NISCC (National Infrastructure Security Co-ordination Centre) 145
NPA (New People's Army) 110
NRC (Nuclear Regulatory Commission) website 115
Nye, Joseph S. Jr., on soft power 47–8

Oklahoma City bombing (1995) 26
OpenNet Initiative 83, 84
OSCE (Organization for Security and Cooperation in Europe) 107–8

Panopticon prison 51
Patriot Act (US) xii, 77, 106
PayPal 81
Paystone 81–2
PCCIP (President's Commission on Critical Infrastructure Protection) 26, 132, 135, 139, 142–3
Powell, William, *The Anarchist Cookbook* 118, 119
power
  changing nature of 29
  concept 13–14
  redistribution, alleged 30–2
  research on 46, 47
  see also meta-power; soft power
PPPs (Public-Private Partnerships), information sharing 142, 146
print, Anderson on 52

realist theory ix
  as self-fulfilling prophecy 59
reterritorialisation, cyberspace 75
RFID (Radio Frequency Identification Systems) 85, 86
  and post-9/11 threat environment 86–7
risk
  assessment, security 159–60

definition x
management 131
Rumsfeld, Donald 114

Said, Edward, on technology 51
search engines 109–11
security
  concept 13
  constructivism 35–6
  and culture 54–5, 57
  deterritorialisation of 75, 88–9
  European constructs of 56
  and global surveillance systems 87
  and hacking 73
  and ICT 71
  and identity 54–5
  national, vs networked security 56
  risk assessment 159–60
  stakeholders, increase in 32–3
  and territorial space 58
  see also cyber-security; information security
Singh, J.P. 45–65
SITE (Search for International Terrorist Entities) Institute 113
SMEs (Small and Medium-Sized Enterprises)
  information sharing 131, 142–6
  associations 142–6
  cost-benefits 143
  government aid, lack of 144
  UK, WARPs 145–6
soft power
  critique of 30
  definition 29, 47
  Nye on 47–8
sovereignty, and cyberspace 14
state
  controls, internet content 77–9, 84–5
  see also China; France; Germany; Iran; UK; US
  role
    cyber-security 154–5
    information age 151–60
    see also nation-state
status quo, transformations, overlaps 54
Suter, Manuel 129–49

Tamil Tigers 100
TDFs (Trans-Border Data Flows) xii
technological determinism 20
technology
  contested role of 51–3
  nature of 74
  politics of 74–5
  Said on 51
territorial space
  ambiguities 68
  and cyberspace 58, 68
  and security 58
  vs hyper-space 53
terrorism
  European responses 57
  and internet 98–101
  and internet governance 14
  US responses 57
  see also cyber-terrorism
Terrorism Act (2006), UK 107
Toffler, Alvin 1

UK, information control 106–7
UN Declaration of Human Rights (1948), Article 19 101–2
uncertainty, acceptance of 160
Uruguay Round (1986–94)
  cultural exception 59
  developing countries, inclusion 60
US
  CIP 26
  information control 105–6
  responses to terrorism 57

war on terrorism see GWOT
WARPs (Warning, Advice and Reporting Points) 145
Wendt, Alexander, on constructivism 48–9
Westphalian topology, internet 84
WGIG (Working Group on Internet Governance) 97, 98
Windows Vista 78–9
WSIS (World Summit on the Information Society) 97, 155

Yahoo! 110